FAUX
FEMINISM

WHY WE FALL FOR
WHITE FEMINISM
_{AND} HOW WE CAN STOP

SERENE KHADER

BEACON PRESS, BOSTON

BEACON PRESS
Boston, Massachusetts
www.beacon.org

Beacon Press books
are published under the auspices of
the Unitarian Universalist Association of Congregations.

27 26 25 24   8 7 6 5 4 3 2 1

This book is printed on acid-free paper that meets the uncoated paper
ANSI/NISO specifications for permanence as revised in 1992.

Text design and composition by Kim Arney

*Library of Congress Cataloguing-in-Publication
Data is available for this title.*
Hardcover ISBN: 978-0-8070-0827-0
E-book ISBN: 978-0-8070-0828-7
Audiobook: 978-0-8070-3513-9

CONTENTS

FAUX
FEMINISM

THE SECRET
LIFE OF AN IDEA

I had always imagined that I would remember exactly where I was when it happened. That the moment my phone buzzed with the text heard round the feminist world would be forever burned into my memory.

But apparently, you only remember the arrival of calamitous news when it comes out of nowhere. The final blow to abortion rights that summer day in 2022 was instead utterly expected. The media had already been conducting postmortems of *Roe v. Wade*, the 1973 case that decriminalized abortion nationwide, for several months. As for me, my entire political *life* had been haunted by the knowledge that this moment would come. I had never known a time when abortion rights and access were not under attack. Still, the overturning of *Roe* had once seemed distant enough that I could joke about it. I remember my teenage self laughing that if the government wanted my uterus so badly, I would just send it to them.

So, on that hazy June day in 2022 when the Supreme Court ruled that there was no constitutional right to abortion, one thing was clear: this had been a long time coming. Feminists needed to roll up our sleeves. We needed a long-term plan. And we couldn't just assume that what we had been doing up to this point was working.

The Court's decision in *Dobbs v. Jackson* may have been designed to send pregnant people back to the 1950s, but the oral arguments surfaced an idea that could only be at home today. It was the idea that abortion was no longer necessary. Things had changed since 1973, one Supreme Court justice pointed out in their only question. There may have been a time when women needed the right to abortion, but not now. Today women were *free*.

The source of this "freedom" was about as ghastly as it gets. "Safe haven laws" allow birthing people to abandon their newborns in places like fire and police stations without facing criminal prosecution. If it was so easy to abandon a newborn, wasn't the ability of abortion restrictions to "hinder women's access to the workplace" . . . "take[n] care of"?[1]

This question, from a Supreme Court justice, seemed to echo the words of an amicus brief filed the year before, one that pulled no punches in its argument against abortion. "Safe Haven laws," it said, "give women total freedom from burdens of unwanted children."[2]

Much of this argument—its erasure of the pregnant body and trivialization of the experience of pregnancy and the adoption decision—was straight out of the conservative playbook.

But what hit me was not the familiar misogyny. It was hearing a staunch abortion opponent claim that women were free. Since when were conservatives saying that women were free? And since when did they seem to be conceding that we *should* be?

I'm a political philosopher (yes, this is a job—I've even managed to convince my parents), so I'm trained to notice ideas. My superpower is seeing "through" public life and cultural trends to the values that animate them. And this time, I couldn't help noticing that the 2020s were a new era: one where it was no longer politically risky for a conservative darling to suggest that freedom from the responsibility of raising a child could be a good thing.[3]

The idea that women deserved freedom was decidedly *not* from the conservative playbook. The conservative side in the abortion debate had long been spouting versions of the idea that women needed to stay where we belonged, whether that meant accepting the "consequences of our decisions," remaining in the kitchen, or as the alt-right would have it, accepting that "America belongs to its fathers and is owed to its sons."[4] But instead, here was an abortion opponent suggesting that "forced motherhood" (yes she used that term, and yes it was a she) was not something women should have to undergo.

The only way I could make sense of this seeming about-face was to think about the person who had argued that safe-haven laws respected women's "bodily autonomy" in the first place. She was a pearl-wearing mom of seven, drafted to the Supreme Court from a Catholic law school, known for seeming to weave a very demanding form of motherhood seamlessly into a high-powered career. It was these bona fides of traditional white femininity that made her popular with her conservative Christian base.

But Justice Amy Coney Barrett and her supporters had long been presenting her as something other than traditional. Barrett, in the eyes of her supporters, represented a new kind of woman.

Barrett was the type of woman who made her own rules. She showed up to her confirmation hearing in a fuchsia-colored dress, as though to make a statement about how femme presentation belonged even in the halls of power. The conservative theater surrounding her confirmation hearing portrayed her as a gender warrior, someone who should be celebrated for not fitting into the conventional mold of what a Supreme Court justice looks like. Never mind that she had been part of a religious group that referred to women as "handmaids."[5]

Republican Senator Marsha Blackburn had used Barrett's confirmation as an opportunity to scold "paternalistic" progressive critics for "not entering the hearing with an open mind." Blackburn, who refers to gender-affirming care for trans youth as "child mutilation,"[6] was suddenly all about criticizing gender roles. Barrett's critics, Blackburn said, must believe "only certain kinds of women would be allowed into this hearing room."[7] Senator Joni Ernst, also a Republican, went so far as to suggest that feminists were like fundamentalists, punishing Barrett, just as "women all over the world" are punished, "perceived and judged based on who someone else needs or wants us to be, not on who we actually are."[8]

Barrett herself liked to insist that she wasn't a woman who let other people tell her what to do or who to be. The academic and professional "victories" that led her to become the sixth woman ever nominated to the US Supreme Court had happened because she was not the type of person to be cowed by sexism. It "never occurred" to her "that anyone would consider girls to be less capable than boys," she said during her confirmation hearings. She had feminist advice ready at hand for those who, like the school-age granddaughters of a Republican senator, would ask for a memento. In their pocket constitutions she had scrawled the words, "Dream big."[9]

Once I learned about Barrett's advice to young girls, she no longer seemed to belong to some topsy-turvy nightmare. Her words could in fact be heard on any given evening on my living room couch. I was dispensing the same advice to my daughter—literally.

When I was pregnant with my first child, I had been gifted all the cliché bookish Brooklyn mom swag: Books with titles like *Baby Feminists* and *A Is for Activist*, and ironically—especially in light of the fact that the *Dobbs* decision was around the corner—multiple books about Barrett's liberal predecessor, Ruth Bader Ginsburg. Even a bib that mimicked Ginsburg's famous "dissent collar."

One book in particular had become woven into our bedtime ritual. It was filled with pictures of intentionally diverse women overcoming obstacles—Harriet Tubman facing down the night with a lantern, Zaha Hadid with a pencil behind her ear building skyscrapers, Florence Griffith Joyner winning multiple gold medals. Its jewel tones, prominent faces, and bold lines were irresistible. So was its singsong refrain.

It was called *Dream Big*.

Barrett's embrace of freedom for women wasn't from the conservative playbook. Barrett was taking pages from the *feminist* playbook now. The same one I was reading. The same one I was reading to my daughter.

The call was coming from inside the house—my house, to be precise.

And any long-term strategy feminists were going to craft after *Dobbs* was going to have to face this fact.

Feminist ideas are powerful, perhaps more powerful than they have ever been. This means, on one hand, that my daughter gets to grow up in a world where there are children's books full of women, including queer women of color, doing amazing things. It also means, though, that there are plenty of women who, like Amy Coney Barrett, are doing amazing things without my or my daughter's interests in mind. And, as my own children's book choices show, it's sometimes hard to tell the difference. Seemingly feminist ideas can be harnessed for causes like misogyny and white supremacy, and it's not always obvious when that's happening.

Whether the unprecedented power of feminist ideas will actually be harnessed for social justice does not just depend on who gets ahold of them. It depends on what those ideas *are*. Barrett was able to write the words *dream big* unironically because she really did embody a certain feminist ideal. She made choices her own mother certainly wouldn't have been able to make, and she embraced political power. She rejected many stereotypes about women. If getting in a 4 a.m. workout, as she was purported to do when her children were little, was what it took to show that moms could do it all, Barrett would do it.

When Barrett argued that the illegality of abortion was compatible with women's freedom, she was using a feminist idea to justify throwing the majority of women under the bus. When she portrayed herself as brave enough to defy sexism, and when her supporters painted her as the victim of regressive gender stereotypes, they affirmed the idea that "representation matters." The price the rest of us have to pay for that representation is not just lack of control of our bodies, but also judicial decisions that have eroded protections for workers, immigrants, and defendants.

But I would be lying if I said that I didn't also think that it was important to challenge certain stereotypes about women. I, who have been teaching and researching feminist ideas for more than fifteen years, have also been known to give public talks in pink dresses and heels just to stick it to the norms of my white male–dominated field.

If we want to understand how we got here—to a world where abortion is illegal in fourteen states, where the final nail in the coffin was hammered by the "ultimate dystopian girlboss," and where public support for feminism is at an all-time high—we need to understand that lines of reasoning like Barrett's are not so dissimilar from those advanced by actual feminists.[10] Feminists have long been aware that arguments and strategies we pursue sometimes serve the few at the expense of the many. We have coined terms like *white feminism*, *neoliberal feminism*, *lifestyle feminism*, and *girlboss feminism* to acknowledge this fact. But using these words is not the same thing as being able to reliably spot faux feminisms. As my own experience inadvertently girlbossing up my daughter shows, most of us have yet to fully recognize the logic that allows mainstream feminism to become a tool of power.

Dobbs, and certainly Barrett's question, were made possible partly by familiar feminist ideas. Mainstream feminists have long framed abortion rights as an issue of choice.[11] It should not be totally surprising, if abortion is just like any other choice, that someone saw fit to argue that moving the choice forward a few months to the end of a full-term pregnancy wouldn't be that big of a deal. Nor should it be surprising that Barrett trivialized the adoption decision. The right to parent, brought to light by the reproductive justice movement, has not figured prominently in the mainstream feminist picture of reproductive rights at any point in my lifetime.

Similarly, generations of feminists holding up the professional woman as *the* image of women's liberation laid the groundwork for the idea that we don't need abortion rights. If feminism aims to free women from the expectation that they parent, or that they primarily or only parent—rather than, say, to secure an equal right to sex for pleasure, or the ability to parent without that becoming a huge liability—it's unsurprising that we have ended up with arguments that say we are already pretty close to having what we want. In the background of Barrett's argument was the idea that technology keeps moving the timing of fetal viability closer and closer to the moment of pregnancy. As anti-abortion conservatives would have it, this technology means that the burden of pregnancy keeps lessening and lessening; forced gestation and birth can be characterized as just asking pregnant people to hang tight a few weeks beyond the moment when they would otherwise have had an abortion.

Other feminist arguments have played into how we got here too. Arguments that it's unfeminist to judge women for their choices, or even—as the meme half-jokingly puts it today—that feminism means celebrating women's rights and women's wrongs, have enabled conservatives to claim that it's hypocritical to judge Amy Coney Barrett, even for her policies.

The idea that feminism is about rejecting the stereotype that women are less capable made it difficult to criticize a high-powered mom of seven. None of this is to suggest that feminists bear responsibility for the evisceration of abortion rights in the US. We have a long, concerted, well-funded right-wing war on women to thank for that. But the arguments that could have stopped the war on women have made their way into mainstream feminist discourse only partially, and alongside arguments that may not be helping our cause at all.

In other words, feminist arguments and images sometimes lead to political strategies that harm women—especially, but not exclusively, nonelite women. The idea that pregnancy is a choice, legal scholar Dorothy Roberts argues, has functioned to support the criminalization of pregnant Black women, who are seen as "choosing" to endanger fetuses by doing things like taking medication.[12] The idea that feminism is about "dreaming big" has not had much to say about the dreams of all the nannies and daycare workers who care for the children of women who manage to make it into the corner office.

This is not what feminism has to be like, and feminists, especially, nonelite ones, have been offering alternative visions for generations. Women of color have been arguing against the "choice" framing of abortion for decades, largely because we have known that this framing will not give us what we need. We have been denied both abortion *access* and the right to parent—in ways ranging from coercive sterilization to the separation of moms from their children at the US–Mexico border.

"Choice" was never going to be able to fix these things.[13] Poor and working-class women (who are often also women of color) have long resisted the idea that feminism is about getting women into the workforce, since the jobs available to them have never been very liberating anyway. Even elite women have not been terribly well-served by the vision of the professional woman as the feminist goal. The loss of abortion rights was a loss for all of us, and even the most privileged women still do more housework.

———————

This book is about how to recognize feminist visions that harm and exclude, and how to stop ourselves from falling into them. One of these visions is white feminism, but I argue that many bad and faux feminisms, including right-wing cooptations of feminism and what might be termed "dream big" feminism, draw their force from a single idea. This idea is as ubiquitous as the air we breathe. But it's not the only idea out there, and we can break up with it once we expose it for what it really is. It's an idea we *have* to break up with if we are going to make feminism work for all women, and if we are going to stave off its potential to become a tool for maintaining the racial and economic status quo.

I'm talking about the idea that feminism is about freedom. Freedom unites many seemingly disparate ideas that end up causing harm or exclusion: that abortion is about choice, that paid work actualizes our human potential, that we shouldn't judge women, that the cultures and communities of women of color are holding them back. Freedom is also at the core of the idea that consent is sufficient for sexual liberation, and the idea that it's good to be a "strong woman," and the idea that beauty standards harm us by saying we have to conform to someone else's standards.[14] There is undeniable power in the idea that feminism is about opposing barriers that hold back individual women. But it is taking up way too much space in contemporary feminism, and is the source of many policies and political strategies that we are coming to regret.

I call the idea that feminism aims to free individual women from social expectations "the freedom myth." It's a myth, not so much because social expectations never harm women, but because it often masks other sources of harm, including social structures that perpetuate inequality. Feminism does not just harm women and gender-expansive people by preventing us from doing things or telling us what to do; it harms us by pushing us into inferior positions in an unjust hierarchy. Buying into the freedom myth also pushes us toward feminist strategies that do nothing about—or even worsen—white supremacy and economic injustice.

The freedom myth is also a myth because of the way it takes hold of our imaginations. It's not something any of us needs to believe in explicitly in order to be kept in its thrall. The "dream big" idea is so powerful in part because it seems so innocent. And it seems so innocent in part because it is in line with cultural ideologies that are so deeply held that they don't seem like ideologies at all. The idea that social progress comes from undoing restrictions, that individual potential has an almost magical power, that a difference made by one is a difference for all—these are among the cultural truisms that the freedom myth taps into.

I am going to try to convince you that the freedom myth is a major reason we fall into providing support for faux feminisms and feminisms for the few, such as white feminism and neoliberal or "girlboss" feminism. I am using the word *we* on purpose. I think actual feminists—that is, people who are committed to dismantling gender-based oppression in all of its intersectional forms—end up thinking in terms of the freedom myth pretty often.

This includes me. I've already told you I read *Dream Big* to my older child (the one who is old enough to have a gender). My academic and activist commitment to feminism has gotten me to a point where I can call myself out in spaces like this book, and where I can Instagram jokes about how you should come to my house for "neoliberal feminist story time." It has not made me immune.

Many of the ideas that make up freedom feminism are genuinely appealing. In the course of writing this book, I thought often about a conversation that a friend and I had about feminism during a Sunday morning coffee-shop hang. As the debrief of the weekend's late-night happenings slid into a debrief of the week, my friend began to share some of the challenges she was facing as an activist. She was organizing against the normalization of sexual harassment and assault on her law school campus. She wanted to talk about how to talk to people about feminism. Like many activists organizing in this new terrain in which we are finally having culture-wide conversations about the pervasiveness of sexual harassment and assault, she was spending a lot of time supporting people who were figuring out feminism for the first time.

At this point, the conversation veered into territory that is, for me, something of an occupational hazard. People ask doctors to diagnose their illnesses. People ask me (not *that* kind of doctor) to help them define and connect concepts. My friend asked, "How do you define feminism, when people ask you?" When I posed the question back to her, she said: "I say it's about radical self-determination." As is probably clear by now, I didn't love this answer.

But the answer was working for her, partly for reasons that I, and likely you, can readily identify with. Many of us come to feminism from the realization that we have been socialized in ways we are not happy about. The details of this socialization vary from person to person. Maybe we were told to stay home when our brothers could go out, or we realize that we are in the habit of apologizing for everything or thinking we are incomplete without a mate, or we feel pressured to present as femme when we don't feel very femme. Realizing these things often brings a feeling of needing to finally break free of what we have been taught. The Indian feminist Nivedita Menon analogizes becoming a feminist to hitting the "reveal formatting" button on a document. Once we recognize the extent of this formatting, it can definitely seem like the solution is to become unformatted.

The idea that feminism is about freedom also promises to bring people in. Perhaps there was a time when you felt like feminism was into dragging women—telling us we couldn't have long nails or that we should be standing up for ourselves more or that it's wrong to listen to hip-hop. Perhaps you've had a conversation with someone who really didn't like categories, who thought that racism and sexism boiled down to putting people in groups. Or maybe you have thought that because so many women have discovered feminism in the last ten years, the best way to leverage more power is to adopt a "big tent" feminism, one with no litmus tests about what you have to believe.

Clearly, though, the desire to bring everyone in has been a double-edged sword. When the *New York Times* found itself running a podcast asking whether we could have a big tent feminism after Dobbs, the answer had to be no.[15] As cultural critic Tressie McMillan Cottom argued in that podcast, women of color had long been arguing for an abortion politics that was more demanding, not less. Similarly, the idea that we shouldn't see people as members of social identity groups has been exposed as an "I don't see color" view that makes it hard to listen and respond to people's experiences of racism.

These problems with freedom feminism are logically connected to it, albeit in ways that may not always be easy to spot from the beginning. If we think that describing people as members of social identity groups boxes them into oppressive social expectations, we are going to have trouble telling the difference between calling out racism and engaging in it. If we think feminism is about resisting social expectations, Barrett has shown up to resist ours, shaping the lives of millions through her jurisprudence while calling us on our bluff.

My friend was asking me for help defining feminism because I am a philosopher. But as a philosopher, I am not just trained to *notice* ideas; I'm trained to see logical connections among them, to think a step ahead and see how things that seemed like good ideas at the beginning might lead to some unexpected places. I am the kind of person who reads a random meme and says stuff like, "That's only true if you have the idea of democracy they had in nineteenth-century France" or "The writing has been on the wall since that policy settled on this definition of this word." This makes me not the funnest companion for sharing internet content with. (It also apparently makes me not the funnest friend to confide your activist struggles to, but you've already figured that out.)

But being a philosopher has also taught me that none of us are infallible. Seeing what our ideas entail, and the associations they trigger, is hard work. But it's work that we need to do if we want to craft a feminism that leads somewhere other than where we are now, if we want to build a feminism that is genuinely, as bell hooks famously put it, "for everyone." In the coming pages, I try to expose freedom feminism, and the often unseen harm it is causing, in hopes that we can reject it once and for all.

There is another reason that my friend's claim that feminism is about self-determination, and the idea that feminism is about freedom more generally, have never sat right with me. I am a woman of color from a cultural background where the idea that social expectations are harmful doesn't always resonate. When memes appear in my feeds about it being feminist to cut off communication with our toxic relatives, as they do pretty much on the daily, I both agree that we should when they really are toxic, and also wish we could talk in some cases about how we might learn to navigate conflict while preserving relationships and valuing our elders and ancestors.[16] I may be reading books about dreaming big to my daughter, yet when my second child was born my South Asian immigrant father shared with me a different idea about why it can be hard for women to "succeed." Part of the challenge was that I was having my babies in a country where parents were "on their own." I was alone partly because I wasn't in a context that believed that taking care of parents was everyone's job.

It is not just that many women of color value our roots. We have also been harmed by feminisms that claim to "free" us from our communities.[17] This is one of best-selling author Mikki Kendall's major grievances against white feminism. She grew up as a brainy Black girl, adored and supported even by those who jokingly called her "Books." But in adulthood, when she entered the world of white, middle-class feminists, adoration was less forthcoming—at least when it came to her Blackness. The idea that, as she puts it "the hood hates smart people," was everywhere. White feminists, Kendall says, continue to insist that smart Black kids are discouraged from doing well in school by a culture that does not value them. Kendall's own experience was quite the opposite: "The same kids who called me Books now pass around my books and tell me how proud of me they are."[18] But social policy keeps emphasizing the need to separate high-achieving Black kids from their communities. Apparently, one can't dream big and be rooted at the same time.

The racial dimension of freedom feminism also shapes Western interactions with women in and from the Global South (the world's poorer countries). I have spent the bulk of my academic career studying ideas that shape Western interventions in the lives of poor women in Asia, Africa, and Latin America. It has been particularly hard to ignore the role of freedom feminism in justifying racial, economic, and gender injustice in the lives of these women of the global majority. The idea that "other" women would be better off if they could escape their cultures and their men is woven deeply into Western misunderstandings of the problems that women in the Global South face.

I realized just how deeply when I read the comments on an article I had published in the *New York Times* in 2019. The article was about women and poverty. I argued that the idea that women in the Global South are oppressed by their cultural customs prevents us from seeing how global economic policy—often set by the US government and US corporations—is a major cause of the fact that over 380 million women and girls around the world live in extreme poverty. The "don't read the comments" rule doesn't apply when you're the author, and the commenters were not happy. The commenters, and also the random emailers, claimed that they, like me, were concerned about women. But they were more concerned about my argument.

Over and over again, they repeated that I was letting local traditions and men of color off the hook. The idea that these play *a* role in women's oppression was not something I had denied. But these commenters seemed to need a piece about women and global poverty to be about things like child marriage (which, by the way, is exacerbated by war and climate change) and opposition to girls' education. This was likely the only article many of them had read about how the global economy increased gendered work burdens. But one article, it seemed, was one too many.

This all left me wondering why the romance around freeing "other" women from tradition had such a strong hold on Western feminists that we couldn't even pause to acknowledge how gender injustice is sometimes increased by the forces we associate with modernity. It seemed clear to me that a woman's oppression is worsened when she adds to her already onerous household labor the need to walk miles to find unpolluted water. It also seemed clear that asking a woman who is already working twelve hours a day to attend a sewing workshop isn't a feminist success story—and certainly not a career choice my readers would recommend to their own daughters.

The answer, I came to think, was that the idea that feminism was a movement to free individual women from social expectations took on a particularly dangerous face when it came to the lives of women in the Global South. The anthropologist Saba Mahmood argued that an "imaginary of freedom" structured most Westerners' understandings of feminism.[19] In this imaginary, tradition and culture were imposed on women from without. Underneath these lay a world of feminist possibilities waiting to be unleashed. But unleashing them would have to mean breaking with expectation, finding something deeper and authentic, going out on one's own. It was difficult to fathom patriarchy as something other than a force that holds us back, or the source of patriarchy as something other than tradition.[20] Western feminists were shoehorning nearly every possible bad thing that could happen to women into a deprivation of individual freedom.

If you are a feminist today, you are probably aware, at least vaguely, that there are wrong ways of doing feminism. You may have heard the term *white feminism* and know it is to be avoided, and heard that feminists have a history of advancing the interests of privileged women while ignoring or harming others. You know we want to avoid repeating this history. But it is not always obvious how to do this. We can talk about privilege and we can learn about history, but we also need to be able to see flawed ideas for what they are. Ideally, we want to be able to recognize flawed ideals regardless of who is presenting them and *before* they do harm. This is especially important in our current political moment. Our ability to harness the skyrocketing potential of feminism for genuine social justice depends on it.

Our increased awareness that feminism can harm and exclude has also meant an uptick in callouts (and call-ins) of mistakes feminists have made. This is mostly a good thing. Callouts, when they are based in a correct assessment of the situation, are important opportunities for learning. But hopefully we are learning more from callouts than how to apologize. We should be learning how to do better next time, not just as individuals, but as participants in movements for social justice. Doing better next time means being able to spot the logics that made the mistakes seem like a good idea at the time—logics we can't always comfortably distance ourselves from.

We need to be able to hold ourselves accountable for making feminism better. Terms like *white feminism*, *Western feminism*, *corporate feminism* and *girlboss feminism*, *neoliberal feminism*, and *femonationalism* are indispensable to the future of feminism.[21] Privileged women's voices and priorities still dominate mainstream feminist conversations. If you are the housecleaner or nanny of a woman who uses your labor to subsidize her ability to go to the office, the idea that feminism was about freeing women from the expectation that we stay home probably never looked that great to you. Ditto if you are a working-class woman who was told that your main problem was people thinking women couldn't be presidents (or Supreme Court justices), and not the lack of paid parental leave.

But talking about privilege cannot substitute for directly discussing politics and the ideas that motivate them. At some point, or ideally at various points along the way, feminists have to ask ourselves what we should do. And we can't do this without evaluating actual political proposals and the extent to which those proposals match up to the ideals we believe in. We don't need to look far to see that the injunction "Check your privilege" has confused a lot of privileged women.

Part of the reason is, of course, that they need to check their privilege more. But as the stories I'm about to tell will show, inadvertent feminist complicity in political strategies that throw the majority of women under the bus sometimes comes from the fact that we are not always clear about what feminism's goals are. It is not always obvious how our politics end up justifying harm or oppression—or what it is possible to think and do instead. Yes, feminisms for the few sometimes emanate from privileged women consciously or unconsciously fighting for changes that will only benefit them. But other forms of feminist complicity arise from being steeped in bad ideas whose consequences are not obvious, sometimes because of one's privilege and sometimes not.

As the philosopher Olúfẹ́mi Táíwò argues, the goal of identity politics has always been to develop better ideas and translate them into better political strategies.[22] Indeed, the notion that we need to talk about ideas and not just privilege is especially true for those of us who lack privilege along some vector(s), who are not white women or girlbosses or able-bodied, or straight or cis, or members of the middle class. We are the ones for whom the injunction to check your privilege is the least likely to tell us something new, but we cannot expect our identities to protect us from ever becoming instruments of power. Our social positioning may expose us to better political ideas, but it does not make us immune to internalizing and promulgating the harms caused by the freedom myth.

I'd add that calls to check privilege are, at the end of the day, hopes for a certain kind of outcome—one that attacks the source of privilege itself. Privilege is one manifestation of unjust social hierarchy. It is not a form of unfreedom (it's maybe even having *too much* freedom). To care about privilege is already to think that the problem feminism needs to solve is largely a problem of inequality.

Part of what it means that feminism is at a crossroads is that we have a choice to make, a choice that we cannot make without thinking deeply about values. It is a choice about what feminism *is*. What feminism means is largely up to us. When I say this, I don't mean that everyone has their "own truth" about feminism. Feminism is about changing the world, and we can't do that without forming communities and changing shared practices and meanings.

I mean that there have always been many strands within feminism. Feminism has always included more conservative and more radical strands. It has contained within it, at the same time, people who believed that a feminist reproductive agenda was about keeping the "unfit" from reproducing,[23] people who believed it was about keeping the government out of the doctor's office, people who believed it was fundamentally about wresting control of our lives from men, people who believed it was about the right to parent, and many, many other things.[24] There have been people who believed that specific work protections for pregnancy and childcare were politically regressive because they undermined the idea that women could do any job men could, and people who believed that they were dismantling the assumption that men's work was the only socially valuable work, and all kinds of people in between.[25] Feminists converge on the idea that there is gender injustice and that we should fight against it, but we have not always agreed on what this injustice consists in or what should be done about it.

But sometimes we have to agree on some fundamentals about what feminism *is*, and this is one of those times. It is either a goal of feminism to demand abortion rights or it isn't; it is either a goal of feminism to fight for choice alone or to fight for more; it is either a goal of feminism to tell individual women to dream big or to question the economic system that makes dreaming big so important to begin with. In all of these cases, and many more, what feminism is depends largely on what we decide right now. What the term *feminism* means to those a generation from now will largely be a product of how we resolve debates about what feminism demands of us today.

This also means we can't hide our heads in the sand when people start claiming that arguments for hustling or girlbossing or wellness, or for freeing women of color from our neighborhoods or our hijabs, are just misinterpretations of feminism. I get why many of us want to do this, why there is an impulse to just say that feminisms for the few are not "real feminisms" and call it a day. This is the most common criticism I get when I tell people what this book is about.

The uncomfortable truth is that feminism is partly what people associated with the feminist movement do. We don't just get to decide who is and isn't a feminist based on who we do and don't like. Nor do we get to disavow the conclusions of arguments, or the imagery associated with them, once they go somewhere we didn't anticipate.

Work-life balance may have started off seeming like an idea that would get women more leisure time, but it has turned into the idea that you need to use your leisure time to craft a perfect body and family, and that buying adaptogens will help.[26] The idea that abortion was about freedom from the government was undoubtedly politically effective for certain demographics, but it just can't furnish arguments for why you might need support to have children or to get an abortion. Arguments and imagery that feminists have used are sometimes directly linked to gender injustice. The world where white feminism and other feminisms for the few don't really count as feminism is a world we have yet to create.

In this moment when we are finally talking about the fact that many feminists have been active supporters of oppressive systems, we should feel very keenly that we don't get to pick and choose. Many of the same feminists most of us were taught about in history books were at some point allies of white supremacy, colonialism, capitalist exploitation, ableism, cissexism, and homophobia, even producing as feminist goals ideas that supported keeping these other systems of oppression in place. From Elizabeth Cady Stanton and Carrie Chapman Catt's very public statements that women's suffrage was compatible with (and could perhaps even strengthen) white supremacy[27] to Betty Friedan's claims that women needed to free themselves from "biological living," as though no one would have to pick up the slack of caring for children or cleaning houses,[28] feminisms for the few have been with us for a very long time.

Most of us fall into freedom feminism at one point or another, inadvertently contributing to the harm and exclusion of the majority of women. But freedom feminism is not our only option. This book is ultimately about how to think toward something else—a feminism for the many. If there have always been many strands in feminism, this book is largely an invitation to pick up another strand.

But in a world in which one strand threatens to strangle the other, we have to start with some serious unlearning. The freedom myth shapes our thinking in surprising ways, so the first section of this book is about unpacking freedom myths so that we can spot them more easily. I start out by assessing the state of play in feminist discussions around beauty and sex. I ask how well the idea that sexism harms us by restricting us—an idea I refer to as "the restriction myth"—has been serving us. The answer is not very well, especially not for women who are marginalized by more than just gender. In fact, the restriction myth has left many of us unable to even name or notice what patriarchy is doing to us.

The harms of sexism are harms to an "us," but this is something freedom feminism encourages us to forget. The individualism myth, which I tackle in the book's second chapter, tells us that feminist progress means that individual women are better off than they once were.

But this understanding obscures two important facts. One is that being better off isn't a feminist success if men are still reaping the benefits. The other is that individual women sometimes make progress by leaving other women behind. This isn't the exception, and often is not conscious or ill-intentioned; it is baked into our society's understanding of work, and of women's work in particular.

In the third chapter, I illuminate a backdrop of feminist discussions of freedom that often goes unnoticed. It's the backdrop of white supremacy, upheld by generations of colonialism. Concern with freeing women from social expectations is not an equal-opportunity concern. We have inherited centuries of associating people of color with "primitive" culture and tradition, and associating Europeans with "civilization" and liberation from these forces. The "culture myth" often leaves feminists pointing the finger for patriarchy at the wrong source in ways that are catastrophic for women of color.

In the fourth chapter, I focus on a myth that gets in the way of feminists' ability to change the world. The judgment myth tells us that feminism is about respecting women's choices. But sexism has never been about women judging other women, and celebrating women's choices is not enough to make sexist oppression go away. In fact, as I show through a discussion of sexual harassment in the food industry, women have lots of good reasons to *choose* to do what sexism demands. We have to change the menu that structures women's choices, not just refuse to judge women. And, I argue, sometimes we need to judge women, especially privileged ones who are weaponizing the idea that they should be free of judgment, harming and exploiting others.

The last two chapters of the book are about how we can imagine feminism beyond the freedom myth. Chapter 5, "Equality and Intersectionality," takes us on a journey to an important crucible of feminism for the many, the universes of Black feminist politics in the 1960s and 1970s. Figures like Frances Beal and Johnnie Tillmon hoped for a very different feminist future from the one we have ended up in. They fought for reproductive rights, but not in terms of choice, and they fought for women workers, but not the idea of freedom from the household. They also understood feminism as a movement similar in kind to movements like anti-racism and socialism. I explore the concepts they developed that are alternatives to freedom feminism, like the importance of prioritizing the goals of the most oppressed members of the groups we belong to.

In the book's final chapter, I explore what feminism for the many looks like today. To fight for a better future for feminism is not just to pick up a strand of feminism forgotten somewhere in history. It is to pick up a strand that has survived, and that is having a renaissance in feminist movements all over the globe, from high schools in Washington, DC, to the streets of Buenos Aires. I describe practical principles we can take from these movements, in the hope that we can get working on the long-term plan that feminism needs if it is going to bring about deep social change.

That long-term plan starts with a different idea.

CHAPTER 1

THE RESTRICTION MYTH

Is Oppression the Same as Telling People What to Do?

The speaker was unabashed about her positionality. "I am a woman of color," she began, her big gold hoops swaying as she spoke. She wore her black blazer open, revealing a tiny gold cross and a T-shirt emblazoned with a purple fist. "I am a mom," she continued, letting her shiny stilettos carry her from the marble corridors of her workplace to her children's art show. "I am a cisgender millennial who's been diagnosed with generalized anxiety disorder.

I am intersectional."[1]

I wasn't at an activist meeting or an academic conference where such declarations would have seemed right at home. I was lying on my couch. Just like the minimalist clothing ads that are the price of streaming TV, this content had been handpicked for me. Clearly, I had triggered the "woke millennial" category in the algorithm, and this commercial was my eerie reward.

"I am unapologetically me," she continued. "I want you to be unapologetically you, whoever you are."

And then I realized *who* she unapologetically was: a strategist for the CIA. I was watching a recruitment video for the CIA. Yes, that CIA. The one that helped install the Taliban as the government of Afghanistan, the same one that backed coups that quashed feminist movements and violently ousted pro-feminist governments all over Latin America.

But, the protagonist suggested in Spanish, joining the CIA was a way to defy expectations. Because "mija, you're worth it."

The protagonist was Stephanie LaRue, and at the start of the video she had all the trappings of a contemporary feminist icon. Like Justice Barrett, she was there to break the rules, to defy expectations. Her shirt had a fist on it, but she was there to give the finger to anyone who thought she couldn't be tough as nails and a mom, or that a Latina couldn't make it that far. Unlike Barrett, she was using terms like *intersectionality* and speaking Spanish and wearing the symbol of the power of the people. A seemingly progressive woman of color millennial working for the CIA was not supposed to be confusing. The unexpectedness was the point. Part of what it meant to break the categories—to intersect, if you will—was to be a complicated, self-contradicting package.

Part of the package just happened to be doing work that undermined women's movements around the globe.

LaRue was carrying on a long feminist tradition of refusing to be what society expected—one not so different from the idea that feminism was about "radical self-determination" that had emerged in the coffee shop conversation with my friend that I described in the introduction. "Well-behaved women rarely make history" the bumper sticker tells us. "Bitches get things done."

Women refusing to fall into line, we have been told for the last several years, will change the world. In a recent essay inspired by the successes of #MeToo, Rebecca Solnit recalled a geographical metaphor from the fantasy writer Ursula LeGuin. "We are volcanoes. . . . When we women offer our experience as our truth, as human truth, all the maps change. There are new mountains."

But LaRue seemed both utterly willing to shatter assumptions and happy to leave the mountains where they were, thank you very much. There is no guarantee that individual women asserting themselves against the weight of social expectations will change the world. The CIA clearly gets this, but when will we?

———————

When conservative or shallowly feminist women present themselves as rebels who refuse to be defined or disciplined, they carry a familiar feminist line of reasoning to its logical conclusion. According to this line of reasoning, patriarchy harms us primarily by imposing restrictions. Feminism is individual self-determination, resistance to being told what to do or who to be. Freedom feminism characterizes the force working against self-determination as something like "socialization," or "culture," or "expectations."

I call the idea that feminism is a fight against social restrictions the "restriction myth." Of course, restriction *can* be a tool of patriarchy. You need only get on the bus and see how many men happily occupy two seats to realize that sexism confines us, sometimes literally. But to reduce sexism to a set of restrictions, especially social restrictions on individuals, is to court various kinds of political danger. This danger goes beyond conservative edgelording that tries to call our bluff by telling us that CIA agents or right-wing supermoms like Amy Coney Barrett are going against the grain (or, while we are at it, that racists are victims of racism because someone dared call them racist or even just noted that they were white).

Feminists can fall for the restriction myth unintentionally, and when we do, we can end up failing to see oppression for what it is, or adopting political strategies that are at cross-purposes with ending it. After all, if feminism is about refusing to be told what to do, it is indifferent about the *effects* of our refusals. It is indifferent to whether our refusals to be told what to do end in endorsements of sexism, or to whether they end up reinforcing capitalism or white supremacy.

To start to see why the restriction myth so often ends up reinforcing oppression, we need only recognize a simple social fact. Everyone is restricted. Being part of a social world means being told what to do: to drive on one side of the road, to make (or not make) eye contact when we speak to each other, to hold the door open for the person coming behind you, to use forks or chopsticks or fingers for eating. Restrictions are not always bad. Sometimes, like when we agree to drive on one side of the road, restrictions help us live together. Restrictions may also give some people benefits they do not give others. If you've been at a family gathering where you've heard a man be told he dare not enter the kitchen, you've seen that restrictions can even become gifts. The prohibition on doing the dishes is, under another description, the privilege of getting to hang out on the couch and watch the football game.

The idea that oppression is the same thing as restriction, and that feminism aims to free women from restrictions, obscures these facts. Our society's system of restrictions produces winners and losers, and this is the thing we need to see. The restriction myth has also drawn us into political strategies that undermine our attempts to fix this problem. We need to do something about systemic inequality. But if oppression is the same thing as restriction, then everyone is oppressed.[2] And if everyone is oppressed, we lose sight of the differences in power and status that feminism is supposed to be trying to change in the first place.

WHY WE FALL FOR THE RESTRICTION MYTH

The restriction myth encompasses more than the idea that patriarchy boxes us in or prevents us from doing things. It's the assumption that all the harms of sexism can be understood as restrictions on individuals, that sexism is the same thing as women being told what to do or pushed in one direction rather than another. It's the idea that every wrong that sexism inflicts on women boils down to us being prevented from doing things. It's the idea that the path out of oppression is to stop doing what we are told—and maybe also to get out of others' way. It's the set of metaphors that, to borrow words from the otherwise radical body liberation activist Sonya Renee Taylor, tell us that ending oppression is about creating "a superhighway free of debris" and "removing ourselves as barriers to others' self-love."[3]

Even genuinely radical activists like Taylor can fall into the restriction myth because it is rooted in something very real. Sexism does harm women by limiting us, as anyone who has been socialized to take up as little space as possible can attest to. The problem is that this is not the *only* way it harms us. Even the norm that women fold their hands and cross their legs does more than tell us how we should sit. To be socialized to take up less space is to embody the idea that we should be smaller and weaker—that we deserve less. To be socialized to take up less space is also to be recruited into the role of seeming not to work (why would women need big or strong bodies, or to stretch out after a long day?),[4] like the custom of men opening doors for women as a show of "respect." The restriction myth tells us that we can stop our feminist analysis at the point where we recognize we are being told to sit one way and not another. But that should be just the beginning.

The restriction myth is also difficult to disentangle from a certain set of metaphors. These metaphors are about excess, about being more than what can fit into society's limiting norms. When we say, for example, that our ideals of beauty are too restrictive, we seem to mean that the diversity of people is too great to fit into the confines of those ideals. When the CIA officer says that she is "unapologetically" her, the insinuation is that she is too much for those who think they can tell her what to do (or who expected her to apologize in the first place). The restriction myth encourages us to "dream big" about what liberation looks like. Loosening restrictions means unleashing energy and possibility.

The lure of these images is undeniable. We live in the era of celebrating the woman who is "too much." The more general sense that every woman has been restricted by sexism opens up an easy path to making the case that every woman is a feminist, or that the path to being a feminist is to do the unexpected. But unless we are okay with the idea that the CIA officer is a feminist role model, we have some soul-searching to do. The attractions of the restriction myth have always been based on a misunderstanding of what inclusive feminism is about, and the politics that result leave a lot to be desired.

Many of us have bought into the restriction myth because we think it will solve the very real problem of feminism being too exclusionary.[5] When Jessica Valenti noticed the disturbing trend of conservative women claiming feminists are hypocrites, she realized she had to point the finger partly at herself. The cofounder of the once go-to blog *Feministing* realized that her work "to make feminism more accessible" had made her an enabler of sexism.[6]

In Valenti's telling, there was a time when feminists just wanted to help "young women who said 'they weren't' really feminists' but who believed they should be able to make the same amount of money as men or be able to attend a campus party without fear of being assaulted" see themselves in the movement. I remember this time well. In my first year of college, I found myself defending feminism to a friend in my dorm whose unshaven legs I was convinced made her a shoo-in. Instead, she told me that feminism was not something we needed anymore. Even a few years later, when I began teaching college, I would ask how many students in a women's studies course were feminists and see only two or three hands go up.

But times have changed. We are all feminists now. Beyoncé, Taylor Swift, Meghan Markle, Ariana Grande—even Barbie. Also the UK's conservative, short-lived third female prime minister Liz Truss (who cited Destiny's Child's "Independent Woman" in a tweet)[7] and right-wing political commentator Tomi Lahren.[8] That same college dorm-mate wrote to me out of the blue soon after Donald Trump's election in 2016 to tell me that she, too, had come to see the reality of sexism.

The restriction myth plays an important role in explaining the ascendancy of this "everyone can be a feminist" ethos. Many, probably most, women chafe at restrictions they face, like not being able to go to a campus party without worrying about rape. A quick way to help these women connect with feminism was to call feminism a movement against restrictions. But, by not saying enough about why sexist restrictions are bad, we opened the door to people railing against restrictions in general. By saying that feminism was opposition to harm that literally everyone faces, we did manage to reduce barriers to entry. But we may have reduced them too much.

Today, feminism is ascendant, powerful, and in danger of losing its meaning. We need to consider the possibility that the restriction myth was a response to a mischaracterization of the problem of exclusion. Of course, we want feminism to be a movement for all women. But feminism seeming "scary," as Valenti puts it, has not been the dominant barrier to feminism faced by poor and working-class women and women of color. They have instead found mainstream feminism exclusionary largely because of its priorities—its debating of leg shaving instead of safe neighborhoods to raise one's children in, its emphasis on nondis-crimination over paid parental leave.[9]

The restriction myth, however, promised to kill two birds with one stone. If our main hurdle was telling women what to do, the problem of exclusionary (white, middle-class) feminism and the problem of priv-ileged women rejecting feminism out of fear were one and the same. Refusing to tell anyone what to do would ensure that women of color did not have to listen to white women's sanctimonious opinions about their decisions—opinions that are genuinely annoying but do not form the heart of women of color's objections to white feminism. It would also ensure that no one would feel like feminism was asking them to change or give up too much.

Including their privilege. Or, to be less abstract, the benefits women can gain from colluding with capitalism and white supremacy.

RESTRICTION OR RANKING?

If we think the restriction myth is a way of unsilencing women, we may be surprised to discover it does plenty silencing of its own.

Tressie McMillan Cottom experienced this form of silencing when her inbox began to fill with "affirmations" from white women she didn't know. Cottom needed to "love herself." She was "cute as a button."[10] What had provoked this outpouring of love notes from complete strangers? Cottom had broken the rules about what was permissible to say out loud. She had said the unsayable.

What the now-celebrated cultural critic did to deserve this was make a simple observation. She hadn't even gone as far as saying the "u" word. She had merely stated what she saw as a bland social fact about herself as a fat Black woman. "I am not beautiful."

The statement, far from a confessional about Cottom's self-esteem, had been embedded in a viral blog post about a music awards show. At the time she wrote it, Cottom was a sociology grad student turning her aca-demic killjoy gaze on what was, by all counts, a very strange pop cultural event: Miley Cyrus taking the stage at the 2013 VMAs with "life-size teddy bears, flesh-colored underwear, and plenty of quivering brown buttocks."

Cottom argued that slapping the asses of fat Black women on stage evoked a trope that went as far back as slavery, using the perception of Black women's bodies as animal to build up white women's beauty.[11] But what seemed to stick in America's craw was that Cottom had described a hierarchy between thin white bodies and fleshier Black ones. And she had not just mentioned it in the more comfortable abstract; she had dared to place herself in the latter category.

There's a word for when someone tries to convince you that something is not true that you know is true: gaslighting. In Cottom's view, all she had done was point out a truth, or as she put it "call a thing a thing."[12] Beauty was a social hierarchy, one that existed independently of how Cottom felt about herself. Beauty was white and Cottom was dark. Women who looked like Cottom, the data showed, were "more likely to be punished in school and receive higher sentences for crimes, less likely to marry, and less likely to marry someone of equal or higher economic status."[13]

This was the truth, but it was a truth that could not be spoken from within the framework of the restriction myth. If feminism is about breaking free from social norms, the idea that beauty exists outside any woman's head becomes an existential threat to feminism. Cottom's unwanted pen pals were getting an important return on their investment in the restriction myth, whether they realized it or not: faith that women could undo oppression just by changing the way they thought.[14] The idea that white supremacist beauty standards would chug along regardless of whether Cottom loved herself could only be a sign that she hadn't heard the feminist gospel.

There was another, deeper reason that Cottom couldn't be understood in a feminist ecosystem dominated by the restriction myth. Cottom was not really saying that beauty harmed dark-skinned Black women by *restricting* them. She was saying that white supremacist beauty standards helped make Black women vulnerable to some not-great life outcomes, including harsher criminal sentences and loss of income. The devaluation of dark skin, especially dark Black skin, was part of a much bigger picture.

The bigger picture was beauty functioning to keep Black women below white women. Beauty made white women *desirable*, and white women could use their desirability to get things.[15] They could get attention, they could make money, they could marry the right "upwardly mobile" man, they could be believed when they spoke. Beauty also sorted Black and white women into different places in our social world, literally and metaphorically. Cottom doesn't use this example, but one need only look at who works in the front and the back of the restaurant to get a sense of how beauty can exempt white women, and women with greater proximity to whiteness, from certain types of exploitation.

In other words, beauty is a racial hierarchy. It ranks white and Black women relative to each other, helps support social practices that reserve better outcomes for white people. To try to characterize this hierarchy as a set of restrictions is to grossly distort it. For starters, the jury or the doctor who doubts the Black woman's claims about her own experience isn't really telling her what to do. They may not even be consciously stereotyping her; they're just taking an extra second to respond to a complaint about her pain or doing their "due diligence" in response to her testimony.

But more to the point, beauty standards do not just tell Black women what to look like. They tell white women what to look like. All women are receiving social messages about how to be beautiful. But they don't get the same things from acting on those messages when they try. Beauty helps white women consolidate racial and class privilege, literally.

When Cottom talks about dark-skinned Black women being more likely to end up with partners with lower incomes, she is referring to the fact that marriage is increasingly a vehicle for people in the middle and upper classes to remain where they are in the class hierarchy. People today are much less likely to marry someone from a different class background than they were in the 1950s, and this means that wealth is increasingly clustered in families in which both adults are middle- or upper-class.[16] One study even showed that a significant part of the economic benefit of a college education came from the increased ability to attract a richer mate.[17] Meanwhile, a body of evidence is beginning to show that Black people are particularly vulnerable to downward class mobility.[18]

The idea that beauty is attainable by everyone, according to Cottom, benefits white women in another way—by making it seem like there is some kind of meritocracy determining who gains the benefits of beauty.

The white women writing to Cottom were not just gaslighting her by denying that beauty existed outside of her head, they were gaslighting her by assuming her relationship to beauty was the same as theirs. This has everything to do with white privilege, but it also has everything to do with the restriction myth. To emphasize social restrictions as the harm of beauty is to emphasize the harm that everyone subject to those restrictions faces, irrespective of their location in our social hierarchy. It is #AllLivesMatter to those who are trying to draw our attention to a deeply unequal status quo.

In other words, Cottom's well-meaning correspondents were exploiting the same vulnerability in the restriction myth that conservative feminists do, but in service of an additional harm to Black women. They were erasing the fact that beauty is a hierarchy and that white women benefit from it. Society tells *everyone* what to do. So long as we describe feminism as a fight against restrictions, inequalities will continue to recede into the background, or even be actively concealed by those that benefit from them. As Cottom puts it, "self-definition" is a pretty meager form of critique, because it "hides the power being played out in the theatre of our everyday lives." The idea that we just need to redefine ourselves, and the fantasy that we can, "only serves that power. It doesn't actually challenge it."[19]

FEMINISM NEEDS A TOPOGRAPHICAL MAP

Cottom and other intersectional feminists are asking us to remake the map of the social world that the restriction myth has created. The restriction myth map is made largely from the voices of privileged women. It distorts the world by flattening it, by denying the reality of inequality.

At its most basic level, a new map must reflect oppressions besides sexism. It is a map where, as legal theorist Kimberlé Crenshaw observed when she coined the term *intersectionality*, we should expect women living at the junctures of more than one oppression to be oppressed in distinctive ways.

The map that intersectional feminism offers is also a different *type* of map from the one freedom feminism consigns us to. It's a map with depth, with mountains and valleys, that begs us to ask questions about who is at the top, who is at the bottom, and the social processes that got (and keep) them there.

It makes perfect sense that women of color would put the concept of hierarchy back in the center of the feminist toolkit. After all, we bear the brunt of a form of oppression that is undoubtedly hierarchical: racism. It's hard to even think of racism without the concept of hierarchy or inequality. Racism is an institution that treats certain bodies as though they are worth more and works to ensure that those bodies get more. It's not that no one tries to characterize racism as restriction; it's just that it's hard to deny that the effect of racism is that it gives some people more power, money, and respect than others. White supremacy is just that, a form of supremacy—where people of one race get, and are treated as though they matter, more.

Once we see that beauty as a fulcrum of racism, we can't *not* see it as harming women by maintaining hierarchy. The ability to "read" bodies as beautiful or ugly in a split-second glance is part of an elaborate, and effective, social sorting mechanism that makes it easy to divide people into deserving and undeserving. Beauty is capital, and white women's attempts to accumulate it ensure that some will have it and some will not. (If everyone is beautiful, Cottom reminds us, then beauty can't do its social job of telling us who belongs where in the pecking order.) Beauty lets us know in an instant who we should treat as though they belong at the top of the mountains on the map, and who we should leave to try to scramble their way up.

But, as we well know, beauty is not only a tool of racial or economic hierarchy. It is a tool of gender hierarchy. This idea has been at the center of feminist analysis for decades. The 1968 Miss America protest that gifted future generations the term *bra burning* was largely about the role of beauty standards in creating a hierarchy among women.

The (mostly, but definitely not all) white members of New York Radical Women, who threw various accoutrements of femininity into a trash can that day, were demonstrating rage at the physical restriction of bras and girdles.

But they also saw beauty as a symbol of the general subordination of women to men. The choice of a beauty pageant as the site of their protest was not a coincidence. Beauty, they thought, was a means of making women compete with each other for male attention—the only, and yet also deeply unpromising, gateway to success. To emphasize this point, they did not just throw bras and girdles and makeup into the trash can. They threw symbols of women's work and its generally less prestigious status, including typewriters and diapers. Women, they argued, were all fighting to be the best in what was ultimately a losing game; we were all Miss America.

These feminists from the 1960s did not fully get that beauty was a form of racial capital, but they were not completely unaware of it either. They wrote in their manifesto that the only person with a real claim to the title would have to be an Indigenous woman. They criticized the competition for only ever having chosen white Miss Americas.[20] And they pointed out something that would be radical even today: Miss America was always white because Miss America was a "support our troops" icon. Here was sexism working with racism and capitalism, which were fueling the war machine.

So, Cottom's analysis of beauty both corrects a racially incomplete picture of the function of beauty and reminds us of a concept feminism has never been able to do without: the concept of hierarchy or inequality. Beauty illustrates the concept painfully well because it involves visible ranking—whether it's a literal beauty pageant or Miley Cyrus holding herself up as the "real" beauty. To be beautiful is, by definition, to have something other people can't have. Beauty is what economists call a "positional good," one that gains its value from being inaccessible to many—not so unlike an $80 "status candle" or a real Louis Vuitton purse.

Beauty ranks women relative to one another and also ensures their inequality with men. Cottom refers to beauty as "bad capital." Beauty is bad capital, in one sense, because of its moral emptiness. But it is also bad capital because attention from men is an unreliable form of currency in so many ways. Even elite women who have used beauty to consolidate race and class privilege enjoy a precarious source of security. Everyone gets old someday, and men have whims. For all women, beauty is a source of susceptibility to sexual violence and blame for eliciting it.

Cottom shares that the day her "waist caved in" was the day she stopped being allowed to wait for the bus alone.[21]

Beauty does not just keep women below men by making us dependent on male approval; it ensures that we will literally have less than men. The beauty standards that were once straightforward pathways to male approval have not eased since 1968. If anything, they have become more demanding. Girdles are called "shapewear" now, but we are also supposed to look great without them—and to engage in new practices like Botox and special exercises that will help us avoid "tech neck." Women are now less economically dependent on men, but beauty is still important and tied to women's ability to achieve economic stability.[22] You still have to be beautiful, or at least look like you tried to be, to get the job, to be seen like you are really "showing up" at work in most industries, and to be seen as worthy or desirable by the wider public.

And since beauty doesn't happen on its own, at least to any but a few unicorns among us—we are losing a lot of time and money in our pursuit of it. A few years ago, I was surprised to see that a friend had given up her trademark straight bob for a head of short curls. She, the philosopher Heather Widdows, had begun research for a book on beauty and had learned something she couldn't unlearn.[23] Over a lifetime, she was going to spend almost an entire year of her life straightening her hair.

In case you aren't a habitual hair straightener, she also did some other math that may apply to you. Spending just two minutes a day applying face products adds up to twelve hours a year, and nearly a month over a lifetime.[24] And given the current trend toward skincare layering, many of us are talking about much, much more. Whatever your poison of choice is, spending twenty minutes a day on beauty after the age of fifteen (and I don't know about you, but I started much younger) translates to almost an entire year of twenty-four-hour days by age seventy-five.[25]

As the saying goes, time is money. Beauty is also a 500-billion-dollar-a-year industry, in which 80 to 90 percent of the purchases are made by women.[26] A recent survey revealed that women were spending an average of $8 a day just on their faces.[27] This adds up to $300,000 over a lifetime. Meanwhile, the average woman has saved just $34,000 for retirement.[28]

The idea that beauty is capital is not just metaphorical. But the metaphor of capital can help us make sense of harms that are hard to articulate in the freedom feminist vocabulary. Capital circulates; it doesn't restrict. When it does restrict, it's because some people have more and some people have less. It gains and retains its value from collective practices of valuing that are not always consciously coordinated, and whose origins cannot be easily identified.

Oppression works by putting some people above others. If feminism is a map, in the sense of an orienting tool, replete with landmarks and meanings, feminists like Cottom are asking for a map that helps us see the mountains and the valleys, not just the lines.

WE CAN'T GET THERE FROM HERE

Cottom's point is about more than just beauty. The restriction myth also crumbles in the face of intersectional feminism when we focus on other issues, like sex. In 2018, philosopher Amia Srinivasan wrote an article with a title that was bound to go viral: "Does Anyone Have the Right to Sex?" The title of the *LA Review of Books* piece was provocative enough. More incendiary still was *whose* right to sex she seemed interested in.

Srinivasan was writing about incels, a group of mostly white, cishet denizens of the manosphere who blame their lack of sexual success on the fact that women have rights now. Srinivasan's article began with the story of Elliot Rodger, who in 2014 stabbed his housemates, shot three women on the lawn of a sorority, and then went on a shooting spree around the community of Isla Vista, California. In the hours between murdering his roommates and his suicide, Rodger uploaded a video to his YouTube channel expressing his rage about his view that "the females of the human species were incapable of seeing value in me." He described his intention to target the sorority because its members were the "very girls who represent everything I hate in the female gender . . . hot, beautiful blonde girls . . . spoiled, heartless, wicked bitches."[29] Rodger, who was half-Asian and who had chosen Asian men among his murder victims, had earlier described his anger at Asian men who had the audacity to speak to white women.[30]

Before I say more about what Srinivasan *meant* by the title of her article, let me just observe that, if the restriction myth is true, incels are right that they are as victimized as women. A subset of incels, for example, emphasizes the fact that men, just like women, are subject to restrictive beauty standards. In the extreme practice known as "looksmaxing," incel men instruct one another in how to reshape their faces and bodies, sometimes suggesting surgeries that involve the breaking of cheek and jawbones—surgeries that both sound grotesque when sought by men and are not so different from surgeries routinely sought by women.

Incels appeal to the restriction myth for the same reason conservative women do: everyone is, in fact, socially restricted. Men who are told that they deserve power and that the prize of that power is being able to fuck and display "beautiful" women don't just believe this out of nowhere. They, too, are at the mercy of society's expectations. Focusing on being told what to do allows incels, who are mostly white, to present themselves as being in the same position as women, or even as victims of them.[31] All the while, they erase the real goal of changing how they look: to enable them to wield power *over* women, a power they deeply believe they deserve.

Srinivasan, of course, did not think incels were right in claiming that they were victimized by women, and by feminism. But she was arguing that they were onto *something*. There was, and is, a hierarchy of what Srinivasan calls "fuckability." Incels are not dismantling that hierarchy; they are asking to return to a time when the hierarchy favored them more—when women "knew their place," or were so economically dependent on men that they would have little choice but to sleep with men like them. As they saw it, there was a hierarchy in place in which some people were deemed desirable, and hence worthy of experiencing sexual pleasure and relationship, and some were not.[32] But the incels were wrong about how that hierarchy was structured and whom it served. And they were, of course, wrong for endorsing the old version of the hierarchy, the one in which nerdy guys like them didn't have to "make it in Silicon Valley" to be on the winning end of the deal.

It is tempting to respond to the ickiness and violence of incels by saying that no one should tell women who to sleep with. This is, in fact, how many feminists responded to Srinivsan's piece, sometimes telling her, in no uncertain terms, that it was time to stop asking the questions she was asking.[33] And it is definitely true that no one should tell women who to sleep with. No one is entitled to anyone else's body. Once again for the people in the back: no one is entitled to anyone else's body.

But this response is at once true and plainly inadequate. It is out of touch with reality to talk about the incel picture of the world as though it just denies the importance of consent. It is a picture of the world in which women are fundamentally less than men, exist to serve men, and are often talked about as less than human. It is not just that incels don't respect women's refusals; it's that their vision positions men as deserving control, even ownership, of those whom they see as belonging in a lower place on the social (or they think, natural) hierarchy.

Incels are wrong, Srinivasan thinks, to long for the bygone days when almost any man could get a woman to depend on him and perform sexual service for him. But perhaps they are not wrong that being marked as undesirable, or as desirable only for degraded or degrading forms of sexual experience, can be a form of oppression. When placement on the sexual hierarchy is intertwined with other modes of systemic oppression, this is all too clear. It is at its most glaringly obvious in the lives of women, queer and trans people, and people of color. A quick perusal of the dating apps, Srinivasan tells us, is all it takes to see expression after expression of blithe devaluation of certain bodies. "NO DICKS, NO FATS, NO BLACKS, NO ARABS, NO RICE NO SPICE, MASC FOR MASC."

Famously, these are codes for sorting potential interests out of one's GRINDR profile, but sexual preferences like these are by no means exclusive to gay men. If anything, Srinivasan argues, the reason many of us non-GRINDR users have heard about them is likely that queer people are used to having their sexual lives criticized, and are thus, for better or worse, likely more capable of turning a critical eye on themselves.[34] The idea that TINDR is better is laughable. Data about race and app-based dating are certainly not any prettier, revealing that Asian men and Black women (Tressie McMillan Cottom pen pals take note) are the subjects of a disproportionate number of left swipes.[35] Until 2020, when TINDR decided to do something to respond to the murder of George Floyd, TINDR users could literally filter out entire ethnicities.[36]

To call "preferences" like these racist, misogynistic, and transphobic is almost euphemistic. But it is unclear where there is even room to name them in the language of restriction. It's not as though such preferences result more from social shaping than preferences that do less harm, like preferences for funny partners or ones who also like science fiction—or just preferences for ice cream over cake. It's not even obvious that any individual is restricted by them. Being less desired than others needn't mean that one is being told to be or do anything.

Think, for example, of the harms that some women face as a result of being rendered either unfuckable, or as too fuckable. Black women, for example, do not just face the problem of disproportionate left swiping; they face the problem of being seen as *too* available for certain forms of sexual encounter. Since the time of slavery, the image of Black women as especially desiring of sex has contributed to the idea that they cannot be raped.[37] As Srinivasan puts it, the "bodies of brown and Black women—especially when they belong to women who are also poor, incarcerated, or undocumented," are, "in an important sense seen as supremely fuckable."[38]

Think also of those who are approached frequently by racial fetishists, such as Asians of all genders who find that their partners expect submission. Think of disabled people, especially women, who encounter both fetishists and the reality of desexualization by a world that infantilizes them, sometimes sending them partners who just want to "take care of them."[39] Everyone is restricted by our limited notions of which bodies are desirable, but not all of us are equally bearing the consequences.

The restriction myth does not just make it difficult to see or name these harms by making them the same as those faced by people in dominant groups. It makes it difficult to imagine a future without them, where the hierarchy of desirability does not have a stranglehold on how we relate to one another. This is because the restriction myth comes with a type of perverse power: the power to make feminist criticism look like oppression. The conservative "feminists" draw on the same perverse power to call actual feminists hypocrites; Cottom's pen pals draw on it to reduce her cultural critique to a lack of self-esteem. The rub is that it's difficult to change a system of value without (kind of, at least) telling someone they are doing something wrong. But if telling someone what to do is always oppressive, feminism is inert.

This is particularly evident in conversations around sex. Sex positivity, an idea that originally included the idea that fighting for women's sexual pleasure meant transforming the dominant culture,[40] has become reduced by many to the idea that we cannot interrogate sexual practices as long as they are consensual.[41] This has been a response to two very real, very important facts about sex in a world that is both sexist and homophobic—that women have been expected to give sex regardless of whether they desire it, and that shame around sex can burden those who have already been discouraged from seeing themselves as worthy of pleasure. But the sexual hierarchy Srinivasan is talking about bumps up against the shortcomings of treating consent as a border beyond which we ask no questions. Should we really dismiss attempts to rethink our desires in less hierarchical ways as fundamentally, problematically restrictionist?

If it is, then feminism cannot say anything about those who, for example write "no rice no spice" in their profiles, or who see Black women's bodies as spaces for enacting their racist fantasies. It is true that the solutions here are not simple. It is also true that attempts to legislate around them have been wrapped up in a racist, sexist, homophobic, and transphobic carceral system. But should our rejection of carceral solutions extend to a rejection of cultural critique? If it does, it's all too clear whom feminism is leaving out. As Srinivasan puts it "a feminism that totally abjures the political critique of desire is a feminism with little to say about the injustices of exclusion and misrecognition suffered by the women who arguably need feminism the most."

There is a difference between saying that individual people need autonomy in their sexual lives and refusing to criticize *hierarchical patterns* and the society that produces them. Yet we have to try to move the needle, with however light a hand, on our prevailing systems of value. And this is, in fact, what radical activists challenging the sexual hierarchy are trying to do. Fat activists, Srinivasan points out, challenge people to see themselves as beautiful. For many fat people, this requires unpacking years of internalized fatphobia, usually entwined with both racism and capitalism in complicated ways. The process for self-reprogramming has to be sought, often with help from the community, but anyone who has internalized these messages knows that this reprogramming also requires changing what one already thinks.

The call to reprogram the self to dismantle the hierarchy of desire has a long history in a movement that Srinivasan mentions briefly, the movement to recode Black bodies as beautiful. This movement, which began in the 1960s, saw something about beauty and sexuality that today's watered-down version of sex-positive feminism has eroded: the deep connection between aesthetics and politics. To wear a hair pick or an Afro, in the 1960s, was often to declare allegiance to the Black power movement, a movement that sought political sovereignty and fundamental changes to our economic system. The white-dominated aesthetic was an expression of broader white control over the system of value. To assert Black beauty was to wrest control over our cultural system of value from white hands.

The restriction myth casts movements like fat activism and Black is beautiful as enemies that forever saddle us with more and more *shoulds*. If shoulds were the same thing as oppression, the right answer would be for feminists to tell these movements to stop. But oppression does not just harm us by telling us what to do. It demands labor and time from some in the service of others, says that some people matter in ways that others do not, subjects some groups of people to deprivation and violence. We need a feminism that is willing to ask questions about our existing systems of value, and who they set up to win and lose. It's hard to imagine a way of confronting these questions without being open to sometimes telling ourselves, and even others, that what we are already doing is not great.

To ask questions about hierarchies of desire and desirability immediately leads us into questions about whose interests our current sexual order is serving and whose it is not. The politics of desirability tell us a story about whose interests are shaping the social order; being desired is a gateway to a number of things, ranging from financial stability and the consolidation of class privilege to love and affection. But training our gaze on questions of hierarchy also reveals, perhaps surprisingly, that being desired is not always a clear gateway to the thing it might most clearly seem to facilitate: pleasure. At least not for women.

I was reminded of this during a late night of hate-watching. The show was *GoopLab*, a Netflix front for Gwyneth Paltrow's pseudoscience/lifestyle brand. The episode was called "The Pleasure Is Ours." It depicted something I had rarely seen onscreen before, a woman masturbating to orgasm. It was not a simulation, not really done for an audience, and certainly not done for the male gaze that is the intended audience of most mainstream porn.

The show's schtick was, on consideration at least, to make old things seem new and even sciencey (ayahuasca for white people, anyone?), so perhaps I should not have been waiting for a recipe for pleasure as earth-shattering as the scene itself. But I was not prepared to find the guru of this episode to be the same one I had read about in books describing 1970s radical feminist workshops. Betty Dodson was her name, and I had plenty of memories of looking at her sex manual secretly as a preteen, plucked from any number of my friends' mothers' bookshelves.

Dodson, who left the world later that year, was, by anyone's account, a fierce feminist whose activism for sexual pleasure should go down in history. She fought for women's right to sex, or more precisely sex they actually enjoyed, by transforming her Manhattan apartment into a space where she taught literally thousands of women how to achieve orgasm. But I was puzzled about why she was still boundary pushing in 2020. Perhaps it was still the case that most women believed in vaginal orgasms or thought it was wrong for them to enjoy sex.

Or perhaps this was another problem-solution mismatch that we had the restriction myth to thank for.

The truth was that it was probably a bit of both. One thing was clear, though, and this was why there was a market for the episode to begin with: cis women having sex with cis men are having bad sex. Like, really bad sex. A recent study of fifty-two thousand adults revealed that 95 percent of straight male participants revealed reaching orgasm at their last sexual encounter, compared to just 65 percent of women.[42] A representative study in Canada found the number to be 86 to 62 percent.[43] Slightly earlier studies report gaps more like 90 percent to 40 percent.[44]

Bad sex is bad enough, but just as beauty is not just about beauty and desirability is not just about desire, pleasure is not just about pleasure. Indifference to women's sexual pleasure fuels rape culture. A culture that normalizes heterosexual sexual encounters that are indifferent to women's pleasure—as ours unmistakably does; researchers continually find young people reporting that men "need" orgasms and women do not—ensures that the line will be gray between "regular" sex and sex that women do not want to have.[45] Similarly, the idea that women do not really need sex, and have to be "coaxed" into wanting it, has propped up many a nonconsensual encounter.

But to start to tell this story is already to chart terrain that the restriction myth is unprepared for. Today's social world is not as restrictive around sex as the one Dodson and her peers navigated when she started giving workshops in the 1970s. There are obvious indicators: More women have sex outside of marriage. *Sex-positive* is a widely used term. Rather than sleeping in separate beds, couples on TV are depicted mid-encounter, even in primetime. The internet abounds with mainstream porn. It makes accessible with a click an unprecedented number of resources about sexual health and hosts communities for people with non-normative modes of sexual expression. Adolescents' knowledge about sexuality is not limited to a single off-limits book on a friend's parents' bookshelf. None of this is to say that sexual restrictions no longer exist, nor reasons for women to feel shame; depictions of women receiving oral sex are still the exception rather than the rule, and even I had to wait for Goop to show me an image of a woman having an orgasm whose intended audience was not straight men.

But there are some less obvious indicators that women are no longer being told to abstain from sex, or abstain from enjoying it. In today's pop culture women talk about wanting to be perceived as sexual, irrespective of whether they are actually having fun during sex. In a particularly gross episode of the top "feminist" podcast *Call Her Daddy*, Sofia Franklyn and Alexandra Cooper celebrate the agency involved in "using your ranking" to hook up. Beautiful women, they say, should feel free to "starfish" and receive pleasure. But, if you're a four, you should give as much as possible and rush out before asking for anything for yourself. They even joke that that may mean accepting a request to exit through the window. Women also report frequently faking orgasms, citing the reason that the ability to come and come quickly is part of pleasing one's partner.[46]

One of the landmark cultural moments of #MeToo wasn't a story about rape or sexual harassment. It was a piece of viral content in perhaps its rarest form—a seven-thousand-some-word short story from the *New Yorker*. In *Cat Person*, the fictional twenty-year-old Margot dates a lowkey angry man in his thirties whose pickup line is "Concession-stand girl, give me your phone number."

Somewhere in the middle of their cringey sexual encounter, she decides she doesn't want to keep going. But she doesn't tell him—largely because she doesn't feel like she can find a way to say no that doesn't make her seem like she ordered food at a restaurant and is now sending it back. She has been acquiescing in someone else's narrative all along, and the inertia of the scripted encounter combined with the need to seem nice carries her through a sexual encounter she wishes she were not having.

The story went viral because women recognized themselves in the sex. They even joked that the author, Kristen Roupenian, had recorded their inner monologues. The cultural conversation we've been having since about bad, unwanted, but consensual sex offers an implicit indictment of the restriction myth that echoes Srinivasan's. In these stories, women consent to sex they find creepy, boring, bad, or just not fun. And—if their taking to the internet is to be believed—they want to talk about it and change the conditions that give rise to it. They are not questioning whether consent should be the floor of sexual experience.

They are suggesting that consent is not enough—and that our view that anything consensual is beyond cultural critique is getting in the way of our ability to imagine the world differently.

The bad sex these "consent is the floor" critics describe has a particular flavor, not so much defined by feelings of shame or lack of bodily knowledge, but rather by partners who don't get it: who use sex to preserve their egos, who don't bother to check whether orgasms are real or fake. These women complain, not so much about feeling like they can't explore or enjoy their bodies, but about feeling like men are not on their team, at least where pleasure is concerned.

Women's depictions of bad sex gesture at a bigger world that is not on their team, not so much in telling them not to be sexual, but rather in the sense of constructing their sexuality as subordinate. Sex researcher Sara McClelland asked women to describe negative sexual experiences and found that women used certain words that men did not. One of these words was *degrading*.[47] More generally, McClelland found that there was a "bottom" to women's bad sex that wasn't nearly as frequent for straight men. Women's bad sex was not just unpleasurable; it was also likely to involve pain or the reliving of past sexual trauma.

In other words, the orgasm gap reflects gender inequality, not just the restriction of women's sexuality. It no doubt reflects other inequalities as well; it is not as though the hierarchies of desirability stop at the door to the bedroom. Women of color narrate a variety of ways that racist fetishes interfere with their ability to experience pleasure, such as being hypersexualized, or being expected to be submissive when one isn't into that.[48] Structural racial inequalities play a role too. As I'll discuss in chapter 5, Black women have long noted that social services like welfare and foster care interfere with the ability of poor women to have sex with the people they actually want to have sex with.

With all of these facts in sight, our single-minded focus on the "learn to pleasure yourself" solution seems to reflect our commitment to the restriction myth more than our willingness to really encounter the problem. To the extent that cultural expectations are driving the orgasm gap, they aren't just women's expectations; they are a toxic combination of women's and men's expectations. It's not rocket science that to see that an orgasm *gap* means that some people are getting more and others are getting less—not just that some people aren't getting enough.

But it's just this more/less relationship that the restriction myth turns our eyes from, and it's to the detriment of women in more ways than just preventing orgasms.

DO WE HAVE TO BE VOLCANOES?

A not-so-long time ago in a not-so-faraway place, there was no orgasm gap.[49] Eighty percent of women having sex with men reported that they experienced orgasm during every single sexual encounter. In some metrics, women even seemed to have a slight sexual edge over men. When asked if they had left their last tryst happy, 75 percent of women said "yes," compared to 74 percent of men.[50]

These stats are not from a science fiction novel. They are from Europe in the 1980s. But this isn't your typical progressive "everything is better in Europe" story. These sexually satisfied women were, at the time, unicorns even among the Europeans. A literal stone's throw away lived women whose sex lives were much more similar to ours; only 63 percent of these less satisfied women reported reaching orgasm during every sexual encounter, and only 52 percent said their last encounter made them happy.[51]

The difference between these two groups was not that women in the first group were watching more shows about how to find and name their body parts. It was the Berlin Wall. The secret ingredient in women's pleasure seemed to be . . . socialism.

The above statistics came from research studies by Kurt Starke, Walter Friedrich, Ulrich Clement, and scientists at the Gewis-Institut Hamburg, part of a larger trend in Eastern Europe during the twentieth century of devoting public funds to the study of women's sexuality. In nearby Poland, a country known for the prevalence of Catholicism, an entire discipline of sexology emerged in the 1970s and 1980s as the practical arm of a similar research program. According to anthropologist Agnieszka Koscianska, Polish sex therapists and academics developed a "holistic" understanding of the role of sex in women's lives, an understanding that included not just biological arousal but also conceptions of love and intimacy and which "stressed the importance of social and cultural contexts for women's pleasure."[52]

Kristen Ghodsee, chair of Russian and Eastern European Studies at the University of Pennsylvania, has extensively researched the lives of women in Eastern Europe and has come to a simple conclusion: socialist women had more fun. The reason was not, to be clear, the brutal form of one-party rule that typified twentieth-century state socialism. Their sexual fulfillment resulted from a set of public policies, many of which might not initially seem to have anything to do with sex at all. They included investments in basic needs, like food and healthcare, pursued partly from an understanding that people deserve access to leisure. Among the policies more directly tied to gender were maternity leave and subsidized childcare, access to reproductive healthcare including abortion, and even inducements for men to do more housework.[53]

In other words, socialist countries were investing in equality—gender and otherwise.

Because these societies saw inequality as the problem, they recognized solutions that are not readily visible to those who see the pleasure gap as a problem of restriction. The orgasm gap was recognized as, well, a *gap*: a difference in access to well-being between two groups of people. But even orgasm "gap" is a bit of a misnomer, since it's not just that cis women who have sex with men are having less pleasure than men; it's that their lack of pleasure is partly due to men's behavior.

The socialists did not need to shoehorn the orgasm gap into a form of restriction, because their interest in inequality gave them the conceptual resources to see it for what it was. Inequality is a relationship, and in this case, it is a relationship in which one group having more partially causes the other group to have less. As the saying goes, it takes (at least) two to tango. I'll say more about this in chapter 2. Recognizing that inequality is a relationship means recognizing that changing the world for women is not always about changing *women*. Sometimes it's about changing men.

The policies pursued by these socialist countries reflected that awareness. As early as the 1950s, socialist governments were concerned about the gender division of labor in the home and tried to get men to do more housework. (When men were recalcitrant, they didn't give up on the idea that women needed to do less of it; they tried to socialize it.)[54] Even when they gave up on getting men to do more housework, they did not give up on changing men's hearts and minds. In the 1970s and 1980s, the Polish government distributed free booklets about women's anatomy . . . to men.[55] As Ghodsee notes, it's hard not to think about the light in which this casts the contemporary US, which can't even seem to provide comprehensive sex education in public schools, let alone education about pleasure.

The idea that men doing housework would lead to better sex for women, an idea available to Eastern Europeans in the twentieth century, was the topic of a more recent spate of headlines on this side of the Atlantic. A 2016 study showed that, among mixed-gender US couples, men that did between 35 and 65 percent of the housework had the most sex.[56] A 2022 study in Australia revealed that couples with greater household equality experienced greater sexual desire for their partners.[57] (Consistent with the idea that men's behavior partly causes the orgasm gap, the study also found that women who did most of the housework had diminished desire for their partners, but not for solo sex.)

These headlines got as far as joking that men might be motivated to do more housework if they knew it would help them get some, but mostly didn't connect the dots to *women's* sexual pleasure. The joke was that men who did housework were hotter (and they probably are, to their partners), but there's also the fact that women who do less housework are probably just less tired. Women do almost twice as much unpaid work as men.[58] Recent evidence shows that men spend about twice as much time at leisure than women. The old sitcom trope would have us believe that a nation full of women saying "not tonight, honey" are just cold fish, but maybe they are just too damn tired. Maybe they actually do have a headache.

The lesson of better sex under socialism is partly a lesson about what feminists can gain from thinking in terms of changing distributions instead of removing restrictions. To ask ourselves the questions, "Who has more, who has less, and why?" saves us, not just from the flattening effect of the restriction myth (everyone is oppressed because everyone is restricted), but also from its tendency to remove material conditions and dominant groups from our arsenal of potential feminist strategies. The strategy of bubble baths and jade eggs puts the onus on women to change, not men. It gives women extra homework and more to spend their money on.

But it doesn't have to be this way. The sex and socialism story teaches us that changing material conditions—not just amorphous social norms—can help end oppression, even when the goods at stake are intangible, like sexual pleasure or desirability. But intersectional feminism also invites us to think even more deeply about distribution—to adopt a willingness to question whether the things we are distributing are actually worth having at all. When we think in terms of equality, we can start to think about whether inequality is being maintained, not just by some having more and some having less, but by our understanding of what is of value in the first place. Sometimes, what is unequally distributed is the power to set the standard of value to begin with.

This is part of Cottom's point about beauty, race, and capital. Part of white supremacy is the ability to *define* beauty so that it is definitionally not-Black, and to establish a set of social practices around it. Thus, beauty is "bad capital." Notwithstanding the proclamations of teen magazines and Cottom's correspondents, beauty is defined by the fact that everyone cannot possess it—and the standard of value is defined in a way that guarantees that members of oppressed groups will never have enough. The path to dismantling inequality is to explode that system of value.

We can turn this lesson about inequality back on the orgasm gap. It seems clear that women are not getting what they deserve in the realm of sex, but who defines good sex to begin with?[59] The entire idea that we can measure the goodness of sex in terms of the presence or absence of orgasm seems, in the face of this question, a little bit sus. The idea that sex ends with climax—that climax is its ultimate point—seems to derive from the assumption that what feels good to cis straight men with penises is what feels good for everyone.

So prevalent is this view that straight people, even in the 2020s, have trouble defining sex as something other than penile-vaginal intercourse.[60] This, in turn, results in culturally coding sexual practices like oral sex, which are more likely to give women orgasms, as "foreplay" rather than the "main event"—as if there has to be one main event at all. Women who have sex with men cite "just wanting the encounter to end" as one of their reasons for faking an orgasm.[61] It is difficult to overemphasize not just the sexism but also the heteronormativity of this picture. Many of the "unrestrict yourself" solutions to the orgasm gap emphasize the supposed difficulty of sexual pleasure for cis women, but 86 percent of lesbians report having an orgasm during every sexual encounter.[62] Yes, women are more likely to know something about other women's bodies, but women who have sex with women are also likely to have different definitions of sex, and the types of pleasure available in it.

Closing the orgasm gap may require more than expecting women to erupt whenever they have sex. It may be about questioning our tendency to assume that pleasure and eruption are one and the same. But this, too, means asking questions about whose experiences get to be the standard for good sex—questions about hierarchy and not just restriction.

Socialists were probably more likely to "get" the problem of the orgasm gap for another reason, one that tells us more about the downsides of the restriction myth than the upsides of equality. To understand it, we need to think more deeply about the hold restriction imagery has on us. We don't just think of women as dormant volcanoes. We also talk about feminine socialization as a "circle of entrapment"[63] and advise women to "break the rules." The image of the home as a space of confinement is the white feminist image par excellence. Even the more radical, intersectional feminists among us can lapse into reducing the ways we can harm each other to being simply "barriers to other people's paths" to "self-love."

But is restriction the only possible way of being harmed, or are we invested in restriction imagery for other reasons? Part of my goal in this book is to persuade you of the latter, that the appeal of restriction imagery stems not from its ability to accurately describe social reality but from our investment in systems of oppression besides gender inequality. In chapter 5, I'll talk about how the idea that culture and tradition restrict stems from colonialism and white supremacy.

But for now, let's talk about capitalism.

The restriction myth comes with metaphorical baggage. The idea of restriction is difficult to unravel from the idea of potential. When we think of being restricted, we often think of pent-up energy, of what might happen if that energy was allowed to be free and express itself. This is the stuff of pretty much every self-help trend—from the idea that microworkouts enable people to exercise more by removing the "time barrier" to the idea that when we let go of that scarcity mindset, we unleash the power to do more.[64] It undergirds generations of feminist messaging about all the unexpected things women will do if we are just given the chance. You can fill in the blank with "play sports" or "become a CEO" or "take off our veils," but the idea that restrictions are dams waiting to burst is everywhere. It shows up in metaphors like breaking glass ceilings and creating "superhighways." To be restricted is to be thwarted, to be unable to do what one would otherwise naturally do.

The idea that that potential will just flow if we give it a chance is at the heart not just of the volcano metaphor but also of our prevailing economic mythology. The idea that if we stop telling people what to do, things will take their natural course is central to the well-worn story about how free markets can supposedly save us from all manner of social ills. Get rid of the restrictions, the classical economic mantra goes, and the market will be able to deliver the desirable social incomes it is almost magically supposed to give us.

Leaning too heavily on this way of viewing the world yields a certain model of how social change happens. According to it, you lift restrictions and whatever is restricted develops on its own. This poses two related problems for thinking about sexism.

First, it shifts the labor of making social change onto those whom the change is supposed to benefit. If your liberation comes *naturally* from being given more space, we don't have to think about the work you put into it as work. This is why we, as a society, have not so much as batted an eye at a set of prescriptions for closing the orgasm gap that is effectively a to-do list for women.

Your average article on the orgasm gap will ask you to do some combination of things like take a bubble bath, masturbate, buy a jade egg, read about the clitoris, spice up your sex life, and talk to your partner. It will say nothing about your paid or unpaid workload, or just how little you are sleeping. It will instead do something more insidious, something cultural theorist Rosalind Gill notes is central to the cooptation of feminism by neoliberalism; it will make acts of work look like acts of leisure. There is indeed an entire sub-industry devoted to getting women to believe orgasm will unleash their potential to be more successful. Katherine Rowland, the author of a book about the orgasm gap, tells the story of receiving a "here's a successful person's morning ritual" newsletter with a twist: incorporate orgasm. Its absurdity was made apparent by the moment she happened to read it in. She was in the midst of serving breakfast to her toddlers.[65]

The idea that unleashing orgasms will improve women's lot is just a particularly mystical version of a common freedom feminist trope. Sheryl Sandberg, author of the early 2010s corporate feminist advice manual *Lean In*, famously said that women needed to resist the "tyranny of low expectations," as though expecting women to work more and harder was the path to feminist change. Betty Friedan argued in the 1960s that working outside the home would unleash creative and artistic power; she seems not to have noticed that work, even of the self-actualizing sorts available primarily to people of the upper classes, was still work—less still that the housework and childcare that these women would leave behind would need to be done, by women of color.

One thing the socialists seemed to be onto, which mainstream feminists are not, is that social change for women does not always need to be accomplished *through the labor of* women. Sometimes the path to liberation is less work, not more. The socialist vision of better sex wasn't just men doing more household chores. It was women spending less time working and less time worrying.

Working and worrying have two things in common: one fuels the other because we are always one accident away from the healthcare emergency that will bankrupt us, and both are notorious orgasm killers. Ask any popular media article on the orgasm gap, and the first advice you will get is to find some time for yourself. The same studies that show that more equitable couples have more sex also show that pretty much all of us are having less sex than a generation ago. We can blame smartphones, or we can realize that our overwork culture is taking its toll. It's amazing to imagine the time and space a person might receive from a social safety net—bodily time and space, and mental time and space. But we won't even be able to see the need for rest if we think that women's work flows forth naturally and does not need to be compensated, just unleashed.[66]

Unfortunately, having time and space to yourself, let alone a social safety net, are impossible to make happen on your own. This brings us to the second problem with the "lift restrictions" theory of social change. Often, making change for women and other oppressed groups requires something other than leaving alone; it requires active social support. By making the process of social change seem natural and inevitable, and by focusing on lifting restrictions to the exclusion of other strategies, the restriction myth draws our attention away from the fact that fighting inequality often costs money.

On the ground, the restriction myth has pushed us toward "feminist" strategies that don't cost anything—and as a result have been most useful to the most privileged of women. Taking time for oneself for leisurely orgasm exploration is not possible for everyone. Many of us simply do not have the time and space. This is to say nothing of what it would take to recover or discover pleasure if your body is broken from unsafe work, or if you need therapy to process your trauma history. Work, for many of us, is unrelenting, and therapy isn't free. (This isn't the Poland of the 1970s, after all).

The restriction myth emphasizes (minorly) changing minds to the exclusion of active support, leading to a feminism that prioritizes elite women across a variety of feminist domains. It's hard in a post-*Dobbs* world not to pine for a time when most people thought abortion should be unrestricted. But we shouldn't forget that framing abortion only as a private choice, one the state shouldn't restrict, does not make abortion access a reality for all the people who need it—less still does it offer an argument for a full spectrum of reproductive healthcare. Lifting restrictions doesn't do much for the Indigenous woman who can't get an abortion because of the Hyde Amendment, which prohibits the use of federal funds, including funds to the Indian Health Service, from being used to fund abortions. Nor does it assist the trans guy who needs to freeze his eggs in order to be able to have a baby when he is ready.

The restriction myth does not just crowd out responses to oppression that cost money; it transforms problems that need material support into ones that just require a change in mindsets. "Tyranny of low expectations" talk psychologizes the structural,[67] even in ways that blame the oppressed for their own oppression. A chapter of Mikki Kendall's best-selling *Hood Feminism* is called "The Hood Doesn't Hate Smart People." As I mentioned in the book's introduction, Kendall names a tendency that runs through not just everyday talk but also educational policy: a tendency to assume that "Black culture" discourages educational attainment. Kendall's own account of being a Black nerd whose grandmother had lived through Jim Crow and would never let her "throw away her chance at a diploma" weaves a very different story.[68] The cause of educational inequality isn't Black people's attitudes about education; it's institutional racism that comprises a lack of investment in schools attended by children of color. But the restriction myth ensures we will think otherwise, while blaming victims to boot.

Perhaps it's time to look for ways to remake the map, other than assuming that women are volcanoes just longing to erupt.

There is an alternative to understanding feminism as a movement to liberate individual women from social restrictions. It is an alternative that is alive and well in the politics of feminists who think about forms of oppression besides gender. We can understand feminism as a movement against hierarchy or inequality, against the structures that subordinate women as a group.

To think in terms of inequality is to center the exact thing the restriction myth encourages us to forget: the fact that our society, including the systems of restriction it puts in place, sort people—not just by naming or categorizing or forming expectations of them, but by slotting them into different roles in a system of benefit and harm, advantage and disadvantage. We are all told what beauty is, but only some of us have to rely on it to be seen as worthy, and only some of us can use it as a tool to reproduce our privileges. We are all told what sex is supposed to be like, but some of us are having orgasms and others are not.

We need to break up with the restriction myth, not just to stop trying to solve the wrong problem, but also so that we can avoid endorsing solutions that, however well-intentioned, get in the way. If social critique, no matter who executes it and how carefully, is always understood as an exercise of restriction, we are stuck with the status quo. If we think social change is a process of unleashing "natural" forces, we will keep coming up with solutions that may serve the most privileged women, but burden the most oppressed.

Still, we might wonder, isn't there something to the idea that patriarchy harms women by restricting us?

Alexandra Kollontai had an answer to this question. The early twentieth-century feminist[69] theorist and Russian revolutionary was no stranger to being silenced for her views about sex. She spent much of her young life in literal exile because of a number of warrants for her arrest.[70] Though she was spared the dire fate of many dissidents because she remained active in the communist party,[71] her criticism of the nuclear family meant that she lived out the last chapter of her life outside of Russia, as Russia's ambassador to Sweden.

Kollontai was a dreamer, and she dreamed about a freer form of love—at least freer than imagined by most people in her time.[72] And she thought that reducing inequality was the way to get there. How, she argued, could women love freely when they were so dependent on men? Women's sex and love lives were dictated by their need to make sure they would not end up dishonored and impoverished when they had children. How could they really love when the idea of love was so bound up with a capitalist concept of property, when people dreamed of "possessing" their lovers, and when women's sexuality had to be highly regulated so that men would know that their heirs were really theirs?[73]

So, Kollontai, along with a cadre of revolutionaries, fought to legalize abortion, socialize laundry and cooking, decriminalize homosexuality, and make it easier to get divorced.[74] But she did not think we could know in advance what sex would look like in a more egalitarian world. Eros, she wrote, "would have to be transformed." But as for what it would look like, "not even the boldest fantasy is capable of providing the answer to this question."[75]

The feminist future is still uncharted territory.

CHAPTER 2

THE INDIVIDUALISM MYTH

Having It All or Doing It All?

It was 7:04 p.m. on a March evening in 2021 when the last roll of toilet paper disappeared from Lily Potkin's downstairs bathroom.[1] It had not been stolen. It had met its end the way most rolls of toilet paper do: someone used the last piece and just went on with their day.

After about twelve hours, a cry came from the bathroom. But Potkin was not going to answer this time. Just like she had not moved the "sausage of death" that had been rotting on the kitchen counter for days or washed enough spoons for her husband to stir his coffee. She was on strike, and it was going down on Twitter.

When the toilet paper reappeared stacked copiously, sloppily, and passive-aggressively in a highly visible "Costco-like fashion," Potkin knew she had touched a nerve. It was almost as though her husband and children had realized that toilet paper does not replace itself.

Every time she was in an office meeting, Ruchiya Tulshyan would start to wonder if she was in an episode of Mad Men.[2] *When it was time to order lunch, all of the heads would turn to her. Taking the minutes? Her job too. Scheduling the next meeting? Also her job.*

But this was worse than an episode of Mad Men. *It was the twenty-first century, and she wasn't the secretary. She was a strategist. But she was the only woman of color in the room.*

───────────

It dawned on Jess Zimmerman one day that there was really only one thing she was an expert in.[3] At least, if being an expert means having spent at least ten thousand hours practicing something. That thing was helping straight dudes process their feelings. She wondered if she should put "agony aunt" on her résumé, especially since she'd been doing this work since high school. She was a much less experienced dog sitter, and she could charge for that. It turns out that those years of late-night texts fielding questions like "How do I make her fall back in love with me?" really do add up.

Everywhere you turn, women are talking about emotional labor. We want to be paid for it (see Lauren Chief Elk's viral hashtag #GiveYour MoneytoWomen). We want it to be recognized as a skill (after all, isn't "problem-solving" supposed to be one?).[4] We are sick of it, like, literally. Women whose jobs demand long hours are three times as likely to get heart disease, cancer, and diabetes, likely because of the additional hours they rack up working inside the home.[5]

A recent *Guardian* column responded to this groundswell by describing emotional labor as feminism's "next frontier."[6] On one hand, emotional labor does seem high on the list of things that women are demanding action about *now*. Women are expressing, all over social media at least, that we are done. On another, though, describing women's unacknowledged labor as a new feminist concern is downright weird. As far back as the 1930s, Black and Chicana domestic workers rallied around the cry that they were workers, not "part of the family."[7] In 1975, in Iceland, women went on strike from paid and unpaid work, which resulted in the outlawing of gender discrimination and the election of a woman president.[8] For decades, feminist academics have been writing about the "second shift," the "informal economy," and otherwise declaring that labors of love are still labors.[9]

In other words, what is now going by the name of "emotional labor" is pretty much feminism's oldest concern. Why, then, does it seem new? One answer is that we have done very little to solve it. There's still no mandatory paid parental leave or subsidized early childcare in the United States. Domestic workers remain the largest category of victims of labor trafficking.[10] Women do a whopping two hours more of housework a day than men.[11] But to notice that the problem persists is just to restate the problem: if the problem is so old, and feminists have been talking about it for generations, why haven't we solved it yet?

The answer is that the feminism that has gone mainstream has forgotten this problem. And the forgetting isn't accidental. The freedom myth has taught us to keep looking away.

If we want to understand why what everyone now is calling "emotional labor" but is more accurately referred to as something like "undervalued labor traditionally assigned to women," has been on the back burner for so long, we need to dig into the ways that freedom feminism is *individualistic*.[12]

It's not just individualistic in the way that is clear on the surface, in the way that has to do with women self-promoting under capitalism and calling it feminism. Yes, for many women, feminism seems limited to talk of being a #girlboss or a bawse. Yes, we live in a time where girl scammers like the Anna Delveys of the world can say with righteous indignation that they had to commit fraud to get multimillon-dollar loans, because no one on Wall Street would give a young woman a chance. But the fact that mainstream feminism can so easily be turned into an argument for getting rich speaks to a deeper form of individualism at the heart of how we talk about feminism—a way of talking about feminism that even the more woke among us can unknowingly fall prey to.

Freedom feminism sells us a certain understanding of how we should measure feminist progress, of how we will know we have arrived—or are, at least, *arriving*. If the harm of sexism is the way it places restrictions on individual women, the way forward is the lifting of restrictions on individual women. Can women wear what they want? Check. Can they dream of being scientists and presidents? Check. Can they ask for raises? Check.

I call the idea that feminist change happens when individual women are freer than they once were the "individualism myth." The reason it's a myth is almost shockingly simple. Individual women being freer is not the same thing as women as a group getting closer to equality. If we call it a day when we notice that individual lives are improving, we will miss the fact that we are still nowhere near equality with men. Being better off than you used to be is also not the same thing as *all women* being better off than they used to be. In fact, your being better off might happen at other women's expense.

HAVING IT ALL OR DOING IT ALL?

Every few months, an older woman tells me I am lucky to have a career. Sometimes they are making an important point about social class, about how rare it is to have a job that provides healthcare, and a job that I actually *want* to do while raising my children. I get to write this book while my parental-leaved-up husband is taking care of our younger child in the next room, and, though this shouldn't count as lucky, I get that it does.

But most of the time the luck argument is about something else. It's about how I supposedly "have it all." The generations before mine, the story goes, had to make a choice between having a career and having children, they say. I, on the other hand don't have to choose. I am living out the "ultra-glam aspiration" of "a well-oiled life" that balances career and friendship and children and hobbies "with myself at the controls."

We all know that the phrase "You should feel grateful" should come with a warning sign. Whether we are being told we should feel grateful that that catcaller found us attractive, or that we should shut up about pay inequity in the United States because we are lucky not to live in Afghanistan,[13] claims that women should be grateful usually work at cross-purposes with feminism. This "You should feel grateful that you have it all," is no exception, even when unintentional.

In fact, when you're in the thick of it in the 2020s, the phrase "having it all" sounds like kind of a cruel joke. Growing up, I was sold the bill of goods many women raised in the 1990s and 2000s were—and are. "In a bid to undo the generational trauma of women having no agency, we were told to spend our 20s focusing on our careers, leaning in, and working hard, figuring out what job gives us meaning. Everything else—love, kids, home, etc.—would fall into place later."[14] I grew up to find myself instead teaching from the bathtub with no childcare in 2020, and taking work calls covered in toddler food. And because I got to have this experience without fear of losing my job, I am undoubtedly one of the lucky ones.

But it's not just me who thinks that having it all isn't what it was cracked up to be. In 2020, even Michelle Obama said that the idea of having it all was "a lie."[15] The idea of having it all has been replaced with joke after joke about "doing it all." Which sounds about right. And it is taking its toll. The average mom today spends almost twice as much time on childcare each day than her counterpart would have in 1965. Moms are 28 percent more likely to experience burnout on the job than dads.[16] If you, like me, have spent huge swaths of the last years attempting to work with a crying baby in your arms, or a toddler climbing into your lap, you won't be surprised to learn that women were almost twice as likely as men to leave the workforce during the pandemic.[17]

If you haven't, you may still have heard about how moms in the pandemic were doing things like gathering outdoors just to scream at the top of their lungs.[18] Women have since returned to the workforce in large numbers, and professional childcare and schooling have mostly resumed, but many of the industries in which women were concentrated have failed to return to their pre-pandemic levels.[19]

There is clearly a disconnect between the feminist dream of women being free from the expectation that they devote themselves to their children and the reality of taking work calls covered in toddler food. But this disconnect isn't just about reality failing to match our expectations. Me working with a fine powder of rice cracker dust in my hair is not a perversion of the dream. It is that dream turned into reality. If all we wanted was for women to be freed from the expectation that they only be mothers, we succeeded. But if this is what success looks like, maybe something has always been wrong with the dream?

As long as we look at the world through a freedom feminist lens, the problem of women's overwork will not appear to be a problem. This is partly due to the restriction myth. Clearly, I, and most women, need more than freedom from the expectation that I should not aspire to have a career; I need social supports like quality childcare and parental leave. Another idea masking this problem, though—the one I want to focus on here—is the individualism myth. The individualism myth tells us that we can measure feminism's success by looking at the successes of individual women. But we won't know how well women are doing unless we look at something else. That something is men.

Seen through the eyes of popular women's empowerment campaigns, the world has all the eeriness of a ghost town. Wandering the office buildings and the school corridors are unconfident, hapless women and girls. For some mysterious reason, we just can't seem to get it together. Mattel's charitable foundation says little girls don't reach their full potential because of a "dream gap." The Ad Council says women are not in STEM because they are "scared to fail."[20] One particularly galling article about childcare at the beginning of the pandemic bore the title "They Go to Mom First," as though kids are the reason that women bear the brunt of household work. Men are nowhere to be found.

The idea that we will know whether feminism is succeeding by looking at improvements in individual women's lives is embedded in a certain fundamental approach to looking at the world, one that philosophers and social theorists sometimes call "methodological individualism." Methodological individualism suggests that we can diagnose social and political problems by looking at individuals decontextualized from their groups or relationships. Instead of seeing that women as a group are kept down in the workplace though the practice of sexual harassment, for example, the individualist sees isolated instances of "flirting." Instead of seeing that the rich are benefitting from the labor of the poor, the individualist just sees a bunch of different individual people earning different amounts of money.

To get a little bit less abstract about how methodological individualism works, indulge me while I tell you a story about one of my favorite things: baking. In 2015, the internet suddenly seemed to turn against the pillar of an American childhood, the Nestle Tollhouse morsel, aka, the original chocolate chip. User after user complained that the chips just weren't what they used to be. "We used them for decades. DECADES,"[21] one reviewer lamented. Now, suddenly, the chips would not melt.

Not to impugn the integrity of reviewers who have used these chips for DECADES, but nonmelting chocolate usually has one of two causes. The first is that moisture can make the chocolate grainy when its temperature changes. Grabbing that spoon or bowl straight from your drying rack may have serious consequences for your finished product. The second is that the stove or the oven is too hot. We've all experienced that burned, grainy texture of a chocolate chip cookie gone wrong. The moral of the story is this: when a chocolate chip tastes bad, it might not be the chocolate chip's fault. The environment—the chef, the oven, the spoon—all matter, and we won't be able to fix our cookie until we see this.

Eleanor Roosevelt supposedly said that you didn't know how strong a woman was until you put her in hot water. But maybe, just like it's time to look to the hot oven to explain our bitter chocolate chips, it's time to turn our feminist attention to the hot water women find ourselves in. If we do this, we will not be able to avoid noticing that men, and men's resistance to feminist change, are part of the problem. If we are willing to part ways with methodological individualism, we will quickly see that it's not time for feminists to be grateful. It's time for feminists to be angry.

Freedom feminism tells us to ask whether we have more freedom than our mothers did. But what if instead, we shifted to thinking about whether men are doing enough? This is the question equality would make us ask. We may have been told equality means asking "Do we have equality with men in the workplace?" or "How can we be more like men?" But it also might mean asking ourselves: Are men and women doing the same amount of unpaid, unrecognized labor? Are men and women bearing the harms of the unpaid, unrecognized nature of this labor equally? Or, as Darcy

Lockman asked after interviewing forty-seven couples across the racial and socioeconomic spectrum, "Are you being fair to your wife?"

The reality that emerges if we ask this question is nothing short of damning. The split of childcare and housework isn't fifty-fifty. It's not even close. Moms in 1980 estimated their husbands did 31 percent of childcare; in 2000 they estimated it was 32 percent.[22] If you don't trust women's own reports, studies with other methods show that women do about twice as much family care as men.[23] A 2017 study of OECD countries found that men did less than a quarter of the housework and less than half the childcare. A recent study in the UK showed that men had five more leisure hours a week than women.[24] Just think of all the things you could do (or, if you're like me, all the extra sleep you could clock) if you had five extra hours in your week.

The numbers are outrageous. We might even say they speak for themselves. Except that there's something even more depressing that they seem to conceal. It's that, in general, men don't seem to care. They know that they do less and have just decided that they're maxed out on what they can do and that something has to give. A study in 2009 that attempted to study caregiving through a gender-neutral lens ended up finding that men and women were equally committed to their jobs. Yet, women were going to superhuman lengths to make sure those jobs did not interfere with their children, and men just weren't.[25] In case you think men are self-deceived in some way, the men in Lockman's interviews don't mince words. "Let's say we both have to be at work and the kids get sick," Ethan says. "I'm sorry: I don't give it a second thought that my work comes first. That's an entitlement that I feel."[26]

Lockman's interviews revealed that individual men were well aware that they were doing less than their women partners. Sometimes they didn't even feel like this needed justifying. It was just how things are. Other times, they had an arsenal of justifications. They ranged from "My wife doesn't tell me to vacuum" to "She tells me it's not good enough when I do"[27] to "I forgot who my child's dentist is."

And if you are skipping this part of the chapter because you want to have kids with a man but haven't yet, consider the fact that though 65

percent of millennial men without children endorse combined breadwin-
ner/caregiver roles, only 47 percent with children do.[28] Consider also the
fact that polling data from around the world indicate that young women
are becoming more and more feminist as young men are becoming more
conservative. A 2024 poll found that one in five men in the UK aged
sixteen to twenty-nine had warm feelings for self-proclaimed "king of
toxic masculinity" Andrew Tate.[29]

Men's ability not to care, and the speed with which women look the
other way, are made possible by the individualism myth. Men could ask,
"Am I being fair to my wife?" But instead they ask, "Am I a good dad?"
The indicators of this are tickles and bedtime books read and booboos
healed, not comparisons with Mom. (Incidentally, studies also show that
men prefer the "fun" parenting labor over handling poop and vomit, and
who wouldn't?) Men occasionally do push against the individualism myth
and compare themselves with other men. But they stop short of comparing themselves with women. And in a world where the bar for dads is
so low, hopes of reaching equality go out the window. In a world where
even the best dads do so little, it's easy to sit on your laurels because
you know who your kid's dentist is when Brad does not.[30]

It's not only men who refuse to appraise the gender division of
household labor against the benchmark of equality. Women, too, often
tend to ignore the possibility that men could change. One of Lockman's
subjects recounts that it has never occurred to her to ask her husband
to get up in the morning with the kids, and that he waltzes down the
stairs at 7:05 like everything is normal. Another recounts that her mom
is constantly telling her how lucky she is that her husband, unlike her
father, does anything at all.[31]

The weirdest part is that it's not like any of these people would say
they believe women should only be caregivers. They say they believe
in women, that women can do amazing things. Ask them, and they are
extremely against society telling women that they can't be high achieving
at work. And yet somehow, people of all genders seem to believe that
women should simultaneously be free to work outside the home and
perform the bulk of the work inside it.

It seems like these beliefs should be hard to reconcile. Yet, they are easily reconciled in practice because of the individualism myth, with a dose of the restriction myth thrown in for good measure. Sociologists Joanna Pepin and David Cotter summarize our cultural beliefs as follows: we see women as choosing "to participate in either (the public or private) sphere, while trying to equalize the perceived value of a home sphere which [is] still seen as distinctively female." We want to free women from the expectation that they do not work outside the home while refusing to think about the fact that the problem in the home is a *division* of labor.

The world of proposed solutions to the problems of care work and housework is a woman-only ghost town. How do we get women into the workforce? Free women from the expectation that they should be stay-at-home moms. How do we stop the downgrading of stay-at-home moms' work? Free women from negative stereotypes of stay-at-home moms. It's like we just can't see what Ian Bannon and Maria Correia have called "the other half"—or what might be more aptly referred to as "the other part of" gender.[32] Gender isn't just women and gender minorities. Men have to change.

None of this is to say that men are the only reason that women are doing the brunt of the "shit work." To say that would be to buy into a version of methodological individualism, to refuse to see how people of all genders are operating within a set of hostile social structures. The gender division of labor is reinforced by the gender wage gap. If one parent is going to forego an income to care for the children, it's rational—and often necessary for survival—for it to be the person with the lower income. Perhaps more importantly, surviving as a one-income family is impossible for most, and yet our workplaces are structured so that it's kind of impossible to be a full-time worker and have children.

We don't have paid parental leave, and even when we do, it's for a tiny portion of children's lives. We don't have subsidized childcare. School is out for the summer, but work isn't. Since the pandemic, snow days in many districts have been replaced with remote schooling, which parents are supposed to be able to supervise while themselves working remotely. Then add to that, as Angela Davis famously argued,[33] postindustrial capitalism invents housework that is not actually necessary but is treated as such by our status-obsessed culture (do I really need to fluff the eight throw pillows that are required to make my bed look "luxe" or cut the vegetables in my kids' bento boxes into flower shapes?), and you end up with a pretty clear understanding of how anyone who tries to do care work or housework is going to end up exhausted.

At the same time, though, people of all genders are operating within the same structure. With the exception of the gender wage gap, a world that is hostile to workers who have homes and children could, in theory, be equally exhausting to men and women. The fact that it's not suggests that men are an important part of the story and an important lever for change. Understanding that men are operating within larger social structures is especially important for considering what causes women of color to be disproportionately involved in unpaid, unrecognized labor. The relevant structures go beyond gender.

For example, mass incarceration of Black men[34] forces Black women to take on more labor, including childcare and housework—in addition to managing strain on families and themselves, and the labor associated with things like visiting family in prison and paying for phone calls.[35] Most Black men who are incarcerated were their family's primary income earners, and most are parents of minor children.[36] When Black men are victimized by the criminal justice system, the demands of Black motherhood increase, in many cases, to a breaking point—the "strong Black woman" stereotype notwithstanding.[37]

Up to this point, I have been talking about how the individualism myth conceals the ways in which women have not made as much progress as one might think. But it also obscures something else: the ways in which men *benefit* from seeming improvements in women's lives, and even ways in which seeming improvements are not improvements at all. In some ways, gender inequality might be increasing as a result of apparent feminist change. Yes, I said what you think I did: women being freer than they used to be sometimes also manifests in women being less equal.

The authority on this topic is the recently deceased geographer Sylvia Chant, who spent the 2000s and 2010s interviewing women all over the Global South about how their lives have changed since they started working for income. The story of Teeda, a thirty-five-year-old woman in Gambia, is fairly typical. Teeda is now "empowered" because she is making money running a fruit stand and dying batik fabrics. If you think this means Teeda is now an equal in her home, think again. Instead, her husband has decided that her money is for the household, and he can spend his as he pleases. As she puts it, "If men pay for breakfast, women pay for lunch and dinner. Women pay for the school lunches. . . . At the festivals women are selling and men are not working."[38]

Working for income has not just increased work burdens on women by creating the dreaded "second shift" of care and housework on top of one's paid work. It has also created a new division of responsibility that is less favorable to women. Part of this division of labor is women's increased work literally subsidizing improvements in men's lives. Now that women work, men can work less, drink and gamble more, even pay for sex workers or seek to bring additional wives into their households. Another part of this division of labor is that some tasks that men used to do now fall under the rubric of "women's work." The classic example is paying for children's school expenses. This used to be the job of men, because men were the only ones with income. Now this is another job of women. This produces a triple hardship for women. The first layer is that they have to do more work than they used to do. The second is that their income is perceived as family income, not income they can spend for themselves. The third is that because their work outside the home is now considered "women's work," it is valued less than it used to be, and its contribution to the household is thought to count less.

Chant has named this phenomenon "the feminization of responsibility and obligation." And treating women like they are responsible for pretty much everything, including an increasing proportion of "shit work," is happening in the world's rich countries as well. Think, for example, of how the division of parenting labor has changed now that more men are invested in dadding. As I mentioned above, the result of men getting more involved in parenting is that the crappier (literally and figuratively) parenting tasks fall to women. Moms are changing the diapers and handling the middle-of-night wakeups, and dads are cuddling before bed.

Dads are coaching the soccer teams while moms are making the soccer snacks and washing and buying the uniforms.

Think also of the fact that men's participation in housework and parenting is seen as worthy of copious and public praise, while women's is thought to be expected. When our first child was born, my spouse and I marveled at how many strangers would compliment him doing the truly commendable task of . . . walking down the street wearing a baby. When he and I cowrote an article about this phenomenon, which we called "the daddy dividend," he got fan mail, and I got criticism . . . including a special email addressed to just me and sent on Mother's Day.[39]

In both rich and poor countries, a new form of emotional labor falls on women when they start working outside the home—that of preserving men's egos.[40] Women's increased achievement outside the home seems to threaten men. Women know this and are saddled with the role of preserving men's self-conceptions. A study of women in Mexico revealed that those who worked outside the home sought their husbands' permission by offering to do even more housework than they were already doing.[41]

In the United States, women also go to great lengths to preserve fragile masculinity: Women whose husbands are unemployed do more housework than their spouses.[42] Women who work in stereotypically male occupations, like law enforcement, go out of their way to do more dishes. Stay-at-home dads do less childcare than working moms.[43] Women who earn more have husbands "who sleep more and watch lots of television," while men who work long hours have wives who do more childcare.[44] The going hypothesis for why all of this happens: women are trying to ensure they don't jeopardize men's senses of entitlement.

To understand how far we have left to go, and to understand the new forms of inequality that are emerging, we need to abandon methodological individualism. We need to look at social structures, and we also need a lens that encourages us to compare women to men—not in a way that takes men as the standard, but in a way that tells us it is not okay for men to consistently have more, get more, count more. Freedom feminism will never be that lens.

Freedom squares well with methodological individualism partly because it is what philosophers would call a "nonrelational" value: a value whose presence or absence in a person's life can be assessed without knowing much about anyone else's life. Knowing how much freedom a person has is like knowing how much money, or how many pairs of shoes, that person has. I don't need to look in anyone else's closet to know that you have seventeen pairs of neon sneakers, much like I don't need to look at whether anyone is listening to you to know whether you have freedom of speech, or see others freely practicing their religion to know whether you do. We won't see the disproportionate harms to women of household labor, caregiving labor, and emotional labor unless we are willing to make comparisons and look at relationships. An equality lens tells us to look at these things; a freedom lens does not. Women are free to work outside the home, but there is a gross *inequality* in how much labor men and women do. Women have more freedom than they used to have, but men are getting *more* out of the new arrangement than women are.

If we remain in the grip of the individualism myth, we can't see how far women have left to go, or the new forms of inequality that are emerging. And if we can't even see the problem, because our refusal to look at men and larger social structures makes us think that things are better than they are, we certainly won't be able to solve it. We will continue to think that the solution is to fix women instead of fixing the world. For reasons we are about to see, that solution is even worse than it sounds.

SOMEONE STILL HAS TO DO THE DISHES

One of the viral articles that launched today's emotional labor craze was accompanied by a picture of a hand clad in a yellow rubber dish glove giving all of us the finger. In it, journalist Gemma Hartley announced that she, like most women, was fed up.[45] But it wasn't that she was tired of housework and childcare. She was also tired of what we now call the "mental load" of managing these things, of asking for recommendations, making phone calls, scheduling. It wasn't that her husband wouldn't clean. It was that she didn't want to have to *ask*.

The solution to the problem that served as the hook for Hartley's article was not asking her husband to clean the house, but to *find a housecleaning service*. On one level, she was just asking for her husband to do a task that involved researching, finding, and scheduling. But on another, she was inadvertently revealing the Achilles heel of mainstream feminism. She wanted to be relieved of women's work by having that work done by. . . another woman. We can try to cover it up with the abstract term *cleaning service*, but we all know who works in the services Hartley is talking about. The housecleaning industry is predominantly composed of immigrant women and women of color, who are three times as likely as other workers to live below the poverty line.[46] Rather than giving the finger to a world in which it's acceptable to pay domestic workers twelve dollars an hour without benefits, Hartley was simply asking for someone else to put on the dish gloves.

Hartley's solution to her problem was hardly unusual. In fact, our entire society's proposed solution to the ongoing necessities of housework and care work is basically Hartley's solution writ large. Transfer undervalued labor from elite women onto less privileged ones. Haven't heard of this solution before? If you haven't, it's because we are used to calling this solution something else, something a whole lot more flattering: "leaning in," being a "girlboss" or a "bawse," prioritizing "self-care" and "me time." We call transferring the unpaid work we are expected to do onto other women "being independent." Pushing labor onto other women and not "relying on men" are two sides of the same coin.[47]

My point is not that we should be dependent on men. It is also not that it is unfeminist to do domestic or care work, or to hire someone to do it for you. That work is important, most of it is necessary, and pretty much all of it is undervalued.[48] I would certainly not be able to write this book if it were not for the labor of professional care workers. My point is that the version of feminism that circulates most widely in our society asks us to strive for a type of independence that is literally impossible. As the philosopher Eva Feder Kittay points out, all of us, you included, managed to grow into adulthood because we were cared for by others. Those others were usually women. Those of us who manage to grow into old age will need care then, and at various times in between. We might try to escape being the ones who do the caring. But someone has to do it.

Once we make the point explicitly, it seems so obvious. But how can something so obvious have been so well concealed for so long? Why does celebrating independence seem plausible in the first place? The answer is that the individualism myth obscures the ways women rely on one another, the way our fates are intertwined. When we assume that we can measure feminist change in terms of individual women's achievements, we don't look at the relationships that make those achievements possible, or the new relationships those achievements create. Our need for care is so deep and ineradicable that any individual achievement is produced partly by the labor of others. Our idea of the successful worker is built on the image of a man who, though he might think himself independent, only got here because someone changed his diapers, and only stays here because others cook for him, feed him, clean his house, raise his children. Any feminism worth its salt should have a plan for what to do about the work that goes unrecognized because it is done by women. Freedom feminism doesn't.

Not only does the individualism myth tell us we needn't recognize how we depend on the labor of others, but also that we needn't track how attempts at feminist change affect women *as a group*. At its best, freedom feminism tells us that the success of individual women *is* all women's success. At its worst, it just ignores the larger context of all women, telling us that whenever a woman does something for herself, that's feminism in action. "Self-care," a term Audre Lorde[49] coined to mean making sure you have enough left at the end of the day to keep fighting for social justice, has been rebranded as getting a manicure or an expensive sound bath. Even those of us who are critical of the corporate rebranding of feminism are probably guilty of sometimes confusing feminism with individual women doing what is best for themselves. How many times have you heard someone say that an act was feminist because a woman "chose" to do it?

Sometimes, though, we hear explicit claims that the acts of individual women are acts *for* all women. This claim is central to the idea of shattering the glass ceiling; when one woman gets somewhere women have not been before, the next woman supposedly won't have to bang her head on the way up. But this line of reasoning moves too fast. Even if we put to one side the concern that an unspoken rule may not be the only force impeding women (restriction myth, anyone?), we have to wonder whether there is room for everyone at the top.

When Taylor Swift became a billionaire in 2023, she was celebrated for "taking a hammer to that glass ceiling—and blazing a path for the next generation of female artists."[50] The 2024 Superbowl saw a host of memes about how men couldn't handle one second of jumbotron on Taylor Swift, and how a nation of little girls were watching. And it's true that Swift has done more for other women than many in her position would do, such as using her power to demand that Apple Music pay artists better and suing radio host David Mueller for sexual assault for groping her, for damages of one dollar, so that she could "be an example for other women."[51]

These moves are absolutely worth celebrating, but they were not ensured by Swift's extreme wealth and could have happened without it. Swift's wealth, like every billionaire's, is not necessarily something feminists should be celebrating. We can love many things about Swift without loving the climate carelessness embodied in her storied private jet use (in just one week of 2024 her plane likely emitted fourteen times as much carbon dioxide as the average US household emits in a year).[52] We can also acknowledge that a world that celebrates billionaires and refuses to tax them even 5 percent more is leaving on the table amounts of money that could bring two billion people out of poverty,[53] the vast majority of them women.

When A-list celebrities like Alyssa Milano and Salma Hayek broke the silence about Harvey Weinstein, they unleashed a conversation about workplace sexual harassment and assault that women across the economic spectrum experience. But in the immediate aftermath, women in low-wage jobs wondered if this would do anything for them.[54] Following the revelation, seven hundred thousand women farmworkers, who knew firsthand the experience of being expected to endure assault to keep their jobs in packinghouses and fields, wrote a letter pledging solidarity to the actors. The celebrities responded with Time's Up, a foundation whose feminist work to transform the workplace ranges from a campaign for greater workplace safety to a fund that enables victims of harassment and assault from across the economic spectrum to seek legal redress.

But there was no guarantee that it would go that way. Nothing about the fact that celebrities spoke out against assault guaranteed that physical safety in the workplace—predominantly an issue for low-income work-ers—would become part of the fight. It could have just as easily ended with actors using their plentiful resources to lawyer up against their abus-ers, leaving those without access to the legal system with little more than #MeToo inspo. It is likely the bottom-up expression of solidarity by the farmworkers that made the difference.

In recent years it has been commonplace in more woke feminist circles to point out that most women are not high-powered actors or corporate CEOs. Exponentially more women are cleaning the bathroom than sitting in the boardroom, working in the fields than on the screen. But it's not im-mediately clear what the solution is to this vast inequality among women. And in fact, the most common solution suggested by the "get women in the boardroom" set is to claim that representation is not enough. More women need to be educated, mentored, and supported, so that more of them are in the boardroom.[55]

But even this solution is limited—and it's limited because we are be-holden to the individualism myth. This time the myth comes with a new twist: we are not ignoring men, or even ignoring women as a group; we are ignoring the structure of the society that women as a group find our-selves in. Our society is characterized by dramatic economic inequality. It's not just that most women are not CEOs or actors or politicians; it's that they can't be. The reason they can't be is not that women are not smart enough (in case you buy into the idea that CEOs are particularly smart). The reason is that our society is so stratified that there just isn't room at the top for everyone. The whole idea of making it to "the top" supposes that society is a pyramid with a special (and tiny) pinnacle reserved for the winners.

And this is to say nothing of the fact that the "winners" are not in-dependent and never were. The winners need support—support that has always come from the invisible fund of women's unacknowledged labor. The imagined world in which every woman is leaning in is also a world in which there are no babies or children or elders to care for, no houses that need cleaning, no office parties to throw or broken hearts to help mend. Our society happens to be structured so that the people who do that labor can't be the winners. Not just because there are too many of them but also because the work they do is not seen or valued. As the journalist Ann Crittenden once put it, if motherhood is the "most important job in the world," why are our bank accounts full of zeroes for the time we put into it?[56]

It's one thing to say that most women need more help to make it to the top because they need more support to get there, and another to acknowledge that our society is designed such that the top will always be the place for the few. The individualism myth tells us that the feminist battle can be won by individual women fighting to the top. If society is like an apartment building, the penthouse is tiny, and its oversized white couches are in constant need of maintenance. We can add a room or two, or exile a few men to the lower floors, but it's just never going to be very big. Those couches are never going to shampoo themselves. To tell the truth, the strategy of trying to get individual women to the higher floors is not very promising, given that the middle class is shrinking, jobs that pay a living wage are rapidly disappearing, and women spend an incredible amount of time doing work that no one recognizes as work.[57] The only way to improve the situation of women as a group is to change the shape of the house, and to make sure that the people who clean it also get to live there, and live well there.

The crassest versions of the individualism myth leave us thinking that the path to feminist change is for all women to become presidents or CEOs. But even those of us who can call out the privilege implied by "lean-in" or girlboss or neoliberal feminism spend considerably less energy noting the fact that it is literally impossible for everyone to devote themselves full time to the type of work that the bosses do. We have already talked about how women can lag behind men even as things seem to be improving. We have talked about how individual successes do not necessarily lift up all women—and why, in an unequal world that devalues women's work, they literally can't. But there's another reason we need to stop assuming the success of individual women is the success of all women, one that is deeply uncomfortable to talk about.

It's this: women sometimes benefit from contributing to the oppression of women. Sometimes we talk about women hiring other women to do housework and care work as an example of this dynamic, but I think that's overly simplistic. To assume that people should not pay others to do this work is to fall into the individualism myth all over again—to assume it would be possible for this work, and for our dependency on others, to just go away. Women who hire other women need to not exploit them and need to fight to improve their working conditions, as do the movements we will read about in chapters 5 and 6. Imagining away the work that women have traditionally done doesn't do anything to help women who work as nannies and housecleaners; keeping it invisible is a step in the wrong direction, a step back from ensuring a fair wage for women who earn their livelihoods doing this necessary work.

Women hiring other women is not an example of individual women benefitting from the oppression of other women. What is oppressive is rejecting the idea that women's work is work to begin with. Elite women who don't acknowledge how their work rests on the work of other women participate in spreading a model of success that will never work for all women, and very rarely serves even them. Saying you can "do it all," and that anyone else can, invisibilizes the labor that makes your work possible.

Lauren Chief Elk, Yeoshin Lourdes, and Bardot Smith started the viral hashtag #giveyourmoneytowomen in 2015. Women used it to demand pay for everything from the smiles that catcallers request, to art, to sex work. The most vocal backlash came, in their words, from "mainstream feminism."[58] If the "real" feminism, as these critics claimed, was about "earning" your money and being "independent" in the ways men are, then those who put up their PayPals and Cash Apps were literally asking for "cash for nothing." In other words, it was not just the patriarchy but also supposed feminists telling us that emotional labor was worth nothing at all.

Women thinking it is feminist to deny the value of other women's work is the individualism myth on steroids. It is the idea that people are independent—and thus the systematic erasure of the work women do to sustain the social fabric—combined with the idea that one's own success is enough. Nowhere is this dynamic more evident than in views of the most "taboo" forms of women's labor, transactional sex and sex work.[59] Simply put, women who are not sex workers invest an awful lot of energy into distinguishing themselves from sex workers.[60] I don't just mean in their direct attitudes about sex workers, which often portray them as "better at sex than anything else" or "kidnapped" and "without agency"—read, their work is not skilled or complicated like "ours."[61] I also mean that women who criticize or belittle sex workers succeed by portraying themselves as better than sex workers, as being women who earn their money legitimately. This can happen even when the term *sex worker* is not said at all; it is part of what's going on in everyday acts of slut-shaming, like when women point out that *they* dress "professionally" and don't "use their sexuality to get ahead," or when they point out that they have "real jobs" when other women don't.

There is a certain structure to women's oppression that makes possible this form of selling out other women, in the realm of emotional labor and beyond. To understand it, we have to let the individualism myth fall away and remember that oppression is about hierarchical relationships between social groups. Women as a group have worse options than men as a group.

But it doesn't follow that individual women have no routes for making their own lives better. In fact, as I have spent much of my academic career arguing, the best way for a woman to get ahead in a man's world is often to prove that she is not like the other women.[62] She is not like the others who use their sexuality to get ahead. Or, she is not like the other feminists who can't take a joke and will report you for sexual harassment. Or, she can put in the long hours at the office, because she is not like the others who need to leave work by 5 p.m. to pick up their babies from daycare.

A woman who knows that she can't change standards for success that are rigged against her has good reason to do the best she can under those existing standards—prove that she can play the game. As the saying goes, if you can't beat 'em, join 'em. The problem is that playing the game—especially when you have the kind of power and privilege that *could* change it, or at least poke holes in it—can make the game harder for others. Pointing out that you don't need to use your sexuality to survive stigmatizes those who do—even when we know that sex work is many women's actual best option. Pointing out that you don't "use your sexuality to get ahead" blames women for the fact that many men can't seem to handle the presence of women in the workplace. Pointing out that you made it to the top by working late hours and being childless makes light of the real fact that so many women can't, and obscures the fact that men are "allowed" to have children and careers.

Feminists who tell women they *should* be able to get ahead by becoming independent do the same thing en masse. They throw the majority of women under the bus. They don't just ignore the fact that most women are not in a position to be CEOs or presidents. They do it by making it seem like something is wrong with the women who aren't or who don't want to be. Instead of turning our attention to why most women are not "high powered," which would require us to look at capitalism and the devaluation of women's labor, they make the issue into one of women's individual failures—about what women aren't doing that they supposedly could and should be doing. One of the grave dangers of the idea that one woman's success is all women's success is that it obscures the fact that the success of one woman can make other women's situations worse. This won't just happen by accident; it is baked into the structure of sexist societies that women have incentives to sell out other women.

We need to recognize these places where women are incentivized to sell each other out. But we can't be so long as we keep thinking feminists can get where we need to go if each individual woman fights for herself. Once we see that fighting oppression means fighting for women as a group, and once we see that privileged women moving up in the social hierarchy often happens at the expense of other women, it becomes clear that this battle isn't going to be fought one "boss" at a time. It might seem like individual success brings everybody up. But up to where, and at what cost?

The story of mainstream feminism overlooking the priorities of less privileged women is, in many ways, a story about labor. We forget emotional labor because men do not even recognize that it is labor that they are asking for from women. But it's not like women are immune to failing to recognize the labor of other women.

The woker footnotes to the mainstream feminist playbook will tell you that the way to fight "lean-in" and "girlboss" feminism is to acknowledge privilege. But once we acknowledge the individualism myth, we can see that this is only a tiny piece of the puzzle. Acknowledging one's own privilege is not the same thing as working to dismantle the system that anoints some people the privileged ones in the first place. To dismantle that system would mean seeing that we are all dependent on labor that women are currently doing for free or for very, very cheap. It would mean paying for, or otherwise finding a way to materially support, that labor. And it would mean accepting that feminists are not winning unless the strategies on the table are *for* the women who do this work, just not the elite women who manage to partly benefit from this labor being unacknowledged and poorly paid.

Trying to write and teach from my bathtub "office" with a toddler banging on the door during the COVID-19 pandemic was genuinely grueling. But undoubtedly, it would have been more grueling if I, like so many of the daycare workers I was used to depending on, had needed to appear at work in person without having care in place for my own children, was living with elevated fear of illness because I had no health insurance, or was living in constant fear of job loss as my industry seemed to be disappearing as more and more children stayed at home.[63]

Feminism will be not just for the few, but for almost *no one*, if its path to change is a string of individual successes. We need to change the shape of our *relationships*. We need to change flows of labor, from women to men, and from women to other women. Otherwise, winning will continue to look an awful lot like doing it all or forcing someone else to do it all. And I'm pretty sure that's not a game any of us wants to win.

CHAPTER 3

THE CULTURE MYTH

*Freedom Feminism Is
White Feminism in Disguise*

I t wasn't clear what exactly pushed Sue to start reporting her colleagues to the authorities. But it definitely had something to do with women.

When the students stopped sending each other Christmas cards, Sue may have missed the Yuletide cheer, but she held her tongue. When she started hearing talk of a teacher spreading dubious ideas about sexual consent, she threatened to go to the press until the school held an assembly to correct them. But when boys' and girls' gym became two separate classes, and teens going out dancing was no longer considered a legitimate part of the high school weekend trip, she again began to wonder if things had gone too far. Then, a male teacher disrespected a woman volunteer on the school bus. Now was the moment for Sue to act.

Sue began by reporting the teacher's sexism. Then came anonymous letters to the educational commission and the city council. She hit the interview circuit and testified at government hearings.[1] She was not the only "whistleblower" who was leaking similar complaints about her school and schools nearby.[2] Spurred by a similar complaint, the government began conducting emergency investigations, including one by the head of counterterrorism at Scotland Yard. It was high time the UK's counterterrorism policy developed an educational arm. Teachers became

charged with identifying teachers and students who might become terrorists.[3] They have since reported students as young as four years old.

I don't know about you, but I could tell a very similar story about the
schools I went to. Well, similar up to the ending. I took girls-only "PE,"
euphemistically described in the course catalogue as "aerobics." We gos-
siped as we rolled our eyes at the screen where a has-been supermodel
led us through an even-then retro series of fire hydrants and sit-ups.
Teachers reinforcing rape myths were a constant feature of my education.

I still remember the day in seventh grade when I was told to change
shirts because my "cleavage" was "distracting" the boys. (I was eleven
and had to look up the word *cleavage* in the dictionary to be sure what
it meant.) As for the school assemblies, I remember those being mostly
about "school spirit," which, as far as I could tell was about having girls
cheer for boys' football and basketball. Once, a girls' team ran out to a
Top 40 song about how girls were both cute and useful for housework,
but I guess that was ironic? As for male teachers disrespecting women,
well, the incidents were too numerous to be memorable.

Still, as far as I know, the press and the counterterrorism experts
were never called.

You see, Sue wasn't just concerned about any women. She was concerned
about *Muslim* women. Her story, which you may recognize from the
Serial creators' *Trojan Horse Affair* podcast for the and the *New York
Times*, is one of entwined preoccupation with women and "Islamiciza-
tion." Widespread instances of everyday sexism, like the idea that girls
needed different gym classes and teachers making sexist comments,
could pass in my majority-white school.

But they became a national security concern when the girls in question were Muslim in the UK, potential terrorists or in need of saving
from the would-be terrorist men around them. Sue is certainly not the
only person in recent memory whose concern about women has become a smokescreen for Islamophobia. In 2019, in a move supported
by a number of feminist organizations, Quebec followed the example of
France's 2004 ban on the hijab in public schools and also banned people

in public positions of authority from wearing "religious symbols."[4] By 2021, teachers were losing their jobs for wearing hijab.[5] The image of the Muslim woman in need of saving has been, and continues to be, used not just to stoke discrimination against Muslim women in Western countries, but also to fuel war abroad. When it was time to invade Iraq and Afghanistan, the very Republican US government suddenly decried the plight of "women of cover."

Muslim women have been having a moment, but they are by no means the first women of color who find themselves drawn into "feminist" battles designed to undermine their communities. In the 1970s Chicana feminists argued that whites used the idea of machismo as a tool that allowed them to blame Latinx culture for social inequality. Machismo, rather than racism or grossly unequal capitalism, would suddenly arise as a topic of discussion when it became important to explain why Latinx people were failing to "succeed" in US society.[6] Given former president Trump's repeated suggestions that Mexicans are rapists and the continuation of this meme in places like Senator Katie Britt's 2024 rebuttal to the State of the Union address,[7] it seems the feminists of the 1970s were onto something that is still very real.

Similarly, Indigenous feminists argue that violence against Indigenous women suddenly becomes very important when someone is looking for a rationale to incarcerate Indigenous men, or to deflect responsibility from policies that marginalize indigenous people.[8] Never mind that assault of Indigenous women is overwhelmingly committed by nonindigenous individuals.[9]

There's something that all of these examples have in common, and it's not just racism. It's a fixation on culture. It's the idea that culture is an impediment to women's liberation. It's the idea that women, especially women from "other" cultures are, like the "huddled masses" described in the poem at the foot of the Statue of Liberty, "yearning to breathe free." This idea, which I refer to as "the culture myth," creates a deep, though sometimes imperceptible, connection between freedom feminism and white feminism. Sometimes freedom feminism is a cover for white feminism, and sometimes it is a gateway drug. But the idea that culture restricts women makes freedom feminism an easy ally of white supremacy.

YEARNING TO BREATHE FREE?

The teacher who reprimanded me for my distracting cleavage would never have worn a scoop neck like the one I thought I looked so cute in. Every single day, even the top button of her shirt was closed. As though that weren't enough, she wore a turtleneck underneath, rolled high so that you could hear the fabric bristle against the edges of her short blonde hair.

The word *cleavage* sounded old-fashioned to me, a cousin of the word *bosom* or something. It suited someone who still seemed to think women's collarbones were risqué. I felt sorry for her. Here I was, in all of my adolescent body-positive glory, somewhere between unaware of and intrigued by the idea that I was free to expose as much of my body as I wanted. And here she was, dressed like a Pilgrim.

I was just coming into feminism, and my teacher seemed to be patriarchy personified. She was telling me what to do. She had outmoded ideas about women. And she was *old*. Messages about what women should be like seemed like they were embedded in everything, and they seemed to want to drag me back to the 1950s— or the 1600s. If, as Indian feminist Nivedita Menon says in her book *Seeing Like a Feminist*, becoming a feminist is like hitting the "reveal formatting" button on the document of your life, I was finding out that there was a document history that kept popping up no matter how hard I tried to delete it.

I thought feminism was about fighting against the forces that kept trying to drag women into the past. And I was responding to something very real. I kept hearing the phrase "it's tradition" used as a reason for everything from excluding women from paid labor to banning abortions. Wouldn't it be better if we returned to a world where (white) women were all stay-at-home moms? (Forget the fact that as sociologist Stephanie Koontz puts it, American families were never actually like the 1950s' TV stereotype.) Wouldn't it be better to return to a world where men opened the door for women? (Forget the fact that as the philosopher Marilyn Frye notes, this was accompanied by men never doing the dishes.)

I did not yet know that this was a very selective rendering of the relationship between gender equality and tradition. The idea that feminism is about freedom from culture might seem like it is a harmless tool that empowers us to respond to forces that weaponize the idea of tradition against women. It isn't. It is an idea deeply tied up in colonialism. The idea of culture as impeding moral progress has always been central to Europe's "civilizing mission," and it has been giving white feminists cover for the last hundred fifty years. But let's start with the underside of the culture myth today. Talk about culture restricting women is often the first lever in a game of racist mousetrap that we don't recognize until after the first lever has already been pulled.

"Where do you think all that spicy stuff about Mexican rape culture came from?" right-wing pundit Ann Coulter asked in 2015, taking credit for Trump's repeated attempts to associate Mexicans with sexual assault.[10] Other chestnuts in her book that she assumed Trump (or someone around him) had read included the claims that Latinx people have a "cultural acceptance of child rape that doesn't even exist in the most dysfunctional American ghettos," that immigrants from Mexico are "more dangerous than ISIS"[11] and that Mexicans don't see women as humans with "rights and freedoms."[12]

"It is the symbol of a political project that is hostile to diversity and women's emancipation," said French women's rights minister Laurence Rossignol in 2016, supporting a legal ban on a bathing suit that looks like a wetsuit with a head portion. The swimwear happens to be called the "burkini." To Rossignol, it shares the "logic of the burqa: lock up women's bodies in order to control them . . . a profoundly archaic vision of the place of women in society [translation mine]."[13]

Donald Trump's repeated associations of immigrants (and not himself) with misogyny seemed to work. In spite of a video of him joking about nonconsensually grabbing women's genitals circulating just before the election, he became president in 2016 and continued to claim that immigration restriction would benefit women. He opened his 2019 State of the Union with a claim that women are frequently assaulted crossing the border, while leaving conspicuously unsaid that women are often raped on *this* side of the border by US customs and border patrol agents.[14] His anti-immigrant vision did not limit its "feminist" concern to Latinx women, either. His executive order banning entry of people from several Muslim-majority countries into the United States also required collecting data about "honor killings."[15]

Meanwhile, comments like Rossignol's continue to fuel opposition to immigration in Europe and Canada. The problem of violence against women is repeatedly framed as a problem specific to immigrants. For example, in France, images of teenagers from the banlieues who are raped and forced to veil have been a feminist cause célèbre for many years. Veiling bans have spread all over Europe. In fact, though there are two countries in the entire world that legally require hijab, fifteen countries in Europe ban some form of it. In a phenomenon sociologist Sara Farris has termed *femonationalism*, far-right parties have gotten in on the game, such that conservatives win elections by depicting Muslims as a threat to local support for women and LGBTQ rights.

It was not long ago that terms like *rape culture* and objections to "controlling women" were used only by opponents of oppression. Today, things are no longer so clear. Feminist ideas, and ideas that sound like feminist ideas, are turning into potent tools for racism. The secret ingredient of this transformation has been freedom feminism. Once we see women as yearning to be free from their cultures, cultural destruction and assimilation start to look like benefits, or at least the feminist cost of doing business.

Part of the danger of the culture myth is that it suggests that "other" women really *want* to have their cultures destroyed or their attachment to their communities weakened. The philosopher Uma Narayan argues that Western images of "other" women tend to fall into one of two tropes. There is the "prisoner of patriarchy," who can't wait to escape a culture that is stifling her. There is also the "dupe," whose culture has constrained her so thoroughly that she cannot think for herself.[16] Both images invite the spectator to think of themself as a savior. "Freedom" consists in you, the spectator, driving a wedge between her and her culture. In the first case, you give her what she wants. In the second, you "empower" her to be smart enough to know what she wants in the first place. This is why Rossignol can say with a straight face that Islam, and not the government that attaches legal penalties to modest dress, is "controlling women." It is also why Coulter can present Mexican culture as a force that sees women "as objects rather than human beings with rights and freedoms."[17]

The culture myth is effective in supporting white supremacy because for a very long time Western nations have been in the business of passing off cultural destruction as freedom. From residential schools based on the idea that Indigenous people needed to become "civilized" to the idea that African Americans are poor because of their "culture of poverty," policies based on the idea that "others" would be better off without their cultures (or that their cultures are harming "us") have consistently served the ends of white supremacy.

The power of the culture myth is that it generates support for such policies while concealing their racism beneath the surface. On its face, the culture myth looks like the view that all cultures oppress women by restricting them. The problem is that in the West, this is not the actual background assumption about how culture works. Instead, there has been a "color line" with regard to ideas of culture and tradition that separates the West from the rest.[18] In the hands of Coulter and Rossignol, the idea that "others" have traditions and Westerners are civilized is relatively unsubtle. But theirs are not the only faces of the culture myth. The idea that women's liberation comes about through abandoning culture also lures feminists into supporting white supremacy through other, more insidious means.

CULTURE MYTH V 2.0: WESTERN INNOCENCE

Kakenya Ntaiya, like most 13-year-old girls in her Masaai community, had had her future mapped out for her since before she was born. She would go to primary school until she reached puberty. Then she would submit to female genital cutting, and drop out of school to marry the boy she became engaged to at age five. From that day on, she would fetch water, gather wood, clean house, cook food, and work the farm. It was all planned out, and when a girl's life is planned out, it serves everyone but the girl. . . .

In many rural areas in sub-Saharan Africa, young girls are expected
to obey the customs of their culture, not challenge them, and certainly
not change them.

Change starts when someone says "no."[19]

I would ask if you've heard this story before, but that would be like
asking if you've ever tasted soda or sliced bread. The ingredients for a
story about women in the Global South are almost as standardized. Start
with the image of a girl in Asia, Africa, Latin America, or the Middle East.
Toss in some "primitive" imagery (here it's gathering wood, but it might
just as well be swatting flies from her child's face or prodding a goat with
a stick). Mention an oppressive "cultural practice" (female genital cutting
and child marriage here, but it could just as well be earlobe stretching
or son preference). Then, for the final, inspiring touch, add freedom
feminist imagery. The real harm this girl has suffered is that she "has her
life planned out for her," that she is expected to "obey."

Ntaiya's story is from Melinda Gates's best-selling 2019 book *The
Moment of Lift*, whose arrival marked Gates's very public announcement
that the Gates Foundation was committing $1 billion to gender equality
initiatives. But the story could have just as easily appeared almost anywhere people in the Global North encounter images of women in the
Global South (if they encounter them at all). The Oscar-winning documentary *Period: End of Sentence* tells us that menstrual taboos in South
Asia are undermining girls' educations, and that the solution is for them
to speak up and get some inexpensive Western technology for making
sanitary pads. If you've ever given to a poverty-related cause, your feeds
are undoubtedly full of ads telling you to buy a cow or a sewing machine
for a brown or Black woman, so that for the first time in her life she can
defy cultural norms that tell her she doesn't matter.

These feel-good stories of poor women overcoming obstacles are
another path from the culture myth into white feminism. "The average
third-world woman" with an "essentially truncated life" who stars in
so much contemporary poverty porn is presented as a victim of her
culture.[20] And the customary story about what will happen afterward
is about freedom. Loosen the cultural straits just a little, the story goes,

and unleash potential. These days, the potential is often explicitly capitalist potential. Once she gets a goat or the livestock of your choice, any woman can transform into an entrepreneur, free from internalizing her society's belief in women's inferiority.[21] As the late anthropologist Saba Mahmood famously observed, Western feminists, even the most "critical" ones, seem unable to escape the idea that there is a deep "desire for autonomy and self expression . . . a slumbering ember that is ready to spark" once a woman is able to break free from tradition.

Of all the faces of the culture myth, this one is the most likely to seem benign. It is also the most likely to make any criticism of the freedom myth seem like moral quietism. After all, oppressive "cultural practices" are real. If trying to undo these practices is white feminism, aren't critics of white feminism apologists for sexism? And, if poverty is a genuine problem, what is wrong with wanting women to be able to make money for themselves?

Answering these questions is complicated. But we won't get anywhere if we think that criticizing the culture myth is the same thing as romanticizing "other" cultures. Of course it is true that some practices are genuinely oppressive to women, practices that feminists need to be fighting against, both inside and outside the West.

But the culture myth does much more than just claim that there is sexist oppression in the Global South. It tells a story about the *cause* of that oppression. When we talk about menstrual taboos, female genital cutting, child marriage, and honor killing as the causes of "other" women's suffering, we adopt a particular way of understanding how that suffering came to be in the first place. Much of what gets called "honor killing" when it is done by Muslims is just domestic violence. And many of the reasons girls have trouble accessing education are decidedly less exotic than menstrual taboos, ranging from the lack of safe transportation and parents' need for labor in the home to poor sanitation.[22] Child marriage is caused by climate change[23] and war,[24] but that's not something we hear.

It's not white feminism to talk about sexism in the Global South (assuming one actually knows what one is talking about, which is, TBH, often not the case). What *is* white feminism is to talk *pretty much only* about cultural practices. In the last section, I discussed how the culture myth props up white supremacy by drumming up support for policies that are actively racist. But it also props up white supremacy by making sure feminists talk about "other cultures" *instead of something else*. That something is us. That something is the participation of people in the West and Global North in ongoing colonial oppression of "other" women.

Not so long after the cleavage incident, I stopped to peruse the books in a news kiosk in an Indian train station. Wedged among the yellowing Agatha Christie novels and a couple bestsellers written in English by non-Indian writers was a book that almost seemed planted to stir my newfound teenage feminist sensibilities. Its spine read: *May You Be the Mother of a Hundred Sons: A Journey Among the Women of India*. I devoured it on the ride to my cousins' homes.

I was prepared for a tearjerker, but I hadn't anticipated that so much of the book would be about fire. There was an entire chapter called "Flames." Hindu couples walked around a fire seven times at their wedding ceremonies, it began. Indians burned wheat for luck or to heal a sick cow. They cremated their dead in the Ganges and held baby-naming ceremonies where a flame was supposed to represent the presence and purity of God.

And then there was fire's "special presence in the lives of Hindu women."[25] Indian women, it seemed from the book, were always in danger of being burned. Sita, the consort of Rama, hero of the ancient Sanskrit epic the *Ramayana*, had walked into flames to prove her chastity, but was so pure the flames could not touch her. Roop Kanwar and Surinder Kaur were real people who were not so lucky. Kanwar had died in 1987. Her death had been billed as a sati, a practice that is now extraordinarily rare, where a widow walks onto the funeral pyre of her dead husband. Kaur's husband had been hoping to marry again and secure another dowry, and his family had murdered her by burning her with kerosene.

I had heard about sati before reading the book, but the book presented it as a "tradition" that was continuing even in my own lifetime. The flames stoked by the ancient epic were so powerful, the book suggested, that they continued to pursue Indian women across the centuries. Roop Kanwar had committed sati—or, as the evidence suggests, had been drugged and coerced into performing sati—just ten or so years before I was in the train station. Sati had been outlawed in 1829, but, as the author of the book positioned it, the tradition was potent enough that the spark of Kanwar's immolation ignited a "sati fever" in her town. And though Kanwar's was one of the only satis recorded in recent memory, the flames seemed to keep popping up in other forms. Dowry murders, like Kaur's, were exploding all over the subcontinent.

I didn't know it at the time, but I had just been drawn into a bizzarro game of colonial connect the dots. If someone had told me that the subjection of seventeenth-century witches to the "swimming test," the death of Virginia Woolf, baptisms, and contemporary domestic violence drownings were connected by a traditional Western reverence for water, I would have at least raised an eyebrow. But somehow, the idea that Indian culture had long been burning women seemed normal.

It seemed normal because it reflected a set of well-worn habits in Western discussions of "other" cultures. If Westerners "know" something about third-world women, it is that their cultures are ultra-sexist. "Know" is in quotation marks here because it's impossible to know something that isn't true. The book I was reading wove a story about violence against women in India that left a lot to be desired in terms of accuracy, like most stories Western audiences hear about third-world women.

It's not inaccurate to say that dowry murder is a significant source of gender-based violence in India. In 2019, India recorded more than seven thousand dowry deaths.[26] Many of these still occur by burning, because it is easy to subsequently represent them as accidents caused by the kitchen stove, though today many of these murders are also presented as suicides in the bathroom. Indian feminists have been organizing against dowry murder, and against dowry itself, since at least the 1970s when thousands of women took to the streets all over India. Nor is it inaccurate that Roop Kanwar was immolated, likely forced by her husband's family.

What is strange and inaccurate, as Uma Narayan argues, is the treatment of culture and tradition as the cause of these deaths. I have yet to read a newspaper report that links intimate partner violence in the United States to the various biblical passages treating women as property, or our nation's shockingly high maternal mortality rate (the highest of any industrialized country) to the fact that Eve is cursed with pain in childbirth. Yet, the book I was reading reached back to a book written hundreds of years before Christ to explain sati and dowry murder. Weirder still, patriarchy and fire were the only commonalities between the *Ramayana* tale retold in that book and the cases of Kanwar and Kaur. Sita was proving herself to her lover who was still alive, and her in-laws were not in the picture. As my dad pointed out to me that day on the train, Sita's name is not the origin of the term *sati*, nor is she considered an example of it.

The book I was reading portrayed Kaur and Kanwar as "victims of Hindu tradition." But this, too, was a distortion—and not just because Kaur was actually a Sikh. Or because dowry murder is unrelated to sati, happens to women of a variety of religions, and is not always done by fire. It was a distortion because it is a stretch to describe sati as an Indian tradition, and a further stretch still to treat dowry murder as an extension of it. Indian scholars like Lata Mani and Romila Thapar, who have studied the history of sati, show that far from being practiced continuously since time immemorial, sati was practiced predominantly by members of the higher castes and would surge in different regions in different times, often in response to the political climate. They also show that Indians were far from univocal in their support for the practice; they had been debating the acceptability of sati for centuries. (In case you were wondering, the practice was rare enough by the twentieth century that it was removed from the Indian penal code in the 1950s, with the understanding that it could just be grouped with other murders or suicides.)

How sati went from a practice that ebbed and flowed, and that was the topic of much internal debate in the territories that became India, to the most famous "Indian cultural practice" is a story worth telling in its own right. The TLDR version is that if sati ever ended up becoming an

Indian tradition, it's because British colonizers helped turn it into one.[27] (Something similar is true about dowry murder; dowry transformed into something much more misogynistic once the British installed the notion of private property and excluded women from owning it.)[28]

The British, ever worried about threats to their rule in India, wanted to know whether they could ban sati without causing a rebellion. So, they deputized a bunch of high-caste scholars to decide once and for all whether sati really was sanctioned by Hinduism. What the scholars found was ambiguous, and why they were invested with the authority to decide what Indian culture is, is another key question (would you think a group of elite scholars reading a book could accurately determine what your culture was?).

The story of the transformation of sati into a symbol of India is complex, but the British reason for investing in it is not. It can be summed up in one word: colonialism. As Narayan notes, "Colonial encounters seemed to instigate a process of defining the self in contrast to the other," and there was special colonial value in focusing on practices that were simultaneously relatable (the British admired the wifely devotion they saw in sati) and that were shocking and lurid enough to be presented as completely unlike anything that happened at home.[29] England, like other European powers, saw itself as possessed of a "civilizing mission." The civilizing mission needed a justification. The "other" needed to be inferior so that the British could claim that they were improving it.

But this doesn't yet explain why sati came to be understood as a "cultural practice"; it just explains why the British wanted to portray it as sexist (which it clearly was). To understand that we need to look more closely at two things: the idea of civilization and the actual effects of colonialism. The idea of civilization is, at bottom, an idea about societies being at different stages of development. I would say that Europeans implicitly thought of themselves as at the peak of this development—but they actually said it aloud. Like, really aloud.

Civilization was, in this colonial mindset, a development away from the "primitive." The Global South was stuck in the primitive, still governed by cultures, traditions, superstitions, and religion. Europe was no longer governed by tradition. Europe was, at least according to the self-congratulatory narrative about "Enlightenment" the Europeans spun—which made its way into all our high school history textbooks—governed by reason.

The idea that Europe has evolved *out of* culture as an organizing force is part of why the culture myth is currently so dangerous—and how it continues colonialism even today. Freedom feminism tells us that women are restricted by culture or social norms. But it does so against a colonial backdrop where "we" already believe that "other" women are more mired in culture, and Westerners have evolved past it. This is why Sue can think, without a twinge of irony, that losing the Christmas card box at school is a tragedy, but Muslim prayers in the school assembly are out of line; Muslim prayers seem like part of a culture and a tradition, but the British Christmas cards do not. It's also why it never would have occurred to me to see my Christian teacher's modesty as being forced on her, when Muslim women are constantly assumed to have no choice in the matter of whether they veil.

The idea that the West has evolved out of culture enables not just a sense of European superiority but also a sense of European *innocence*. If bad things, including sexism, happen because of local culture, other possible stories of why they happen disappear. What are these other possible stories? They are stories of colonialism, in which colonialism creates or exacerbates patriarchy. Because, if you step back and think about it, the British created the conditions for the sati of Roop Kanwar, and for its celebration by those who set up a holy site in the village where she died. Sati would probably never have become a symbol of Indian womanhood if the British had not turned it into one in the nineteenth century. To say that Kanwar's sati was caused by Indian culture is to erase European involvement.

When we say that something is part of a culture or a tradition, we suggest that it has been going on since time immemorial and was not caused by external forces.[30] In other words, to say that "culture" causes something is to deny that it could have been caused by colonialism, or the actions of Western nations more broadly.[31] This quality of cultural/traditional explanations reverberates far beyond the example of sati. It's not coincidental that we are constantly taught that the cultural practices or traditions of "others" are the cause of patriarchy in those "other" places. It's convenient for those of us raised in the West to believe that.

It was convenient for the British to believe that local culture, and not themselves, were causing an increase in sati. The author of the book I was reading in the late 1990s wasn't a British colonizer, but we have to ask whether it was also convenient for her—an American journalist—to believe that she, and people like her, had no hand in the suffering of Indian women. We should be asking ourselves the same question when we run into versions of the culture myth today.

But by all counts, we are not. A few years ago, I went to a New York City performance of *Nirbhaya*, a play about the infamous rape and murder of Jyoti Singh Pandey in Delhi in 2012. The incident had been covered all over the world, spawning over 1,500 news items in English.[32] The play was followed by a discussion of sexual violence. "It's unbelievable what goes on *in these countries*," I remember one panelist saying. "It's really a part of the culture," another chimed in.

Singh, a student and the daughter of a baggage handler at the Delhi airport, had boarded a bus with a male friend. A group of young men on the bus beat Singh's male friend unconscious, gang-raped and disemboweled her, and left them on the side of the road. The story was horrifying and gruesome, and it sparked a watershed moment for feminist organizing in India, as thousands took to the streets in Delhi to protest not just Singh's rape but also the culture of impunity around rape and the complicity of the Indian police in allowing it to happen.

Rape apologists criticized Singh for "being out late." This line, like "What were you wearing?," is a favorite chestnut of victim blamers the world over. The same line was used on other Indian women in high-profile rape cases, including a woman who had been kidnapped in 2010 in Dhaula Kuan. Singh had been seeing a film with a friend that night, but it was not her first time being out in the evening. Nor was it the Dhaula Kuan victim's first time.

Both victims, historian Tithi Bhattacharya observes, were workers in Western-owned call centers.[33] Pandey was putting herself through school by working for IBM in the evenings, though the Western media much preferred to emphasize Pandey's flouting of tradition—the potential forbidden romance of seeing a movie in the evening with a man, the fact that her rural family had sold their land to educate her.[34] The workdays of both Singh and the Dhaula Kuan victim needed to coincide with the workdays in the United States and Europe, so it was not unusual for women in their situations to be walking unsafe streets after dark.[35]

These Indian call center workers were far from alone in experiencing increased vulnerability to gender-based violence because of their participation in the global economy. Women are raped leaving factories, not just call centers. Bangladeshi factory workers, for example, today report being beaten by their husbands for arriving home as late as 2 a.m. The fact that their supervisors, seeking to underpay them, punch their time cards so that it looks like they left at six does not help their cases.[36]

Rape and intimate partner violence are perhaps the most cross-culturally consistent forms of gender-based violence. This on its own should have given the discussants of the play I attended pause in calling gang rape part of "these cultures." But some roots of contemporary gender violence are also in global economic structures. The neoliberal reforms that Western countries have led the charge to impose on the countries of the Global South have produced new forms of gender violence. But it is far easier to blame culture than to ask about the ways we—the ones buying the fast fashion and complaining about talking to call center employees when our computers break—are responsible. The role of culture-blaming was, and is, to shift responsibility for the effects of sexism away from the forces of imperialism and white supremacy.

It's not just that the culture myth prevents us from seeing that seeming cultural practices are often created, or reinforced by, Western forces. It's also that the general trend of culture-blaming tells us to look everywhere but the West for the cause of sexism.[37] If I asked you about an issue affecting women in the Global South (well before reading this chapter, at least), you'd be likely to tell me about child marriage or honor killing or female genital cutting. You might not say the word "culture" at all. But the pathways that connect the oppression of women in the Global South with "culture" are probably well worn enough in your mind that they don't lead to other explanations. For very few of us do words like *militarism* and *neoliberalism* pop up when we are asked to think about a woman in South Asia or Africa. And that's understandable when all we talk about are the Ntaiyas and Nirbhayas of the world.

Imperialism oppresses the women of the Global South. To chronicle all of the ways would take another book, maybe several. But if we were to let the scales of the culture myth fall from our eyes, a couple of broad trends would emerge—trends that loom so large that we would wonder how we ever didn't see them. One of these is militarism, both historical and ongoing. We have already seen how British imperialism turned sati into a cultural practice. But if we think this was only going on in the nineteenth century, we are seriously mistaken.

Think back to the fear motivating Sue (and Coulter and Rossignol), the fear of "Islamic extremism." Of course, Sue, Rossignol, and Coulter think that there are way more Islamic extremists in their communities than they actually are. But Muslim feminists all over the world do have to contend with very real patriarchal forces who justify practices ranging from honor killing to the denial of inheritance rights to women with reference to Islam. And it's not just women in the Middle East; by all accounts, the girls attending the school Sue worked in were actually told that Muslim wives could not deny their husbands' sexual requests.

The story of these sexist forces coming to power is also a story of Western intervention. Try as Western pundits might to spin Muslims as having had the same practices since the Middle Ages (when, by the way, they were much more "Enlightened" than Europeans), arguments that the "true" Islam is one that denies rights to women have been on the rise in recent decades. Consider, for example, the 1979 Iranian revolution that introduced laws prohibiting women from walking the streets unaccompanied, instituting sex segregation nearly everywhere, and closing all of the nation's daycares. The government that preceded Khomeini's was a monarchy that the US and the UK had reinstated by toppling a popularly elected government—all to protect their access to oil. The shah's government was famous for its brutality, and for kleptocracy; its power was maintained not by "local traditions," but rather by the CIA. This is just one version of a very common story about the resurgence of sexist "cultural" practices.

As for stories like that of Ntaiya, the poor African girl Melinda Gates says had her whole life planned for her, we also need to look to Western intervention to understand global poverty. Countries that were colonized are, to this day poorer—30 percent poorer overall when the colonialism entailed significant natural resource extraction.[38] But lest you think that these nations have had "enough time" to recover from the effects of official colonialism, it is not like Western policies that exacerbate poverty stopped in the first half of the twentieth century.

In the 1980s and 1990s, the IMF and the World Bank imposed neoliberal economic policies, including demands that poor countries reduce restrictions on trade and cut spending on things like health and education. Though these policies are now widely acknowledged to have contributed to poverty and inequality, versions of them continue under different names. Try as Western discourses might to convince us that poor women are poor because of something about their "other" cultures (I once saw a late-night talk show participant say people in Africa were "still rubbing sticks together to make fire"), it's more accurate to say that economic policies promoted by the world's rich countries are to blame.

These policies did not just cause poverty; they caused gender inequality. The majority of the world's poor are women. Yet women put in longer days at work—four years' more worth of days over a lifetime, to be precise.[39] Western economic policies also cause gender inequalities in other ways. We've already talked about women being subject to violence after late nights in call centers, but that's just the beginning. Neoliberal economic policies demand work from women. (Who is going to care for the sick when government spending on healthcare goes away? Who needs to walk farther to get water when your local water supply is polluted by a foreign-owned factory or mine?) In general, even IMF policies that have aimed to increase women's workforce participation have concentrated them in precarious, badly paying jobs.[40]

In fact, the entire aim of "getting more women into the workforce" is a perverse marriage of the culture myth with the sexism embedded in standard economics. It's just not true that most poor women are not already working. Most of them are grinding on for hours upon hours each day in some combination of childcare, subsistence farming, fetching water and firewood, and informal sector wage labor, like selling peanuts from a cart or sewing garments in their homes. When the IMF imagines women as needing to break out of cultural restrictions that tell them not to work, it ends up increasing the demands that "women's work" place on them.

These demands combine with demands the IMF already puts in place to cut spending on health and education because it's "good economic policy." But people don't stop getting sick and kids don't stop needing somewhere to go during the day. Instead, women end up taking care of them. It's not an exaggeration to say that the Western-led approach to alleviating poverty assumes that there is an inexhaustible fund of women's work that can support social change.

It's really hard to solve a problem when you're deluded about what its causes are. Once we see how the culture myth obscures many of the real causes of gender inequality, it's unsurprising that white feminists fail so often. It is not just that white feminists are arrogant, or that the societies they come from have their own problems these feminists refuse to see. It is that they do not even see the *why* behind the sexism that "other" women face. The culture myth practically ensures that they won't see it.

MISSIONARY POSITIONS AND THE FREEDOM FEMINIST LIE

Author and lawyer Rafia Zakaria didn't look like anyone else in her women's studies course in graduate school. For starters, she was brown. The "ethnic" scarves and piercings the white professor and predominantly white other students sported weren't quite like the long, embroidered tunics she had brought back from Pakistan. The students' skin was exposed; their boho jewelry and scarves referenced cultures from everywhere and nowhere; their hair was unruly as though to symbolize a sexuality that just could not be tamed.

The class itself was about sex, and the participants were eager to show just how liberated they were. Students "rambled on about threesomes, triumphant and unceremonious dumpings, or emotionally attached lovers."[41] Everyone "shared and overshared." Zakaria, who would go on to write *Against White Feminism*, did not. She was a single mom and domestic abuse survivor, mostly focused on the stresses in her life caused by precarious childcare and a recent divorce that had raised concerns about her custody of her daughter.

Zakaria knew how this made her classmates see her. She must be a repressed Muslim woman, whose silence could only ever be evidence of her prudishness. For all they knew, she had been forced to wear a burqa since childhood, and her being allowed to attend the course was all the sexual liberation that one could expect from her. They didn't know that she had been a teen sexual rebel of her own kind back in Karachi, the kind who snuck makeup, flirted boldly with strangers, and wore her school uniform just a tad too short.

To the white gaze, Zakaria was a dime a dozen.

To Zakaria, so were the professor and students.

It wasn't just their "alternative" uniform. It was the striking similarity of their performances of sexual "liberation." Everyone overshared. Everyone was pro-porn and anti-attachment. Everyone performed what the asexual theorist Kristina Gupta would call—in a riff on Adrienne Rich's idea of compulsory heterosexuality (or comphet as it's now nicknamed on TikTok)—"compulsory sexuality."[42]

For people who were supposedly so free, their lives looked pretty scripted.

This isn't a dig at Zakaria's classmates for being unoriginal. They were not alone in having a culturally shaped menu of options; part of being a human is that our lives are, to some extent, scripted. The weird thing was that their script looked like liberation to them.

There was an important reason that Zakaria's classmates needed to see themselves as liberated from tradition to see themselves as feminist: the culture myth. If feminism is about freeing yourself from culture, then your source of liberation has to be radically original. It cannot come from inside your culture. But thinking you are free of culture and actually being free of it are two different things.

The truth, at least as Zakaria saw it, was that her classmates were rebelling into an established subculture, one that didn't deviate from mainstream Western culture as much as they may have hoped. The subculture is familiar enough that we can mentally populate Zakaria's classroom with one-night-stand detail sharers and sex column advice readers (or today's *Call Her Daddy* listeners) without knowing any of the individuals involved. It was a subculture that had the veneer of feminism, and some genuine engagement with both feminist and queer politics, but with accompanying heavy doses of plenty other ills of Western culture—like capitalist self-branding, the reduction of women's sexual pleasure to fodder for the male gaze, and amatonormativity (privileging sexual relationships above other forms of kinship).[43]

We shouldn't be too hard on Zakaria's classmates for turning to their own culture for tools with which to combat sexism. (We should be hard on them for their unacknowledged imperialism, but more about that later.) Where else besides their own culture should we expect them to turn? It is not as though they could just make up new norms and identities out of nowhere. As feminist and queer theorists have been pointing out for an age, we construct our identities from culturally available tools. All politics is a remaking, not a beginning. Remaking can surprise us, so it does not follow from any of this that feminist politics is hopeless.

But it does mean that *freedom* feminism is based on a lie. The freedom feminist dream of women being unshaped by social norms is an impossible one. Literally everything we do, from the language we speak, to the modes of transportation we use, to the times of day we eat and sleep are shaped by social norms. Try as we might to find a "true self" that is underneath all of these norms, we can't. We have been shaped by them since before we were conscious, before we were out of our parents' bodies, hearing their music, absorbing specific pregnant people foods, taking in the rhythms of their language. If we were not shaped by social norms at all, we would lose our ability to relate to each other. This is because socialization is largely a set of shortcuts for interacting;

we cannot speak without a shared language, would have to debate every exchange for hours if there were no norms of purchase or barter, would get into an awful lot of accidents if we were not all adhering to the norm that we drive on one side of the street.

It's difficult to overstate the significance of these facts. The fact that the culture myth offers an impossible ideal should give us enough reason to abandon freedom feminism—even without the resultant racism and imperialism. Freedom feminism tells us that the way to end sexism is to eliminate social influences. But this is something we simply cannot do. We can no more eliminate social influences than we can stop breathing air. Freedom feminism is a lie.

If this sounds bleak, it shouldn't. Feminism doesn't have to be about breaking out of traditional or cultural constraints. Feminists every-where are involved in practices of cultural remixing that are changing the world every day. Zakaria's term paper in that class was one case in point. Many Muslim feminists, she argued, were reshaping their so-cieties' oppressive sexual mores from within. Zakaria wrote about the work of Asifa Quraishi-Landes, a law professor who argued that laws criminalizing adultery and fornication in Pakistan were not defensible in the terms of the Qur'an. She wrote about Amina Wadud who argued that women could reclaim Islamic traditions in ways that supported women's equality.

Zakaria's professor was not impressed. But if the idea of Muslim women fighting patriarchy using tools from within Islam was unimag-inable to her, well, let's just say it says more about her than about Islam.

Zakaria's classmates were engaged in cultural remixing too, a form of it that refused to challenge certain dominant ideas in Western culture. The "sex-positive" feminism they inherited had some distinctly anti-patriarchal ideas, among them that it was okay for women to enjoy sex, and some anti-heternormative ones, like that it was okay to have sex outside of marriage. But their feminism also had some distinctly patriarchal ideas, like that performing the enjoyment of sex was more important than actually being into it (without the performance you might be uncool, or unfeminist) and that being able to produce orgasms (real or fake) was an important part of being able to catch a sexual partner, usually a man.

Sex-positive feminism had also become a commodity as much as it was an identity. Zakaria's class took place in 2006, and she notes that the show *Sex and the City*, with its chosen family of very heterosexually active, very, very, very rich women (including a writer who could fill a closet with Manolo Blahniks?) inaugurated a new marketing category. Perhaps ironically, the need to perform sexuality to be sex-positive had also become another sexual *should* for women, one that marginalized people who wanted to resist sex, or at least the form of sex that was the implicit ideal—commodified, performative, unattached, mostly heterosexual, with little room for asexuality or social support for forms of kinship that are not based on sexuality at all.

The irony is that Zakaria's white feminist classmates fell for all of this *because* they were so sure they were free. What could be more Western than the belief in one's own liberation? As we just discussed, the idea that "we" are free and the "others" are not is as old as colonialism. And the idea that "we" are free because we choose the right cultural objects in the market is, well, as American as apple pie. If you think the right body piercings and pashminas show that you are worldly, or that a closet full of Manolos (or more recently, Louboutins) shows you have invested in yourself rather than a man, it is because someone has marketed to you really well. And Zakaria's story took place in 2006—before the advent of targeted advertising. I can't even bear to think about how much of the time I spend "choosing" elements of my identity is really the effect of big data.

Once we recognize that part of Western culture is seeing oneself as free from culture, we can perceive another way that freedom feminism serves white feminist ends. Western culture trains those who live within it to see it as a transcendence of culture, versus a culture of its own. Because of this, Western women often can't tell the difference between trying to free other women from their cultures and spreading their own.

Narayan called this idea "the missionary position." Western feminists who fall into it believe that only Westerners can name, and do something about, gender injustice. If gender injustice comes from culture, it's only those who are free of it (read: Westerners) who can see through culture enough to criticize sexism. The missionary position tells us that if a woman of color, or a woman in the Global South, wants to criticize or change her social world, there is only one direction she can turn for help. That way is outward, toward the West. She needs Western intervention and Western ideas to save her; there's no way she could see sexism, let alone work to change it, on her own.

Zakaria wrote her paper about Muslim women using their faith to argue for a world that was less sexually punishing to women. Her professor's feedback was that Zakaria didn't use the course texts enough. There wasn't a single text by a Muslim woman in the course.

But, if Western culture is the sole origin of tools for criticizing sexism, why would one expect to find feminist texts by Muslim women? The possibility of Islamic feminism is a casualty of the culture myth, as is pretty much any other feminism grounded in a culture whose members are people of color.[44] It's not that surprising that Sue, who called in the anti-terrorism authorities because of her colleagues' alleged poor treatment of women, never asked a Muslim woman what she thought of the situation. When a reporter asked Sue why she hadn't, she replied that she thought they were afraid of speaking out. It's also no wonder we conceive the remedy to poor women's plight as "saying no" to cultures that degrade them; what could there possibly be in a "rural area in sub-Saharan Africa" worth saying yes to?

The missionary position is yet another way that freedom feminism becomes a justification for white feminism. The culture myth closes off the possibility that feminism can be embedded in culture, that "other" women might be "called to feminism in another language."[45] This in turn hinders something that should be central to any feminist politics worth its salt: solidarity.

White feminism is not just bad because it's imperialist; it's bad because it's not really feminism. Nor is the culture myth really feminist; it leads us to pursue political strategies that won't undo sexist oppression, by limiting our imagination of what a feminist future looks like. If the realities of the contemporary West are the best women can hope for, the best isn't actually that radical. If we want to end oppression, we need to hope that the future can be better than this. Feminists of color have long been arguing that solutions to women's oppression are embedded within their cultures, but the culture myth presents this as impossible.

Zakaria's classmates might have ended up with some more revolutionary ideas about sexuality if they had been willing to look at their own history and culture that shaped their lives and perspectives, rather than assume that they could think themselves free. They might have even been able to see that the perspectives on sexuality they touted were not as liberatory as they'd thought, because of their connections to capitalism and coloniality. They might have seen that less oppressive ways of living sexuality have existed in cultures around the world.

This is what many women of color feminists argue about their own cultures, cultures that colonialism (sometimes with the help of white feminism) have attempted to extinguish. For example, North American Indigenous scholar and activist Kim TallBear argues that the dominant understanding of sexuality is worse for women, and people who are not men or women, than the understanding of sexuality it attempted to replace. Part of the project of imagining a feminist future is looking at Indigenous ways of relating, roots far older than the settler colonial sexual relations that tried to supplant them.

TallBear's journey into thinking about nonmonogamy began when she was a child. It grew out of a conflict between settler images of Native families as "broken," rife with "unmarried mothers," and her own lived experience of kin. TallBear grew up with four generations in her grandmother's house. It was a house full of laughter, of people "overflowing" into the orange linoleum-floored dining room.[46] Nothing about this way of life felt "broken." For a long time, in her own life, she shifted between avoiding monogamous marriage because she was sure she would fail to live up to the ideal of the nuclear family, and avoiding it because she was sure that marriage meant submission to men.[47]

The lightbulb went off when she realized that the idea of marriage she had inherited was a settler ideal. That ideal said that kinship consisted in monogamous heterosexual marriage. Yet as Cree/Metis feminist Kim Anderson puts it, in Native American societies there traditionally was "no such thing as a single mother."[48] This was because of thriving extended kin networks of mutual support, like the many pairs of feet walking in and out of TallBear's grandmother's dining room. The settler ideal of the monogamous nuclear family saw the unmarried woman with children as a "single mother," pathologizing her and denying her support and recognition for the forms of kinship she did have.

The ideal of the heterosexual monogamous nuclear family also subjugated, and subjugates, women in many other ways. Its history has always been about private property. I don't mean treating married women as property, though this is certainly true; I mean the relationship between marriage and land property. TallBear, Anderson, and other Indigenous feminists argue that the purpose of the nuclear family in North America was to create a basis for dispossessing Native people. The only understanding of land in the settler mind was as a commodity that was privately owned. The only people settlers conceived as landowners were men. The only way to know who should inherit men's land was to trace lineage through their children. Since there were no DNA tests back then, there was one way to know which babies "belonged" to which men: control women's sexuality, enforce monogamy, and entrench the idea that there are only two genders.

TallBear's interest in nonmonogamy, though, is not just about excavating the past. It's about imagining the future differently and realizing that Indigenous traditions are fertile with possibilities for such a reimagining. She uses the Dakota word Tiyospaye to describe the types of extended kin networks that long dominated the North American continent. This form of kinship included multigenerational families and households that did not revolve around a single sexual pairing. North American Indigenous societies recognized more than two genders, or what we might call genders through a contemporary Western lens. Some of these genders had recognized social roles, and there was an "element of flexibility in gender identification."

But when TallBear says that Indigenous forms of family and sexuality are more flexible, she imagines something that Zakaria's classmates couldn't quite fathom. They couldn't perceive that in trying to create "new," "free," sex-positive sexual identities, they were participating in an algorithmically identifiable marketing category. While TallBear argues that the dominant form of sexuality in the West is harmful, her solution is not to create new sex-positive identities. Instead, she says that the Indigenous insight is to criticize the idea of identity altogether. Identity is laden with capitalist and settler overtones; the indigenous alternative is *relating*.

This emphasis on relating over identity has been an important part of TallBear's intervention into more mainstream, settler-dominated conversation about sexuality and family in general, and nonmonogamy in particular. She jokes that her inbox is full of notes from two types of people, those who have discovered through a DNA test that they are "really" Native, and those who have recently begun identifying as polyamorous. TallBear says she often responds to the latter, because she actually feels she has something to offer them. Her advice is that it is a mistake to think that being polyamorous is a gender or sexual identity. Thinking of it that way means thinking of it as "something to be held unchanging within one's own body—as one's body's property."[49] She also argues that seeing oneself as always relating allows one to navigate one's relationship to oppression more fruitfully. Relating allows recognition of the reality that one has been formed in relation to harmful circumstances, like capitalism and colonialism, without reducing oneself to that. Instead, there is always the possibility of reshaping relations.

TallBear also argues that there is important feminist potential in the Indigenous idea that the web of relating we find ourselves in is *nonhierarchical*. There are no "special" forms of relation that are worth more than others, or fundamentally different kinds among others. This opens up an idea not available to Zakaria's class: that the assumption that sexuality is a distinct, privileged type of relation is itself worth questioning. Nonhierarchical relating pushes against amatonormativity, the notion that kinship based on a sexual bond should be privileged above all other forms of relating, like friendship or multigenerational childrearing. It also pushes against the idea that monogamous marriage is the only source of a real family.

TallBear's Indigenous criticisms of Western sexuality may sound abstract, but they are also highly practical. To move from the idea that monogamous marriage is the "right" kind of relating to a recognition of what monogamy has done to women and Indigenous forms of kinship means advocating for new social support structures. Concretely, it is about reforming the tax deductions and subsidies we currently reserve for married couples and rejecting the lack of subsidies for childcare and eldercare. It is about supporting a variety of family forms, including polyamorous ones and ones that are not founded on sexual bonding at all.[50] It also translates into practical advocacy for more open custody arrangements—which, if you will recall Zakaria's life story, might have helped her more than an injunction to performatively share her sexual exploits.

TallBear's feminist vision is embedded deeply within the history of North American Indigenous cultures. But it isn't exactly a call for a return to the past. She wants us to resist the idea that we are moving "back to something purer" or "forward to something better."[51] The idea of moving back assumes that the past is no longer with us and that we know exactly what it was; the idea of moving forward accepts the European colonial idea that the future is always better than the past. The culture myth tells us feminists have two choices: return to an anti-feminist past or turn toward a cultureless future that is really just white Western culture by another name. The idea that there are feminist possibilities within longstanding cultures can help us think beyond the false choice given by the culture myth. TallBear tells us that what we need is conversation "in and across what is called in English, time."[52] Feminist change is more complicated than freedom feminism would have it, but it also doesn't require creating from nowhere.

The culture myth is a path to literal violence and exclusion. But it's also a dead end, one that cuts us off from imagining the kind of radical change we really need to build a feminist world. Freedom feminism might have the word *freedom* in it, but it is awfully limiting. It forces to evangelize for Western culture because we are under the mistaken apprehension that it represents moral progress. It traps us within its way of seeing the world because we start from the assumption that cultures, especially "other" cultures, are feminism's enemy.

To accept that culture is not always the problem, and that sometimes it is even the solution, would be ruinous for white feminism. White feminism has always been about saving others from their backward cultures.

Freedom feminism cloaks that idea in what seems to be more innocent language. But once we have seen what freedom feminism actually does to people of color, we cannot unsee it. We need to actively work against the way culture talk allows feminism to be an unacknowledged tool of white supremacy. The first step is to realize that freedom feminism is based on a dangerous lie, the lie that it is possible to be free of culture. The next is to develop a genuinely radical view of what feminism is *for*.

CHAPTER 4

THE JUDGMENT MYTH

The Personal Isn't as Political as You Think

I n 1986, Audre Lorde wrote that caring for herself was "an act of political warfare."[1] She was in the midst of her second battle with cancer,
realizing that overextending herself wasn't helping her or the causes she
was committed to. Lorde was a Black lesbian, but the passage in which
she coined the term *self-care* immediately followed a meditation on her
own privilege. It was her economic stability that had allowed her access
to the cancer treatments that were keeping her alive. She had been able
to make a living as a writer and activist. Having privilege meant using it
for good, and, in her case, empowering others through her writing. "If
one Black woman I do not know gains strength from my story, it has
been worth the difficulty of the telling."[2]

Search the hashtag #selfcare today and you're likely to find legions
of women whose realities seem distant from Lorde's: TikToks of twenty-
somethings going through twenty-plus-step skincare routines to elec-
tropop soundtracks. Instagrams of influencers feeling themselves in fur
vests and Louis Vuitton bags.[3] Minimalist mom inspo of a watering can
held up to nourish one's own flower crown with the hashtag #lookout-
fornumberone right next to #selfcare.[4] Sometimes the self is highlighted
with a "fuck haters" flourish or references to Ariana Grande's call to "be
your own fuckin' best friend."[5] "Completely unconcerned with what's
not mine" is a common follow-up.[6]

In another dark twist on a classic feminist trope, novelist Daphne Merkin defended "women's agency" in a 2018 *New York Times* op-ed. She had taken to the country's paper of record to confide her supposedly unspeakable views.[7] In a piece entitled "Publicly We Say Me Too: Privately We Have Misgivings," Merkin turned feminist ideas about the value of women's agency against us. The term *agency*, now ubiquitous in feminist academia and politics, was introduced in the 1980s to complicate the way women live under patriarchy. We don't just unthinkingly do what sexism demands, the term insisted. We often find creative ways to survive and self-define.

For Merkin, though, "women's agency" became a new type of rape myth, the acceptable liberal equivalent of "but what were you wearing?" She was responding to the fact that women were suddenly posting experiences of workplace harassment that did not include physical violence. They were making complaints about things like receiving (what their superstar bosses euphemistically called) "romantic writings" full of "adolescent passages."[8] They wanted an end to collegial "pats on the back" that ended with hands up under their shirts[9] and repeated sexualizing "compliments" on their physical appearances.[10] Merkin protested that these women were self-infantilizing. She was tired of reading "story after story of adult women who helplessly acquiesce to sexual demands."[11] Most women know how to extricate themselves from these situations, she went on. Those of us who can't figure out the tactful "no" every time, or who dare hope for jobs where we don't have to fight off wandering hands or go through "interviews" in hotel rooms need to stop making excuses for ourselves. Or, more precisely, we make the mistake of treating ourselves as though we don't really have freedom to choose. We, to use, Merkin's other epithet, think we are "as frail as Victorian housewives."

The idea that women are adults who can make their own choices was once a revolutionary point about how the state and men were not better equipped than women to know what was good for us. In the hands of Merkin and many like her (think: the Utah representative who greeted the overturning of *Roe v. Wade* with a comment about how she trusts women to "control their own intake of semen"[12]), the idea now works to shift responsibility for anything that happens to women back onto women. The idea that women, especially women who were multiply oppressed by racism, patriarchy, and heterosexism, needed to care for themselves and each other to replenish their power to organize, was, for Lorde, a powerful reminder that even the most powerful activists are still vulnerable bodies. For today's influencers, "self-care" is a preemptive strike against anyone who would judge them for the $100 facial mist it takes to keep up that #cleangirl aesthetic.

These reversals in the political valence of claims about women's choices and the need to respect them are depressing and predictable. When we insist that we can make our own decisions, and that no one has a right to judge us for them, we are demanding a certain kind of freedom, a freedom to be left alone. In a world in which our menu of choices is rigged, with liberalism and capitalism functioning as our dominant political languages, respect for women's choices doesn't lead where we think it does. A politics that leaves women to make their own choices is, in the world we actually live in, a recipe for keeping patriar-chy, and other oppressive systems like white supremacy and capitalism, intact. Freedom feminism might make for less feminist infighting, but it won't transform society.

One of freedom feminism's most insidious faces is the idea that the goal of feminism is to respect women's choices. The judgment myth, as I call it, lives in the comment section of pretty much any news item describing a woman's behavior. The typical back-and-forth goes something like this: A woman does something (works outside the home or is a stay-at-home mom, has sex or doesn't have sex, eats a cupcake or doesn't eat a cupcake). Someone criticizes the choice, or just takes the choice as an opportunity to make some kind of social commentary.

Cue the "feminist" conversation stopper. Don't judge women, one version goes. It's proof that feminism has succeeded that individual women can make their own choices, goes another, and we should stop getting in the way. Feminism is about letting women make their own choices, and talking about what women do is unfeminist.

There is literally an entire genre of feminist writing devoted to the question, "Can I be a feminist and . . . ?" Perhaps the most common fill-in to the blank is "Can I be a feminist and wear high heels?" If you ever comply with social expectations around femininity, there's a well-worn internet search out there waiting for you. Can I be a feminist and wear makeup? Can I be a feminist and be a stay-at-home mom? Get cosmetic surgery? The title of Roxane Gay's best-selling *Bad Feminist* is a nod to this trope. She opens her important paean to the complexity of living as a feminist by declaring that yes, she is a feminist, even though she listens to hip-hop and loves blow jobs.

Women are worried about being judged by other women and they're especially worried about being judged by feminists. There are some good reasons for this. Feminists, especially powerful and privileged ones, have historically misunderstood the lives of women whose choices and circumstances are different from theirs. One consequence of this tendency to misunderstand can be a quickness to assume that the choices women make, especially ones that involve going along with what the patriarchy expects from women, are evidence of their personal failings.

Middle- and upper-class women may not understand that dressing up for work is sometimes a way to celebrate finally having a job where one doesn't have to wear a uniform,[13] or that wearing internet tutorial–worthy makeup along with one's uniform can be a form of resistance. Cis feminists have been quick to judge trans women who find joy in a trip to Sephora for upholding oppressive norms of femininity. But this is often what it takes to be seen as a woman by others, and trans and cis women alike are navigating a world where things we value about being women are bound up with oppressive gender expectations.[14]

But there is a difference between acknowledging this fact and convincing ourselves that other women's judgments are *the* problem feminism is supposed to solve. If freedom feminism tells us to free ourselves from social expectations, the judgment myth offers a comfortably simplistic understanding of what an expectation is. This simplistic understanding in turn funnels our feminist energy away from political change, or so I hope to convince you. It ensures that we will turn inward and substitute performative critiques of [insert gendered term here]-shaming for critiques of the systems that make that shaming possible in the first place. And it produces a feminism that is so friendly to capitalism that it quickly becomes a rationalization for it.

I have not been immune to constructing my feminist identity around worries about other women's judgments. Like most women, I have made a lot of choices to do what the patriarchy says I should. Like many a femme, I have been known to put on stilettos when I need instant confidence. I get a little bit too excited about wearing matching dresses with my daughter. I volunteer more often than I should to take the meeting minutes and buy the office birthday gifts, and I am definitely in the habit of apologizing before I make a comment. I have responded to more than one catcaller's request that I smile by, well, smiling. In all of these cases, I have felt it necessary to explain to myself how these choices were compatible with feminism.

Part of my explanation has been that most of these choices are more complicated than they seem. I've worked most of my life in highly male-dominated fields where no one would buy the office gifts if I didn't, and I know that women in the workplace face professional and social consequences for not seeming agreeable. As for the heel-wearing, part of my goal has undoubtedly been to dare others in that same male-dominated profession to deny that there is a space for women and femmes in it.

This knowledge about the complicated character of my choices has shielded me from some unwelcome judgments from others. It has helped me be easier on myself. But it has not shielded me from sexism.

I still remember the day I decided to wear red heels to a job interview. In my defense (though the judgment myth is right that I shouldn't have to defend myself) the rest of my outfit was conservative. I was wearing a black business suit. The only skin showing was on my hands and face.

At the end of my presentation, a white man in his seventies approached the podium. "I have a question," he said. I put on my best thinking face and leaned forward expectantly.

"What else do you do in those shoes?"

There were things to worry about besides other women's judgment. There was nothing I wanted less in that moment than for other women to leave me alone.

THE APPEAL OF THE JUDGMENT MYTH

Facing down the patriarchy is easier to do in the company of other women than on one's own. So, it's hard not to wonder how we got to a cultural point where the assertion "Leave women alone" so often works as a kind of feminist trump card. The judgment myth took hold partly because of how it played in a recent political moment, and partly because it appealed to ideas that are deeply rooted in Western political culture.

The historical origin is shallower, though calling it shallow isn't quite right, because it clearly evokes deep feelings in people. The "can I be a feminist and" think pieces speak to the fact that fear of being judged is a real motivator for many women, me included. I have already mentioned part of the reason for this; in feminism there is a long history of women, especially elite women, just not getting it when it comes to other women's compliance with patriarchal norms.

But the fear of being judged by feminists looms large in our minds for another reason too. The idea of feminists as enemies of women, as purists that no actual woman is good enough for, became widespread in response to a political moment that is before my time, and likely before yours. By the 1980s, feminists were, in a certain sense, *winning*. Since 1973, there had been a constitutionally protected right to abortion. In 1974, women became able to get credit cards in their own names. Gender-based employment discrimination had become illegal: in 1978 it became illegal to fire a pregnant woman, and in 1986 sexual harassment was finally acknowledged as discriminatory. In the 1980s, women began to make up half of all college students.

In spite of such significant gains for women, another narrative was exploding all over the media. As the Pulitzer Prize–winning journalist Susan Faludi documents in her aptly titled book *Backlash*, movies and headlines told a story of women afflicted with failure and unhappiness.[15] They concocted an apparent paradox: when feminism had been so successful, how could women be so unhappy? There was no acknowledgment that twenty years of activism (since the second wave) were not enough to undo thousands of years of patriarchy, nor that the right was launching a concerted attack on "working women" and blaming them for a breakdown of the American family—a campaign that would achieve its culmination in the dismantling of social supports for poor women in the 1990s known as "welfare reform."

The real thing that was making women unhappy had to be *feminism*. College-educated women were leading empty lives because they wanted to have husbands and babies, and couldn't reconcile this with the need to become the heartless achievers the feminist "myth of independence" told them they should be.[16] In an argument that foreshadowed Republican senators' insistence that feminists were being too judgmental when they tried to keep Amy Coney Barrett off the Supreme Court, a presidential spokesperson described feminism as a "straitjacket" for women.[17] More generally, anti-feminist politics today borrow heavily from the backlash playbook. Blame the movement that attempts to solve the problem for the problem itself (bans on "critical race theory," anyone?) and portray demands for change as attempts to limit freedom.

In 1990, Wellesley College invited first lady Barbara Bush to give the commencement address. In an act that feels as much 2024 as 1990, 150 students tried to cancel her. Or, to be precise, they signed a petition opposing the administration's granting Bush a high-status platform from which to advise young women. It was inconsistent with the mission of a women's college to bring in a commencement speaker whose main claim to fame was having a husband, the students argued.[18] The students' initial preference had been for Alice Walker, who had recently won the Pulitzer Prize and the National Book Award for her novel celebrating Black women's relationships and resistance to patriarchy and racism.[19] Barbara Bush was a far cry from Alice Walker.

During my college activist days, I would have loved for a mere 150 signatures on any petition to be enough to garner national media coverage. As we well know from today's flood of think pieces about "cancel culture," any number of signatures becomes enough when a college petition touches on the media's current cause célèbre: in 1990, it was the idea that closed-minded feminists were making other women suffer.

The Wellesley event managed to get covered in outlets like *Time* and the *New York Times*.

It also ignited the so-called "mommy wars."[20] Seemingly unaware that Alice Walker was a mom, or that Barbara Bush was the wife of a sitting Republican president, the media and college spokespersons took this as an occasion to chide young women for failing to see the value of motherhood. Apparently, critiquing an honor bestowed upon someone who was famous for her husband's accomplishments—an honor that had previously been given to the likes of Maya Angelou and Gloria Steinem—was indistinguishable from critiquing motherhood itself. (If the college was just trying to make a statement about the value of full-time care work, one wonders why it did not consider bestowing the honor on one of the students' mothers. Or nannies.)

According to the ensuing reportage, women were at war. Feminism had pitted women who were stay-at-home moms and women who pursued careers against one another. If you have a sense of what feminists were actually doing during that time, or any analysis of race and class, it's hard not to regard this whole thing with a giant eyeroll. It is true that the quintessential feminist portrayed in the media was a rich, white, childless achiever who had ignored her biological clock to make it to college or the boardroom. It is also true that many prominent feminists in the mid-twentieth century rejected motherhood. But organizations like Federally Employed Women had been fighting for childcare and flexible scheduling since the 1960s,[21] calling for twenty-four-hour childcare centers to open across the country. And there were longstanding women's movements that campaigned for public assistance as a support for care work, like the Black-led "mother-recipient" welfare rights movement I will discuss in chapter 5.[22]

It's not just that the mommy wars story misrepresents the history of the feminist movement; it also misrepresents stay-at-home motherhood as a choice, in spite of the fact that it is an option available mostly to the rich and white. Women of color and poor and working-class women have always had to work outside the home. Being able to survive on a single income has been the province of the privileged. This is increasingly true today as the cost of living rises. Today's social media tradwives present themselves as making a choice to "rest" at home instead of engage in the hustle culture they associate with feminism and that #girlbosses actually do celebrate, ignoring that having this choice requires a certain amount of economic privilege. (Many of them also link housewifery with hierarchy and privilege in another explicit way: white women need to be at home to transmit "European" culture to their children, their alt-right-dictated responsibility.[23])

If the memes and think pieces of today are to be believed, the mommy wars are alive and well. One alt-right momfluencer famously tweeted that feminism was about encouraging women to "work 9–5 and drink wine every night until their ovaries dry up."[24] Not all manifestations of these judgments are so extreme. During a scrolling break from writing this piece, I read a meme asking us not to judge "working moms" who "all" spend every day feeling guilty. (I guess I'm not a real working mom?) The week before, I read a headline insisting that stay-at-home moms were the real victims of the pandemic. That this stuff managed to survive amid the pandemic's strain on *anyone* with young children in 2020, 2021, and 2022 is a testament the mind-boggling resilience of the idea that feminists don't want women to be moms.

The main effect of all of this feminist blaming has been to change the face of the enemy. What really makes moms' lives so hard remains obscured—namely, our lack of social support for parenting.

The real reason women feel bad about our life choices, at least according to the mommy wars discourse is . . . *feminists.*

Enter the belief that the real thing holding women back is other women's judgment. Enter the judgment myth.

When you think that being too judgmental is the problem, it makes sense to pivot to the view that you won't tell anyone what to do. The message that wifehood and motherhood were oppressive (as society had configured them to require utter dependency on a man) had had its day. It was too polarizing. In the conservative political environment of the 1980s, the environment that birthed "family values" and the Christian right, the idea of transforming marriage into an equal partnership and making childcare public didn't play well.[25] It was far more palatable to the mainstream to describe feminism as the belief that women just deserved a choice.

The upside of this message was that it didn't offend anyone.

The downside was also that it didn't offend anyone. It's hard to make change without making any waves.

Defending women from judgment about their choices around career and motherhood may help us feel a little bit better, but it doesn't disrupt the system that makes motherhood so costly to begin with. It's not women's opinions that have built the modern workplace around the assumption that the worker is a breadwinner whose career trajectory can move uninterruptedly upward, and who can work evenings because he doesn't have caregiving responsibilities. It isn't women's opinions that have given us a society that thinks care work is not worth paying for, or paying for well, or publicly subsidizing. Nor is it women's opinions that have given us a host of state laws that prevent LGBTQ people from adopting. Of course, women hold opinions that support all of these oppressive structures and policies, but women being nicer to each to each other isn't a substitute for awareness of those structures or policies, less still for action that will change them.

The idea of leaving alone—and being left alone—has roots in the American psyche that predate the backlash against feminism by hundreds of years. This deeper root of the judgment myth lies in the political philosophy known as liberalism. Liberalism, the school of thought behind most Western democracies, places a high value on people's abilities to live lives of their choosing. Liberals hold that individuals have rights to live their lives as they see fit, even if others disagree or disapprove, and that the way to respect this freedom is to reduce interference in people's lives. If you, like me, grew up hearing the phrase "It's a free country," meaning "You have to let me do what I want," you have been inculcated with the concept of freedom that underlies the judgment myth.

It's unsurprising that a country of people who have been repeating "It's a free country" since elementary-school recess is fertile ground for a feminism that centers respecting women's rights to do as they please. The conception of freedom as noninterference goes by the name "negative freedom" in the history of political thought.[26] This is by no means the only way of understanding freedom, and it's not one that feminists, or other radicals, have preferred throughout history.[27] But the freedom myth lays claim to a relatively status-quo American understanding of freedom, suggesting that feminism is just about applying that understanding to women; freedom is about being left alone, and women deserve to be left alone too.

I am not saying that the freedom myth is appealing only because of societal brainwashing. Far from it; there are plenty of feminist issues for which the right political solution involves spending less time telling people what to do. Choices about abortion and birth control are obvious examples. So are cases of the government tying public assistance to marriage, or trying to control which bathroom people are allowed to use.[28]

On the other hand, I'll never forget the first time I thought I was approaching an abortion rights demonstration that turned out to be an anti-vax one instead. I had seen a sign with a "No" symbol and the words "My body, my choice." I had to get really close to see that what should have been a coat hanger was in fact a surgical mask.

This experience was a testament to a bigger concern about negative freedom. In our current context, appeals to negative freedom often work against the oppressed and vulnerable. Being expected to wear a mask to protect others from COVID-19 and being forced to carry a pregnancy to term both involve being told what to do, even if their effects are dramatically different. When the purveyors of backlash in the 1980s portrayed feminism as a "straitjacket," they were taking advantage of the fact that it's difficult to make change without taking a stance about what people should do. So were the Republican senators who insisted that progressives were hypocrites when we dared criticize Amy Coney Barrett.

The successful portrayal of feminism as a form of confinement, and Barrett as a victim of feminist narrowmindedness, are telling about why a feminism based on the judgment myth won't lay a path to gender equality. We live in a society in which rich white women with children are held up as paragons of motherhood and work-life balance. The forces that ensure this (from cultural representations of women of color as bad mothers to the inaccessibility of affordable childcare) are sometimes invisible, but they are powerful nonetheless. When these forces are at work, the demand to leave Barrett alone is not an innocuous "You do you." It is—at least when made en masse about women in power and women like her—a demand to leave society as it is.

The same argument applies to almost any existing inequality: the request to leave people alone is ultimately a request to do nothing and leave the inequality intact.[29] A politics with negative freedom at its core is a politics that preserves the status quo. It may seem that refusing to tell people what to do is actually a way of challenging the way things are. Occasionally, it is. But structures like patriarchy and white supremacy are not just a heap of judgments, whose machinations we can stop by simply withholding our commentary. Refusing to criticize them, or the actions that perpetuate them, won't stop them from setting the parameters of what is possible for any individual to achieve in their life, or from sorting society into winners and losers. Social structures work through material rewards and punishments, not just feelings of praise and shame; they are bigger and more powerful than individual judgments.

In other words, there is a certain amount of inertia to the unjust status quo, and the idea of freedom at the heart of the judgment myth is ready to let that inertia take hold. The social machinery is set up to keep producing inequality. In fact, it is set up to do this *through* our own choices.

WHEN EQUALITY IS NOT ON THE MENU

When Rosa arrived at work that day barefaced, she wasn't out to prove a theory.[30] She just thought it would be nice to squeeze in a nap before her dinner shift. But the extra sleep meant she had to rush through getting ready, and she skipped her usual makeup routine.

It was a good night for Rosa's service. The sushi came out quickly, so there were no disgruntled patrons to wrangle. She didn't have that many tables, so she had time to smile and chat and refill waters.

Only one table tipped her the 15 to 20 percent she was used to receiving. Most tipped her only 5 to 10 percent. Her boyfriend had once told her that women servers make more money than men servers because they "look better." Maybe her accidental experiment had proven him right.

Servers have been in the business of leveraging their looks for tips for a long time. Rosa's boyfriend might have "tipped her off" to the not-so-hidden sexual expectations of server jobs, but women often give each other advice on how to navigate them. In the words of Laurie Ter-rell, a longtime server, older waitresses "groomed" her as soon as she entered the industry as a teen. "We serve a basic need, and we need to look cute and be friendly while we do it, so go and get some acrylic nails and put some makeup on," they had suggested.[31]

Sometimes the advice was not just about how to alter one's appear-ance to one's advantage. Sometimes it was about tolerating sexual ha-rassment. "So and so over there . . . if you let him pat your butt after he orders, he will tip you 100%."[32] Laura, a pizza delivery driver talks about how her manager wanted to date her. She refused, and then he made her work life miserable. In order to protect herself from his retaliation, she finessed her technique: "flirting with him, but just enough to stay on his good side."[33]

Other times, it isn't about tolerating sexual harassment but about learning to modulate one's behavior to avoid it. Women working in restaurant kitchens "learn quickly to crouch, never to bend over when grabbing a pot."[34]

These women are exemplars of agency. They are smart and savvy, making calculated decisions that help them succeed at work. Notwith-standing Daphne Merkin's definition of agency as being responsible for leaving or fending off harassment, it's clear that these women's ways of negotiating their workplaces' unfair demands are subtle, effective, and responsible. Alexandria Ocasio-Cortez, who was a bartender before she was a member of Congress, tells a story about her own life that highlights just how carefully women in the restaurant industry have to calculate in order to stay safe and get by financially. She remembers checking what day of the month it was before deciding how to respond to a harasser. If it was the twenty-eighth and her bills were about to be due, it might be time to let that untoward comment slide.[35]

Former server Gina explains her reasoning about her choices to negotiate around, rather than confront, harassers this way: "You need to get that money, and when you get that tip at the end of the day, you know it was no big deal."[36]

Of course, she's right that if you make your money through tipped work, it matters terribly how much money you end up counting at the end of your shift. But even if it feels like "no big deal," needing to tiptoe around these existing rules, day in and day out, takes a toll. Gina talks about how she had begun to blame herself for the days her handsy boss would rub her shoulders; maybe she just looked stressed out? Natalia, another server, says it is mentally exhausting to constantly have to ask herself, *Do I want to tell this man that he's being a pig, or do I want the $20?*

Women who are, or have been, servers also find that the expectation of harassment follows them into other arenas of life. Laurie says the industry gave her nightmares about unwanted touches, and that she had become so hypervigilant that when people she loved put their arms around her, she would flinch.[37] Jade, who is trans, talks about how tables of drunk men posed not just the threat of unwanted sexual advances, but also the threat of being punched in the face.[38] These experiences also follow servers into other jobs. Women who leave the industry—an industry that is so many women's first experience of paid work—find that their habituation to harassment makes them more tolerant of harassment over time and in other work situations.[39] Marlea, a server who went on to make a career in public relations, says that being a server made her feel that it was normal for her workplace to require her to have a certain look, and that to this day, she feels it is a workplace requirement to stay a certain size.[40]

My own ambivalent laugh at the "What else do you do in those shoes?" comment from a harasser in academia had been honed for a long time, starting during my first job in food service. I can still recall the day a customer told me he would get in trouble if he told me what else he wanted, and that it wasn't on the menu.

The women in the restaurant industry whose stories I have just told probably also want something that's not on the menu: to get through a day of work without objectification or harassment.

It turns out that Rosa's boyfriend was wrong. Women don't earn more tips than men. Men earn more tips than women, or at least some research suggests they do.[41]

The reason seems to be that people tip more for service that seems exceptional, and men's baseline service is seen as exceptional whereas women's is not.

To put it differently, women are held to a higher standard. We can speculate about what makes a woman's service stand out as exceptional, but we know that attractiveness correlates with higher tips in general, for both men and women—as well as that women face a more demanding standard for professional appearance than men do.[42] We also know that women are expected to be agreeable on the job,[43] and research shows that the expectation that employees be agreeable increases their vulnerability to harassment.[44]

All of this adds up to women having to pay a beauty and harassment tax just to do their jobs. Servers face a host of unwritten (or sometimes written; in 2006 a court ruled that requiring women bartenders to wear makeup to work did not amount to appearance discrimination)[45] appearance and agreeability job requirements, including wearing makeup and accepting "flirtation." But in the job description for servers, clearly nothing about taking orders, bringing food, or even chatting requires beauty, sexual availability, or what the philosopher Talia Bettcher calls "reality enforcement" for trans people.[46]

As Gina puts it, "You don't need harassment to serve chicken wings."

Every day, women are choosing to (or not to) put on lipstick before going to work. Every day women are making choices about whether to bend over to grab that pot in the kitchen. In spite of this, chicken wings still often come with a side of grope.

Usually, there is nothing an individual woman can do to change that. Telling that man he is "being a pig," slapping him, walking away, sending your colleague to that table, figuring out the level of smile that will keep things chill without escalating the flirting—these are all things individual women can do. Sometimes they are attempts to fight the system, sometimes they are attempts at self-preservation, and sometimes they are both. But any woman doing these things on her own is unlikely to find that harassment stops in her restaurant—let alone in the world at large.

In fact, the woman who stands up to harassment or refuses to put on makeup is likely to be punished. As Natalia put it, every time she tells a harasser he is being a pig, twenty dollars is at stake. She is one of the lucky ones, since others might lose their job for the same behavior. Study after study shows that women do not report harassment because of concern about retaliation.[47] And study after study suggests that how much women are tipped is affected by how much they "look" the part.[48] Any woman who has stopped wearing makeup and been told "Are you okay? You look tired" by every person they meet knows that rejecting appearance-related norms does not mean ceasing to be judged by them.

This is the real reason we can't expect respect for women's choices to get us to gender equality. Women have good reasons to comply with norms that oppress us. Complying with those norms benefits us; it's often the best we can do to get by. If we are getting something out of tolerating harassment and paying the beauty tax just so we can go to work, the large-scale outcome of leaving us to make our own choices is predictable. It's more patriarchy.

To be clear, we are not the reason that patriarchy continues to exist. The judgment myth is right that women shouldn't drag ourselves for putting up with groping or putting on that lipstick. But the reason we shouldn't drag ourselves is also the reason we should expect sexism to keep chugging along if we embrace a feminism that is reduced to respect for women's choices. The menu of choices is rigged. Chicken wings with a side of grope is on the menu, and women have a reason to keep selling that item as long as the penalties for not selling it remain high.

It is tough to come to terms with the idea that women benefit from making choices that do not challenge sexism. If sexism harms women, it may seem that there's no way women could benefit from engaging in the behaviors the sexist system rewards. That seems paradoxical. But sexism doesn't harm women by making all of our options equally awful, or by preventing us from making choices at all.

Instead, sexism harms us by making all of the options available to us worse than those available to similarly situated men. Sexism makes women as a group worse off than men as a group, but that doesn't mean that women can never make choices that benefit them as individuals.

Think about it this way. Men make their choices from one menu and women from another. (The reality here is of course more complicated because men of different races and classes make their choices from different menus, and because the world is not just divided into men and women.)

The MEN-u for the most privileged men is like that of a Michelin-starred restaurant with a twist: the options are delicious, and they're cheap. The menu for women, especially the one on offer to women who face multiple oppressions, is like that overpriced restaurant you go to in the middle of the night because it's the only place open. You have mediocre options, and you really wish you were somewhere else.

You can also think about it like this: patriarchy, and other oppressive systems, offer rewards to the "good" ones, the ones who play by the rules. Servers who wear makeup get tips, women who laugh off sexual harassment get attributions of coolness and agreeableness. Sometimes the rewards are ordinary, like making the maximum amount of money you can at a job that doesn't pay very well or very predictably, like serving at a restaurant. Sometimes the rewards are extraordinary, reserved for the token woman whose compliance can be held up to illustrate the supposed fairness of the system: a seat on the highest court in the land for the woman who challenges neither the expectation that women can "do it all" nor the expectation that women (especially white, able-bodied women) should carry every possible pregnancy to term.

There are rewards for playing by the rules, and costs for breaking them. And the costs are often ones we shouldn't expect anyone to have to bear. Asking women working for tips not to wear makeup or not to confront harassers is an unfair demand to reduce their already precarious incomes.

If it sounds pessimistic to say that women's lives are run by rules they can't change through their individual behavior, it's because we should be pessimistic about *freedom feminism*. We should be pessimistic about the judgment myth. But that doesn't mean we need to be pessimistic about feminism. Women change the rules of the game all the time. It's just that they don't usually do it through uncoordinated acts of individual choice. They do it through collective action.

The idea of changing the rules of the game can sound daunting and abstract, especially when we are used to thinking that our choices are the only things we can control. But sometimes acts that change the rules are small. In 2018, two women in the restaurant industry created an eye-catching poster that restaurants could hang to make clear that there were policies in place to protect servers who were sexually harassed on the job.[49] It read "In the Case of Sexual Harassment You Are Not Powerless," but its purpose was largely to make clear to those who saw it that this was an establishment that took sexual harassment seriously.

On one hand, it's just a poster. On the other hand, the poster makes clear that in restaurants where it hangs, it's not business as usual when it comes to harassing servers. It resets expectations: chicken wings don't come with a side of grope here, and servers won't be penalized for rejecting roving hands. Women in the industry have also organized to make sure supervisors are trained to respond to harassment when it happens. Michaela Mendelsohn, the owner and manager of six El Pollo Loco franchises who has hired more than fifty trans employees in recent years, and is herself trans, was one of many women in the restaurant industry who worked to pass a recent California law requiring supervisors to be trained to recognize harassment based on gender identity.[50]

But some restaurant workers are thinking even bigger than reducing harassment in specific restaurants or responding to harassment that has already happened. They are trying to change the conditions that make it worth putting up with harassment in the first place. Women restaurant workers are relatively unanimous that working for tips is partly to blame[51] for the fact that the restaurant industry is the leading industry for sexual harassment.[52] It sets up a power dynamic wherein the customer expects to be able to use the threat of a bad tip to control behavior.

But tipped labor is part of an even bigger picture than gender inequality or sexual harassment. The reason we tip our servers and people in other countries don't has to do with the fact that tipping is a legacy of slavery. After the Thirteenth Amendment abolished "involuntary servitude," white business owners were still looking for ways to avoid paying wages to Black workers.[53] Enter the idea of the tip for service, borrowed from the customs of European nobles who tipped their servants. Today it is not just women but also people of color who dominate industries in which tipping is the norm. Tipping is an important site of intersectional oppression of women of color; Latinas are nearly twice as likely to work for tips as white men.[54]

In December of 2020, a group of restaurant workers gathered in Albany, New York, to take a stand against sexual harassment and tipped labor. They carried a banner bearing phrases ranging from "My body is virus-free" to "Your eyes are pretty," phrases they had heard on the job from patrons and bosses who sexualized them.[55] They had with them the twenty-four-foot figure of Elena the Essential Worker, a reimagined Rosie the Riveter for our times, a Black single mom working in the restaurant industry, wearing a mask bearing the words "Fight don't starve." They were just one group of the hundreds of thousands of workers organizing with One Fair Wage, an organization whose work has already brought an end to the subminimum tipped wage in two states and the District of Columbia.[56]

These stories about feminist action are not stories of respect for women's choices. If you think about it, they are not really stories about individual choices at all. No think pieces were written about whether you can be a feminist and choose fives and tens with a side of grope over one-dollar bills à la carte. There was no illusion that women's judgment was the cause of harassment or the tipped subminimum wage. The focus was on changing the menu, and that was not something that would come from being left alone.

JUDGING WOMEN AND LOVING WOMEN

Change comes from women working together because individual women, left to their own devices, are likely to comply with sexist expectations in order to survive, not upend them. Yet the idea that patriarchy can work through women's choices is one that feminists have been reluctant to face.

I was reminded of the reason why during my red heel job interview. I had given my presentation, survived a day of back-to-back meetings, and it was time to talk about where we should go to dinner. Some of the options required long walks. There was snow outside, but I had packed my boots. I mentioned casually that I would need to change out of the heels.

"I always wear Birkenstocks," one of my white male companions volunteered. "I teach in Birkenstocks, and they say you should wear to an interview what you wear to teach. I don't know why women have to make this so hard on themselves."

Oh right. I had done this to myself. *Women* were doing this to ourselves.

Blame. It has almost always been the endpoint of acknowledging that women's own choices are an engine of patriarchy. And the blame doesn't just come from nonfeminist white dudes in Birkenstocks. Sometimes it comes from other women, feminists even.

Fear of blame (and blaming) is part of why even the best-intentioned feminists fall into the judgment myth. This fear is a response to something real. We don't have to look far to find "feminists" saying that women's own choices are the cause of just about any sexist practice, including workplace sexual harassment and assault. Daphne Merkin's repackaging of "Why didn't you leave?" as a lament for women's bygone agency was not alone. It was a common response to #MeToo.

In 2018, a group of one hundred high-profile French women published a criticism of #MeToo in France's leading newspaper, *Le Monde*. After a sustained defense of men's right to be awkward, they turned to ridiculing women who thought feminism meant that they shouldn't have to endure groping (their example not mine). Women can demand equal pay, they wrote, without seeing men who rub up against us in the subway as cause for trauma. If we chose to, we could simply transform the unwanted subway touching into "a non-event." In case readers weren't clear on what they thought it meant to acknowledge that women had choices, they ended by noting that they were teaching their daughters to be "informed and aware," and that it was a violation of our "inner freedom"[57] to claim that harassment would harm us. Actor and producer Catherine Deneuve was one of the petition signers. The last feminist petition she signed that made waves on this side of the Atlantic was the

1971 Manifesto of the 343 "Sluts" who confessed to having had illegal abortions. A woman who had fought publicly to make abortion available in the 1970s was now arguing that being "informed and aware" could save you from assault.

Or consider *Atlantic* columnist Caitlin Flanagan's take on a young woman's description of a sexual encounter with actor Aziz Ansari that she described as "by far the worst experience with a man" she'd "ever had."[58] "Grace" described an evening when on a number of occasions Ansari overlooked signs of her discomfort and her feelings of having been pressured into sex. Flanagan seized on the fact that this example was not a clear-cut case of assault, casting Grace as an example of the excesses of #MeToo. Grace was not navigating a complicated power differential; she was, in Flanagan's eyes a "grifter," one who didn't get the point of casual sex. To Flanagan, Grace was setting the feminist movement back by not staying quiet about a crappy one-night stand. Grace didn't get that generations of women had fought for her to be able to have no-strings-attached sex. Flanagan, apparently capable of reading Grace's mind, went on to accuse Grace of using sex as a way "to matter."[59] "Women have choices now," Flanagan seemed to say. "It's time to take responsibility for what happened to you, and for letting the movement down."

With "friends" like this, it's no wonder feminists have wanted to avoid the claim that women's choices could perpetuate patriarchy, or at least leave it intact. But these "feminist" uses of agency for victim-blaming ends are just silly on their own terms. No, being smart enough to make decisions about my life doesn't imply that I can do Jedi mind tricks that turn violent experiences into positive ones. No, it doesn't imply that I should at least try to.

No, insisting that women should be allowed to decide who they want to sleep or flirt with does not imply that it's their responsibility to fight off any man who can't take a hint. Last time I checked, part of respecting people's right to decide was asking them what they wanted, or at least checking in about whether they were on board with what you were doing.

No, acknowledging that women sometimes make choices that are not in line with what the women's movement supposedly fought for does not mean that every such choice "sets the women's movement back." I say "supposedly" because I'm pretty sure the women's movement did not fight for the idea that there was a "right" way to have sex and that it was a no-strings-attached way, but this isn't the place to pick that particular fight. My point right now is just that we can break the link between respect for agency and victim blaming and we can do it without pretending that women's individual choices have magical powers. We just need to acknowledge that women exercise their agency in the world.

The political theorist Michaele Ferguson says we need to stop being so afraid of judging women.[60] In fact, she says, judging women can be a way of loving women. We just need to see that we can love other women without celebrating the choices they make. Ferguson argues that most of us already do. Most feminists *have* made some changes to our own lives to bring them into line with our values, and most of us have friends and family members who have not. I feel strongly about the fact that I didn't change my name when I got married, but I certainly have not dumped my friends and family who chose differently. I have tried to say "no" to more requests for unacknowledged labor from my colleagues, but I don't expect all women, or myself, to do this every time, because I know how hard saying "no" can be.

It shouldn't be surprising that we all love women who don't resist sexism at every turn. It shouldn't surprise us because we ourselves don't always resist it (or at least I don't). I've already confessed to not giving the "What else do you do in those shoes?" guy the finger. It's rough out there. We live in a world that dispenses penalties for resisting sexism, and a job interview is not usually the best place to test whether those penalties exist. We also live in a world that is only "partially transformed by feminism," where some of the penalties are lessening but others still have us in a vice grip, where some feminist ideas are easily accessible and others are not.[61]

Once we recognize that we are all living in a world that faces women with crummy options, we will see that judging women isn't as bad as it seems, Ferguson thinks. Judging looks bad when we feminists start regarding ourselves as the pure ones, looking down on those who happen to sometimes make the office coffee or wear lipstick to get tips. But if none of us is pure, we need to judge and *be judged*. If I'm going to judge others for changing their names, I need to be ready to be judged for not flipping off "What do you do in those shoes?" guy or Birkenstock guy. The idea seems to be that judgment isn't that bad if it's just mutual accountability.

Ferguson helps us remember that with our rigged menu of options, anything we do will either require sacrifice from us, require us to go along with an oppressive system, or both.[62] This is a step up from the judgment myth, which suggests that the only way to avoid victim blaming is to insist that all the choices women make are good. But women aren't unicorns whose only effects on themselves, or the world, are positive. Just like everyone else, our choices are sometimes good, sometimes bad, sometimes neutral—and always shaped by social structures that are outside our control.

Once we see that we are making choices within unjust social structures that we don't control, one wonders why we need to get in the business of judging women at all.

If the problem is with a set of social structures—written and unwritten rules, rigged menus—maybe we need to point the finger at them, instead of at each other. Ferguson argues that we can see judgment as a feminist act once we acknowledge the unjust world that structures our choices. As she puts it, "It is possible to imagine living as a feminist with this dilemma: accepting that being a feminist means loving nonfeminists, and accepting one's own inability to fully embody one's own feminist principles . . . a feminism involving humility and self-forgiveness, an awareness that we are all constrained by the demands of femininity."[63]

There is something to be said for redirecting conversation about individual choices to the systems that shape those choices to begin with. Instead of talking about whether it's feminist to wear heels, we can talk about why beauty is a job qualification to begin with, why it makes sense to get confidence from beauty in a world that rewards us for being beautiful, why it's trivializing to treat heel wearing as something frivolous.

In characteristic mastery of this move, Representative Ocasio-Cortez tweeted a picture of herself standing on bags of frozen broccoli at the end of a long day in 2019. This, she joked, was the price of having worn heels all day while touring the construction at La Guardia Airport and lobbying for solar panels. When Instagram asked if she really had to wear heels, she both asked us to take the heat off her (she was just trying to feel her "jush, okay?") and reminded us that heels, in fact, work for women in power. No, she didn't have to wear heels, but come to think of it, she had "yet to see the Speaker wear flats."[64]

In an interview, Ocasio-Cortez elaborated. "Femininity has power, and in politics there is so much criticism and nitpicking about how women and femme people present ourselves. Just being a woman is quite politicized here in Washington. . . . There's this really false idea that if you care about makeup or if your interests are in beauty and fashion, that that's somehow frivolous. But I actually think these are some of the most substantive decisions that we make—and we make them every morning."[65] To focus discussion on whether she should wear heels (or her signature red lip) is to fail to acknowledge the system that asks women to gain power this way. It mocks women for strategizing within constraints, and for being clever enough to find pleasure in beauty along the way.

Before we get too excited about the idea that feminists don't have to judge women, though, we need to remember that not all women are Alexandria Ocasio-Cortez. AOC deflects judgment of her choices in order to draw attention to the context that oppresses women as a group.

But sexism isn't the only system that oppresses women, and women don't always fight for other women. Ocasio-Cortez knows this and is in the habit of using comments about her appearance as opportunities to promote the fight against other inequalities—most famously when she wore a stunning white gown to the Met Gala that bore the words "tax the rich" on the back. Yet, being aware of gender inequality doesn't guarantee a fight against other inequalities. Women don't check hierarchies like race and class at the door once they start identifying as feminists. The idea that we should love each other because we are all subject to the same patriarchal rules is all fine and good, until we remember that women can reenforce sexist rules on each other, and that sexism is not the only form of injustice.

Chef Naomi Pomeroy tells a #MeToo story from her perspective as a woman restaurant owner. She wasn't always an owner; she was once a restaurant *worker* trying to figure out how to ascend the ladder. It didn't take her long to discover that the way up was to "be one of the guys." She partied with them, let some of them slap her on the ass.[66] It wasn't long before she started to find herself on the other side of the dynamic. Women chefs "learned that the real way of handling it and getting ahead was maintaining (if not even creating) the bro code. Sometimes WE started slapping people on the ass," she says. This phenomenon is more widespread than we may wish to acknowledge; women in male-dominated industries often find that being one of the guys is easier than making waves by calling out sexism.

This phenomenon isn't limited to the restaurant industry or to women who are the literal bosses of other women. Think of Emily Meyers in the movie *Fair Play*, whose hedge fund promotion is cemented by her learning to laugh at jokes about sexual abuse during after-work drinks at the strip club. Merkin and Flanagan seem happy to collect bylines and retweets by mocking women who dare speak out about sex and power. Barrett seems more than willing to use her power to remove abortion rights from other women. Her status as the ubermom does not seem to commit her to caring much about moms whose race and immigration status are different from hers, or pregnant people who don't want to be moms. When asked during her confirmation hearing whether it was "wrong to separate children from their families to deter immigrants from entering the United States," she replied that she couldn't be "drawn into" this issue as a judge.[67]

Judging women isn't the solution to the judgment myth, but it isn't something we can completely get away from, either. One problem with the judgment myth is that it keeps the heat off patriarchy, but another is that it takes the heat off powerful women. We need to be able to tell the difference between choices women make to get by or to get ahead, and choices that are or aren't *feminist*. By reducing feminism to an affirmation of all choices made by women, the judgment myth prevents this. Sometimes, it even actively lends support to systems that oppress women, like capitalism.

WOMEN DOING WHATEVER THE F*CK THEY WANT

If you're trying to escape other women's judgment, there is someone out there willing to sell you the solution. After all, if other women's judgment is the feminist enemy, as the judgment myth suggests it is, you need to armor up. Want to escape the idea that being a working mom means your house is a shambles and your kids are living off self-made peanut butter sandwiches? There's a momfluencer out there hawking bento lunchboxes that will transform the cheese and crackers you packed into an artisanal cheese board, and herbal cleaning products in pristine white packaging that will almost make you confuse mopping the floor with a trip to the spa. Want to escape the judgment that being a stay-at-home mom means not contributing to your family? You can become the momfluencer yourself, or just find a way to sell other moms some combination of "buttery" leggings, essential oils, and costume jewelry.

There is even an entire genre of marketing content riding the coattails of "I'm a feminist but" think pieces. The cover story of an Australian *Cosmo* issue about how Beyoncé is a "feminist in heels" offered a convenient new(ish) marketing angle for their usual array of beauty products, clothes, and yes, shoes. A recent internet profile on how women are transforming the shoe industry repeats the political footwear bromide. "Feminists love their heels," the shoe innovator says, defending her quest to redesign the pump. She goes on to list the names of successful women who wear them.[68] If these feminists are brave enough to stand up to those who tell them powerful women can't wear stilettos, surely we should be brave enough to embrace who we are and buy a pair. In the future, we can even express our devil-may-care individuality by letting the company assign our feet a personalized serial number that makes it easy to buy their shoes without even trying them on.[69]

It's not a coincidence that the era of freedom feminism is also the era of feminist branding. Negative freedom, the type of freedom that we respect by leaving others alone, also happens to be the type of freedom celebrated by defenders of capitalism. Laissez-faire literally means to "allow to do." Freedom feminism tells us that women's real problem is that they are too restricted, that women would flourish if we just "allowed them to do" what they want. Neoliberalism tells us the same about markets, that social problems like poverty would solve themselves if we just let individuals do their own thing. Just as capitalists chide progressives for not understanding that trying to bend the market to moral demands is futile, so too does the judgment myth locate the problem of sexism in moralizing about justice and women's lives. If the judgment myth is supposed to be a path to social change, it must be because the invisible hand of women left to their own choices will result in the end of sexism.

In a society where consumption is the main theater of choice, and where lifestyles are increasingly defined as marketing categories, the judgment myth gives us a privatized feminism. As anyone knows who has spent fifteen minutes poring over the toothpaste labels in the supermarket or hours down the internet rabbit hole trying to find the perfect milk frother or feminist T-shirt, we face a dazzling array of choices when we consume. By suggesting that all of our personal choices as women are feminist, the judgment myth coats everything we do with a political sheen, especially the buying of products that affirm our identities as feminists or choosers.

The problem with a feminism that is so hospitable to capitalism is not just that it tricks us into thinking that consuming is feminist action. The judgment myth also provides feminist cover to class inequality in general, and in particular to women who exploit other women. In a society that tells us that the choices we make rebound to us in the form of individual success, the idea that feminism resides in the choices we make makes it easy to repackage "hard work" as a feminist act.

Women striving—or, as we now like to call it for a grittier vibe, "hustling"—is one of freedom feminism's most recent, and most ubiquitous, incarnations. "Girlbosses" and "independent women" are the judgment myth's avatars, but they are part of a long line of images that equate feminism with working hard and getting ahead, including working on oneself.[70] Such images present as boldly defying the judgment of anyone who would dare stop one from bringing home that paycheck. The idea that choices to hustle are *feminist*, and not just part of the neoliberal grind, makes work within the capitalist system look like it's part of a struggle for justice. In the words of philosopher Nancy Fraser, it supplies a certain "romance" that invests "flexible capitalism with a higher moral meaning."[71] The romance attracts women of various class backgrounds. At one end are those "determined to crack the glass ceiling." At the other are "female temps [and] low wage workers . . . seeking not only income and material security, but also dignity, self-betterment, and liberation from traditional authority." As Fraser puts it: "Harnessed at both ends to the engine of capitalist accumulation."

Women of all classes might be buying into the notion of striving re-packaged as feminist freedom, but not all women are benefitting equally. Women of all classes do sometimes find relief from patriarchy in earning their own incomes, especially when it liberates them from an abusive man. But the hustle that's being rebranded as evidence of feminist daring is mostly not "clopening" (taking the closing shift and then the next open-ing shift, leaving you with a seven-hour gap to sleep and shower and hope that you have someone else to take your kids to school[72]) at McDonald's. It's sometimes the hustle of the middle-class "momtrepreneur" hosting parties for her MLM on social media after her kids have gone to bed. But more often than not, the putatively feminist hustle that is celebrated as "leaning in" or being a girlboss is an attempt to get rich. The repeated message, straight out of the deserving/undeserving-poor playbook, is that the path to success is to work really hard and take no prisoners.

If choosing to work hard and be rich is a feminist act, it's hard to talk about what is unfeminist about the idea that there is a top to begin with. A woman making her way to the top, even if she sells it as making room for other women at the top, is really a move to make room for a few women in jobs that are valued partly because they have been his-torically done by (rich, white) men, rather than a move to change the system of value that devalues jobs that women have historically done. Cheryl Sandberg, the former Facebook CEO and author of *Lean In*, loves to share an anecdote about how none of the men in a board meeting she was in knew where the women's bathroom was. But, as journalist Dawn Foster points out, this can't have been because there were no women working in that office.[73] The women just happened to be employed as secretaries and office cleaners.

In 2000, bell hooks argued that what she called "lifestyle feminism" was having its heyday. Lifestyle feminism, she claimed, was the idea that rage at patriarchy was enough to make one a feminist.[74] The problem was that performative rage at patriarchy didn't require caring about women besides oneself, let alone women of different races or classes. This is also a problem that besets one of the more interesting faces of contemporary criticism of the feminist success aesthetic—the Bimboverse. This online world of women and gender-expansive people identifying as bimbos is partly an affirmation of an over-the-top self-objectifying aesthetic, including the anti-feminist idea that beauty is the most important thing in the life of a femme. At the same time, it also gives the finger to femme phobia and to the idea that feminism means professional success.[75]

When Bimbos explicitly affirm, as many of the most high-profile ones do, that they are leftists, they make clear they are taking aim at the hegemony of the girlboss aesthetic, especially among women who are older than them. In a TikTok video entitled "Who Is the Gen Z Bimbo?" Chrissy Chlapecka informs us that being a Bimbo is about "emotional intelligence."[76] Rather than being out there for herself, the Bimbo is always there for her "shes, theys, and gays" and to "step on Trump supporters." Millennials may not get it, but she is focusing on her looks and not the corner office while scribbling "capitalism is the root of all evil" in block caps in her notebook. Still, as a different viral TikTok that began "I don't have ambition. I only want to be attractive"[77] makes clear, this dream of leisure is reserved for the pretty ones, and the lucky ones, unless it becomes a call to change the social systems that determine who gets work and pleasure and safety, and how.

Before its fall from grace in 2020, the Wing, an enclave of cozy, millennial pink, feminist-branded coworking spaces, sold all kinds of "don't dare judge me" merch, including a key ring with the slogan "women doing whatever the fuck they want."[78] The spaces were supposed to be oases for women in a men's world, but the company's hourly employees, mostly Black and brown women, found their role was to mop up the paradise, not participate in it. When staff tried to use their memberships during their breaks or off-hours, they dealt with members handing them their detritus and chirping that it was anti-feminist not to throw it away for them.[79] Co-founder Audrey Gelman appeared visibly pregnant, a "first" for a CEO on Inc.'s *Female Founders 100*.[80] Meanwhile, the pregnancy of Tahirah Jarrett, an hourly employee in the Wing's Brooklyn location, was far less welcome in the workplace.[81] "Black Lives didn't matter when I told y'all I had a miscarriage and you told me to come into work."[82] Perhaps the Wing had taken the advice on the merch a little too literally?

The Wing's messaging was the judgment myth writ large, not just in its "doing whatever the fuck we want" messaging, but in its insistence that acting for oneself was a bold feminist act. In yet another twist on Lorde's phrase, the company's website sold shirts emblazoned with "EXTREME SELF-CARE," yes, in all caps.[83] Gelman's Instagram once pronounced, "Women go through their lives taking care of everyone & everything, and there is deep relief in entering any tangible space where someone is finally taking care of you."[84] The entire idea that it was feminist to act in one's own interests was borne from the freedom feminism that had made its way into business schools and startup culture, reducing patriarchy to a tendency to judge women for ambition.[85] If sexism was judgment of ambition, ambition could be rebranded as a feminist act.

This is why the #girlboss/lean-in/she-EO lexicon teems with phrases that cast critics as enemies of feminism. If there's one thing a #girlboss knows it's to "fuck all haters." She also knows when to conveniently pull out the sentence "No one would criticize a man who did the same thing." As though the power held by rich white men is not also a problem for women. We're living under a form of capitalism that saves its worst forms of exploitation for working-class women and women of color, so it's not surprising that women who clamor for a place in capitalism's upper echelons end up doing the same exploitation. A feminism grounded in the judgment myth encourages us to celebrate or ignore such exploitation when women are its agents.

In 2021, the white self-help guru Rachel Hollis livestreamed that she worked hard so that someone else would clean her toilets, or as she later clarified, she had a "sweet woman"[86] who did it. When fans called her out for being "f*ing privileged," she decided it was a good moment to double down on her support for inequality. Those who thought her life was "unrelatable," were, she said, getting *exactly* the vibe she intended to project. In fact, "if life is relatable to most people," she said, "I'm doing it wrong."[87] To drive the "let them eat cake" message home, she posted a slew of photos of women she looked up to, including Harriet Tubman. Hollis is the author of a book that is literally entitled *Girl, Stop Apologizing*. Clearly, the idea that women should never have to apologize should never have seemed like a feminist idea to begin with. If it did, or does, we have the judgment myth to thank.

In 2017, a statue called *Fearless Girl* appeared in New York City's financial district. The plucky bronze figure of a preteen girl faced down the sculpture *Charging Bull* that had long graced Wall Street, her ponytail blown back by the bovine's apparent force. The bull has been a symbol of American capitalism and imperialism since 1987, when it was erected spontaneously by a patriotic artist who wanted to showcase the country's resilience after a stock market crash. When *Fearless Girl* appeared one morning, she seemed to burst with positive political potential. "Wall Street" had, in recent years, come to mean corporate greed, the rapacity of the 1 percent. Perhaps she represented the everyday person tired of corporate control of US society. And she wasn't the usual representation of "everyman"; she was a girl, to boot. Maybe she symbolized not just a critique of the rich but also the idea of a truly inclusive economy.

On International Women's Day 2021, though, she became awfully unapproachable for an everywoman. She was surrounded by broken glass, seeming to scream "touch at your own risk." Unapproachability was not the symbolism her commissioners had intended, though. The denticulate panes were meant to be shards of the so-called glass ceiling that keeps women out of the top echelons of corporate America. *Fearless Girl* was a message to the girls of tomorrow. As the plaque accompanying her put it, "Today's broken glass ceilings are tomorrow's stepping stones." The girl had never been trying to break down economic inequality; she had just been looking for a place inside. She had been commissioned by an investment firm. That investment firm had, incidentally, paid out a $5 million settlement for pay discrimination that same year.[88]

The judgment myth tells us to invest our energies in protecting the girl who gets ahead and then faces down the world, daring anyone to judge her. To be fair, it also tells us we shouldn't judge her little sister who decided to be a stay-at-home mom instead. It may even imply we shouldn't judge the girl who "chooses" to be a fast-food worker whose "flexible scheduling" means she scrambles to find childcare before every shift and sometimes doesn't. But we don't talk about her much. Maybe it's because that would make it too obvious that choice is not worth celebrating when all of the available options are bad.

It's no wonder the bull is still standing there, no matter what happened—or happens—to the glass ceiling.

Feminists have long been saying the personal is political. But that phrase was never intended to mean that political change would spring from each of us doing whatever we thought was best for us. The reduction of feminism to a respect for women's choices has always embodied a retreat from politics. Opponents of gender justice have long been aware of this fact—whether they are reproaching women for not saying "No" to workplace sexual advances or reducing women to "haters" for calling out exploitation by other women. The question is whether feminists are brave enough to face it.

CHAPTER 5

EQUALITY AND INTERSECTIONALITY

In early 2022, Keeanga-Yamahtta Taylor wondered in the pages of the *New Yorker* how women could have ended up somewhere besides where we are now.[1] Abortion rights were on the brink of evisceration. But, the renowned scholar and activist suggested, this was not how history had to go. We could be living in a world where abortion remained legal in all US states.

The reason we weren't was that we hadn't listened to Black women. If the nation had framed abortion rights the way they had, instead of in terms of privacy or choice, we would not have opened ourselves to the trivialization of pregnancy and caring for children that was so central to the Supreme Court's decision in *Dobbs v. Jackson Women's Health Organization*. We would know that abortion was a matter of life and death, that taking the abortion decision out of pregnant people's hands would mean that women would count less than men, and that poor women and women of color would count less than white ones. We would, Taylor argued, understand that the fight for abortion rights was a fight for equality.

Taylor's answer runs counter to many popular narratives about abortion, and about intersectional feminism. Abortion initially strikes many of us as an issue about freedom—and it lends itself easily to freedom feminist analysis. What could be a more clear-cut example of the need to free ourselves from social expectations than the demand that we, instead of a society that says we must become mothers, should decide what happens to our bodies?

And then there is the fact that equality has gotten a bad rap in many social justice circles over the last generation. The concept of equality, we are often told, flattens intersectional differences and is the *reason* for white feminism and other feminisms for the few. In the 1980s, bell hooks famously argued that equality was the reason that white women felt no dissonance between calling themselves feminists and reaping the benefits of capitalism and white supremacy.[2] If you have heard that mainstream twentieth-century feminism left out women of color, you were probably told that something called *liberal feminism* was to blame. Look up the term *liberal feminism,* and you'll see it defined as the idea that men and women are similar and deserve equal rights and opportunities.[3]

If equality was the problem that led to feminisms of exclusion, how could it possibly be part of the solution?

But I am here to say just that—that equality is central to the solution. I have spent much of this book arguing that the problem is freedom, that feminisms whose central value is individual freedom have a logic that ends up serving the interests of the powerful. It's time to talk about the alternative. Equality—or, if you prefer, opposition to inequality[4]—has to be the central value of a feminism for the many.

Lucky for me, Taylor is right about the history of feminism. A feminism focused on fighting hierarchy is not something I have to invent. It is all around us, and it has a long history—even if it is a history you weren't taught. Value for equality, understood as the dismantling of hierarchy, has long been central to intersectional feminist politics.

INTERSECTIONS AND BASEMENTS

On a sunny morning in March 1970, thirty-year-old Frances Beal, one of the activists Taylor thought we could learn from combed out her Afro, put on a dress that was a "little too short," and dropped her kids off at her mom's.[5] Beal headed to the offices of the Third World Women's Alliance (TWWA), an organization she had cofounded with a group of Puerto Rican women two years before. By the time Beal and her comrades had made it uptown to join the protest organized by the National Organization for Women (NOW)—which many assumed would take up a single lane of traffic—the protest had taken over all of Fifth Avenue.

An unprecedented fifty thousand women were in the streets demanding free childcare, educational and professional opportunities, and the repeal of abortion laws.

Beal was then a divorced mom of two. But, like many women of her generation, she had once been a teenager bleeding on a stranger's kitchen table. Her life had been saved by a late-night trip to the emergency room.[6] Not everyone she knew had been so "lucky" with their illegal abortions. Her friend Cordelia had lost her life in 1958.[7] And Beal had decided in that moment that she was done with the code of silence around abortion. This was a bold choice given that the law said that discussing "abortion with three or more people was a conspiracy to commit a felony."[8]

Beal was at the march to fight for abortion rights. But the 1969 pamphlet that had made her famous focused on a different medical procedure.

La operacion, as it had simply become known, was the most common surgery on the island of Puerto Rico.[9] Statistics from the 1950s showed that one fifth of Puerto Rican women had had the procedure, many of whom were in their teens and twenties.[10] By the time Beal was at the march it was one in three.[11]

The it in question was salpingectomy, removal of some portion of the fallopian tubes.

It was a method of sterilization. Many who had undergone the surgery reported having been told it was the only way to avoid getting pregnant.[12]

And it was coming to the mainland of the United States, Beal argued. Black and Puerto Rican communities in the continental US were home to "maternity clinics" that pushed sterilization.[13] Women on welfare were being told that their benefits would be cut off if they didn't seek sterilization.[14] Black women were dramatically overrepresented among those sterilized in federally funded programs on the continent.[15]

It had gotten so bad, Beal reported, that Black women were afraid to be admitted to the hospital for necessary surgery because they didn't want to end up with an unasked-for tubal ligation or removal.[16] This wasn't an isolated problem; a few years later, Latinas on the West Coast would win a federal class action suit over involuntary sterilization during medical encounters. Some of them were sterilized during childbirth, or while they were unconscious.[17]

Nor is this battle over. In 2020 more than forty women submitted testimony about forced gynecological procedures while in ICE custody.[18]

Women of color like Beal did not think the issue of sterilization was just about the right to do what one wants with one's body. Nor did they think it was about the right to throw off the social expectation that they be mothers—many of them were outraged about their sterilizations because they wanted to *be* mothers.

The women of color organizing against coercive sterilization thought it was a mode of economic and racial control. Some people were seen as fit to reproduce and some were not. Some people were seen as deserving of resources and some were not. Beal wrote in her famous pamphlet that la operacion was a tool for maintaining the "power imbalance between the white haves and the non-white have-nots."[19] It was one of "the many schemes the ruling elite attempted to perpetrate on the Black population in order to keep itself in control."[20]

In other words, mass sterilization of women of color was a way of perpetuating *inequality*. It was a way of ensuring that some people would reap the benefits of the postwar US economy and that some would not, and that the divide would fall largely along racial lines. It was a way of ensuring that the people of the colony of Puerto Rico, and people of color in the United States, would not get "too much" or grow "too much" in their numbers. It also expressed a classic colonial idea about people of color: that they were not capable of making decisions, and so they deserved to be ruled by their "superiors."

If you have heard of coercive sterilization before, you have probably heard it used as an example of how the barriers to reproductive freedom that white women face are different from those faced by women of color. This is true. Coercive sterilization and abortion restrictions are of a piece in that they violate the bodily autonomy of individual women and other potentially pregnant people.

But this is not all they do. And if freedom is all we talk about, we will miss how they work together and what they do to oppress women of color, poor women, and disabled women. Coercive sterilization and abortion restrictions are two parts in a regime of hierarchy. The effect of abortion and contraception restrictions was to encourage *able-bodied, middle-class, white* women to have more children. To state what should be obvious but clearly is not, as shown by the history of feminism, not all women are able-bodied, affluent, or white.

US policy had long been shaped not just by the idea that women should be mothers, but also by an ableist ideology about which women were fit to reproduce.[21] In the early twentieth century, a number of states passed laws legalizing sterilization of the "dependent" and "diseased." The way ableism and racism intersected rose to national attention in 1973 when doctors at a federally funded clinic performed coerced salpingectomies on Minnie Lee and Mary Alice Relf, who were Black and judged to be "intellectually inferior."[22] Their parents were not asked for consent. The girls were twelve and fourteen. This crystallized a social logic that some women were supposed to have children and some women were not; some women's children were desirable and some were not.

Puerto Rico was effectively a US colony, and coercive sterilization was rampant there, not just because it embodied denial of women's bodily autonomy, but because it embodied the idea that colonial subjects deserved to be ruled. Mass sterilization of Indigenous people all over the US aimed quite explicitly at the genocide of peoples deemed "inferior." It wasn't a coincidence that sterilization was happening at high rates to women on public assistance and disabled women. In all of these cases, in addition to the symbolic inferiorization of, and disrespect for, entire groups of people, the policies were designed to create economic haves and have-nots. As Beal observed, the reproductive politics of her time reflected the idea that the benefits of postwar prosperity should be reserved for the few. The few were white and able-bodied.

The hierarchy of mothers, or of those seen as worthy of mothering to begin with, is far from a relic of the past. One of its faces today is our ongoing Black maternal health crisis. The US already has the highest rate of maternal mortality in the industrialized world. Within that calamitous picture lies a worse reality for Black women, who are three times more likely than white women to die in childbirth.[23] And it seems to be getting worse. More Black women died in childbirth in 2021 than in 2019.[24]

Motherhood is so dangerous for Black women, says Felicia Ellis in the film *Aftershock*, that "a Black woman having a baby is like a Black man at a traffic stop with the police."[25]

It was the image of the Black woman at an intersection that took center stage in the 1989 article in which legal theorist Kimberlé Crenshaw coined the term *intersectionality*.[26] In it she offered a variation on a longstanding theme in Black and women of color feminisms. Beal's 1969 pamphlet was called *Double Jeopardy: To Be Black and Female*. In it, she argued that any feminist struggle for Black women would have to fight racism and class oppression.

Crenshaw developed the image of the intersection to contribute a more specific idea than that Black women have different experiences, or that they face multiple oppressions. It was the idea that people facing multiple oppressions face unique forms of oppression, irreducible to the sums of their parts. The Black woman in Crenshaw's image is standing at the intersection, hit by two cars driving in different directions. The story her body would tell, Crenshaw argued, would not be of two different accidents. Some of her injuries would not be easily traceable to one car or the other. But they were there, and we needed a politics that could do something about them.

For Crenshaw, this would have to be a politics that fought inequality. Coercive sterilization was, and is, an intersectional harm. The bodies of women of color are the site of the reproduction of multiple hierarchies such as gender inequality, white supremacy, ableism, and the division of society into classes. Their gender subjected them to forms of control and risks that men, even similarly situated men, were usually not subjected to.[27] Their race and colonial status meant that they were seen as less deserving of a share in postwar prosperity, as less worthy of decision-making power over their own lives, as less human.

As in all cases of intersectional oppression, these facts bled into one another; it was hard, for example, to tell where the racial inequality ended and the gender inequality began. But the entire idea that they could intersect the way they did relied on the assumption that both were forms of inequality. Crenshaw's original vision of intersectionality was of hierarchies that compounded one another. In addition to the famed image of the traffic accident, she offered another analogy, one that has gotten much less play even in a world where *intersectionality* is everyone's favorite buzzword.

This analogy offers what is plainly an image of hierarchy. Imagine, Crenshaw suggested, that all oppressed people live in a basement;[28] their ceiling is the privileged world's floor. But the fact that the oppressed are all in the basement does not mean that they are all equally oppressed. Some of them are literally stacked on top of each other, with those closest to the ceiling standing on top of those closest to the floor. The danger of neglecting the fact that people are subordinated in multiple ways, Crenshaw argued, is adopting a politics that only benefits those who happen to be closest to the ceiling.

This is one way to understand why it has been so damaging to leave coercive sterilization, and its legacy, out of feminist histories of reproduction. If we formulate what women need based on what middle-class, able-bodied, white women need—as we do when we treat abortion and contraception as our central goals—those women may make it out of the basement. But to get *everyone* out of the basement, we need to be able to see why they are there. And we simply won't see it if we see only gender. Women of color are kept in the basement both by being denied abortion and contraception *and* by being denied the ability to reproduce if they want to.

The focus of mainstream feminism on abortion and contraception is a manifestation of the same deep philosophical problem in our political culture that I have emphasized throughout this book. We have difficulty articulating social injustices as anything but denial of freedoms. Abortion and contraception are easiest to mobilize around because they often take the form of requests to leave women alone. But, as I argued in the chapter on the restriction myth, many needs around reproductive justice require active support, not just noninterference. If you want an abortion you can't get because you are on Medicaid or depend on the Indian Health Service (the Hyde Amendment prohibits federal funds from going to abortion), you need much more than just to be free of social restrictions. Ditto for if you want to have children, but you cannot afford to, or are not safe to do so—whether because of Black maternal mortality risks or unsafe neighborhoods or coercive sterilization or lack of appropriate trans healthcare.

The courts have been more than happy to turn the emphasis on choice against feminists. Just look at the *Dobbs* decision I discussed in the introduction for the receipts. In a particularly cruel moment in the oral arguments, Justice Barrett argued that women could exercise the choice to have a child . . . after it was born. Safe haven laws, which allow parents to drop off newborns at fire stations without fear of persecution might "take care of the problems" of "forced motherhood."[29] But it isn't just conservatives who sometimes don't get that some reproductive injustices don't reduce to being told what to do.

Beale, and other anti-sterilization activists, lived the political heartbreak caused by freedom feminism and its insistence that restrictions are the enemy. White feminists, time and again, just didn't get why someone would want to make sterilization harder. In the later 1970s, when West Coast Latina activists advocated for waiting periods and counseling before sterilization, they were trying to create hurdles for racist doctors and medical institutions, not people who could become pregnant. Yet they found that even NOW activists they had been collaborating with for years wouldn't support them. As Evelyn Martinez recounts, "It was like having someone throw cold water in your face." NOW didn't want waiting periods or counseling because they saw them as barriers, as more faces telling women what to do.

But Martinez wanted the NOW activists to see that doctors were effectively already telling women what to do: "Women were being sterilized without their consent, consent forms being shoved in their face in the middle of labor, in English, a language they didn't understand."[30] And the Latinas identified another problem that NOW just couldn't see—a problem the members of organizations like the Mexican American Women's National Association saw as genocide.[31] The absence of restriction on the powerful was enabling racial, economic, and gender inequality, but this, for white feminists, just did not compute.

There is an added irony that coercive sterilization *does* deny people a type of freedom or bodily autonomy. Clearly, you cannot consent to a procedure when you don't know what it is or what the alternatives are, or if it is performed while you are giving birth or while you are literally unconscious. But white feminists still struggled to see that things like poverty, racism, and lack of access to linguistically appropriate materials could also constitute impediments to freedom. The only thing they could see was the social expectation that women should have babies—and they lacked the nuance to see that this expectation applied unequivocally only to white, economically privileged, able-bodied women.

More importantly, they could not see that removal of restrictions can perpetuate inequality, if inequality is already baked into the structure of society.[32] As Martinez pointed out, unrestricted sterilization *was the status quo*. And it was a grossly unequal status quo, one that subordinated women and people of color. Leaving the sterilization status quo untouched was a way of ensuring that potentially pregnant people would have less control of their lives than people who could not get pregnant. It would work, together with a host of racist and sexist stereotypes, to promote the view that women and children of color were drains on society, less deserving of all kinds of benefits. And it would perpetuate the view that all people of color mattered less, had a lesser right to exist.

Unless we understand how coercive sterilization produced inequality, we won't understand activism by women of color against it. We won't understand that it targets women, and not cis men, for exposure to risk and loss of control. We won't understand that it exposes women of color to higher risks than white women. Nor will we understand why some feminists of color today, and also many disability feminists, focus on a right to *have* children.

Choice language does not only obscure the fact that reproductive control is a mechanism of inequality. Women of color have also pointed out that freedom language can itself cause inequality by changing how people see and frame social injustices. Sociologist, law professor, and author of *Killing the Black Body*, Dorothy Roberts argues that the idea that abortion is a choice is partly to blame for the incarceration of pregnant women for using drugs, or for being suspected of using drugs. After all, if abortion is a choice, so is pregnancy; women have *chosen* to carry the pregnancy to term.[33] If women who are pregnant post *Roe* (and pre-2022) have been freed from the expectation that they be mothers, then they are personally responsible for being pregnant.

In a different twist on a similar idea, women in the Global South and Indigenous women are often subjected to forms of coercive population control while being described as "freed from motherhood." In 2021, the Chinese government tweeted that Uygur women, who are predominantly Muslim and have declining birthrates, "are no longer baby machines" and are "more confident and independent."[34] The evidence is mounting that Uygur women are subjected to forced pregnancy checks and long-acting contraception. This is all happening while the Chinese government has placed one million Uygur people in concentration camps.

OPPRESSION AS A FORM OF INEQUALITY

Feminists have long understood that fighting injustice sometimes means creating a new language. To live as a woman activist in Beal's time (and in some ways today) was to live in a world where the words to call out sexism just weren't available. Reproductive control was called social welfare, sexual harassment was called flirting; the world was telling women that down was up and up was down.

For women of color like Beal, the distorting language that described the injustice she was facing wasn't just coming from society at large. As with so many of the cases I've described in this book, the call was coming from inside the feminist house. At the 1970 protest march, Beal and her comrades from the TWWA had no sooner arrived than they were told they didn't get what feminism was. Like just about every group at the march, Beal and her comrades carried a homemade banner with a simple message. When Lucy Komisar, NOW's then–vice president, saw it, she told them to take it down. The words on it had, Komisar said, "nothing to do with women's liberation."[35]

The banner named one of the best-known women radicals of the time. She remains a household name today—and a household name many of us associate with feminism.

Her name is Angela Davis. Beal replied that their "Hands Off Angela Davis" sign had "everything to do with the type of liberation we're talking about."[36]

The TWWA had known their banner was going to make waves, and they refused to take it down. The waves were part of the point. They wanted white feminists to see connections that were apparent to many radical women of color at the march that day.

Patricia Romney, an anti-racist organizer from the Bronx who became a member of the TWWA on the spot that day later said that it was ironic that NOW tried to exclude the TWWA from the march because the TWWA almost hadn't come anyway. As she put it, the image of the woman that was so frequently at the center of mainstream feminist organizing in the 1960s, that of the frustrated housewife who wanted more, was not one that TWWA members could identify with.[37] Most were moms who worked outside the home. Women of their race and class backgrounds never had any other option.

Angela Davis was partly a riposte to that image. They wanted the organizers to see feminism as "an ongoing struggle against racism, sexism, and class oppression."[38]

Oppression was *the* core concept of feminist organizing in the 1960s and 1970s. Radicals of the era, including not just feminists but also anti-racists and leftists, invented it to describe social relations that were structured to ensure some groups of people would get more, or count more, than others.[39] Oppression meant that some people would be treated as rulers and others as fit to be ruled. It was a myth that where you ended up on the social hierarchy was reducible to your individual choices. Instead, much had to do with the group(s) you belonged to and which floor of the social "house" you were sorted into by our social institutions.

This is the line of thinking that, for example, birthed the idea of institutional racism. Central to that idea was the sense that whites as a group exercised power over Blacks as a group, and that in order to see this, we needed to situate individual racist acts within a larger context. Over time, the idea of structure evolved into the idea that laws, policies, and social practices could ensure that some people would end up counting less, even without individual members of the dominant group consciously pulling the strings.[40]

When activists of that era, especially activists of color and leftist activists, talked about liberation, which they did on an everyday basis, often they were not talking about individual freedom. They were not talking about the right to make decisions about one's own life free from interference. Because they had originally believed that the social hierarchy they lived within was caused by the actions of dominant groups, they were talking about not wanting to be ruled by those who thought themselves superior.[41] Over time, as they saw that social structures included laws, policies, and cultural practices that were sometimes not directly put in place by dominant groups, they talked about *systems* and not just rulers. But to these activists, liberation meant an end to a society where some groups were locked in the basement, to use Crenshaw's image. Liberation also meant also questioning the idea that our society needed a basement to begin with.

In other words, they were talking about liberation *from oppression*. Radical women of the mid- to late twentieth century, including Beal, were developing the understanding of sexism as a form of subordination because they were experiencing sexism in what might seem like an unlikely place: *within* radical movements. Before they founded feminist spaces, they were anti-war demonstrators or leftists or Black power or Chicana activists. They formed feminist groups because they thought it was time to start seeing gender dynamics as similar to other forms of oppression. These other forms of oppression, like racism and class exploitation, were manifestly about hierarchy and control.

The men who were fighting hierarchies like racism and class inequality, they thought, seemed perfectly comfortable demanding subordination from women *within* their own movements. The movements were diverse, but the experience of being expected to provide "maid and steno service"—to take the notes and clean up after the meetings—was nearly universal.[42] So was the expectation of sexual service—be it to reproduce the race, or to show visiting activists from out of town "a good time."[43] Marge Piercy wrote that the New Left was an "economic microcosm" with "women concentrated at the bottom."[44] Beal wrote that some men in the Black power movement seemed to have taken their ideas about women "from the pages of *Ladies' Home Journal*."[45]

If the TWWA wanted their banner to symbolize the organization's alliance with Black power, their existence as an independent organization spoke to a novel diagnosis of the problem with American society. Radicals needed to add gender to their understanding of the types of oppressive hierarchy in need of dismantling. This didn't mean that it was more fundamental or important.[46] Feminists needed to understand that the causes of women's subordination ran as deep as those causing racism, economic inequality, and imperialism. Liberating women of color from oppression would mean recognizing, and fighting, more than one oppression at the same time.[47] Today's freedom feminism is partly a result of our cultural drift away from the insight that oppression was about social structures that ensured *hierarchy*. This cultural drift has come with costs besides an inability to understand harms that happen to women of color. It has affected our ability to see the harms that sexism inflicts on all women.

EQUALITY THROUGH OTHER EYES

A few years before Beal wrote *Double Jeopardy*, an exasperated tweenage Anita Allen scribbled a rhetorical question in her journal. Her mom, she had just learned, was pregnant again. Allen had overheard her mother telling a friend she wished she could have an abortion and was aghast. With all the subtlety of pretty much any adolescent talking about her mom, Allen asked, "How could she not want to have a baby? What else does she think she is for?"[48]

Allen's mother had dared to think that she was for something besides making and caring for children. It wasn't that she didn't want or value kids; it was just that five was enough. Allen's mother had been having babies since she was fifteen. But abortion was illegal, and she had a controlling husband and little formal education. It was only after her sixth child graduated from high school that Allen's mother was able to pursue high school equivalency training and attend a local business college. This was enough to get her to the job that would be the peak of her official career: department store clerk. It was the best-paying job she could find, and she would die soon after she started, "ironically," Allen notes, on her sixth child's birthday.

US society seems to have regarded Allen's mother much like Allen had in that cruel moment of her youth. Her mom was a Black woman who had grown up in poverty, and she had not been quiet around Allen about any of the forms of disadvantage she faced. Yet, Allen reports, her mother believed that it was her gender that had "fixed her fate. Being a woman meant being a wife and mother to the exclusion of other ambitions."[49]

As Allen aged, she inherited the other side of this coin. Allen shifted from believing that a woman's role was to be a mother to believing that she needed to do everything possible to avoid becoming pregnant. There was no way for a young Black mom to end up anywhere but close to the bottom of the social hierarchy. Her mother had taught her that if she became pregnant, "the best part of her life would be over."[50]

Allen grew up to become a professor at an Ivy League university and to write one of the best-known defenses of abortion as a requirement for women's equality. The observation she had made as a child encapsulated one of the very most important, and most forgotten, points feminists can make about why abortion should be legal.

A government that denies women control over our reproductive lives tells women what we are *for*—and that answer is for men, and for reproduction. It tells all people with uteruses and some people without them, that we are for making and caring for babies, that other pursuits are invalid or at least secondary to this purpose. But this is not like other forms of being told what to do, because the thing we are for has little monetary value in our society. Being *for* that thing means not just greater exposure to dependency and poverty, but also the control of our bodies and sexualities by men and the state.

The government tells us we are for pregnancy and childrearing in a society where pregnancy and childrearing create all kinds of vulnerability. Where, as I have already mentioned, having babies subjects you to death at an alarmingly high rate in a country as rich as this one—especially if you are Black. Where being a full-time caregiver means at best seeing half your spouse's income on your social security check and at worst a string of zeroes. Where "planning" is supposed to be really important for making enough money to survive, but where you cannot "plan" what happens to your body.

A decade after Beal marched on Fifth Avenue, but many years before Allen wrote her equality defense of abortion, Audre Lorde wrote that one of white feminists' gravest mistakes was their assumption that women of color could only teach them about the lives of women of color.[51] We absolutely need to see that the bodies of women of color are special sites in the production of racial, economic, and ableist hierarchies. But a hallmark of Black feminist activism has also been that looking at the lives of those facing multiple oppressions can help us learn what will liberate *all women*.[52] The lives of women of color make particularly clear what is at stake for *all women*. It would be a mistake to take from my discussion of coercive sterilization that women of color's lives only teach us about women of color. Looking at the lives of less privileged women is crucial for understanding *sexism*, how reproductive control affects all women.

Allen was writing about her experience as a Black woman to make a point about women in general. Her mother's life made visible something about the importance of abortion that would have been less visible in, say, the life of a white woman with a college degree. As Keeanga-Yamahtta Taylor put it, "No woman can escape the cloud of inferiority that is attached to having no say about when one becomes pregnant."[53] But just what that cloud of inferiority is like is especially visible in the lives of those who can't fall back on race or class privilege to protect themselves from the effects of sexism. Rich and middle-class women might be able to stave off some of the inequalities caused by forced pregnancy by hiring a woman not so different from Allen's mom. But the life of Allen's mom lays bare what it's like to not have these privileges.[54]

Allen's mother had to wait until midlife to complete high school. The "fifty-five-year-old quarrelsome Black lady who chain-smoked," Allen remembers, was "hard to employ."[55] As in all cases of intersectional oppression, it was again hard to know how much was gender and how much was race. But here are some things we do know, and that Allen emphasizes: Allen's mother waited to go to school until after her husband would allow it and after her children were finished. That she thought at least one of her pregnancies was derailing her life in a way she wished to undo. That "her schooling was interrupted by the births and needs of grandchildren, the marriages and divorces of daughters, and the slow deaths of her grandmother and father."[56]

Despite their other differences—and they were vast, both across time and across their location on the progressive ideological spectrum—Taylor, Beal, and Allen had one argument in common. It is that lack of reproductive control prevents a person from enjoying "full" participation in society.[57] The repeat use of the term *full* is striking. Women, and pregnant people, are already participating in society, but on terms that degrade them, terms reserved for those who count less than others, whose lives are *for* others. Their participation in society is contingent on them serving a role of being for others, in service of those who have significant control over their bodies and their fates. Lack of access to abortion did not just mean that women could not control their fates; it meant that they were consigned to a certain one: a fate of care and service. The young Anita Allen had internalized the patriarchy so well that she could articulate the fate it set forth for her mother in a way that few who were older than her would dare say aloud: in a society where women and Black people had to serve others, what else could Allen's mother think she was *for*?

Lack of reproductive control does not just create a class of people who are *for* others; it creates a class of people who will get less than others. In a different society, care and service might not be pathways to economic vulnerability; in a different society, the world might not be so starkly divided into those seen as worthy of receiving care and those seen as fit to give it.[58] But Allen's mom didn't live in that society and neither do we.

Allen's mom's résumé fit her to have a certain kind of interpersonal relationship and slotted her into a certain sector of the economy.[59] The big-picture result of lack of reproductive control—at least in our society of nearly nonexistent social supports for childcare and child well-being— is what is often called "occupational segregation." Women, and increasingly women of color, dominate the sectors of the economy that are more "flexible." These are the jobs one can quit and start again in tandem with the births and illnesses of children, for which a consistent employment history or the perception of accumulated skill are not job requirements. "Flexible," as we know from corporate euphemisms about jobs that are less stable and poorly paid, often just means "worse." Dominating this sector of society is, in the societal big picture, no domination at all.

Occupational segregation is a major driver of gender inequality in the US, and women's lack of reproductive control seems to be an important driver of it. We often hear about the "wage gap," which conjures the image of women doing the same jobs as men for less money. This is definitely a thing. But women are also concentrated in different industries from those where men are, and these industries are (surprise) generally worse paid. This is true across class and race lines, though poor women of color are affected the most dramatically. Studies that try to get to the bottom of why some industries are dominated by women find that working hours and flexibility of hours make a difference. Predominantly male occupations are also the ones that demand more hours and include more opportunities to earn more overtime pay.[60]

Lack of reproductive control affects occupational segregation in another less obvious way. Our association of women with mothering, and our devaluation of caregiving, mean that "women's" jobs are worse paid, regardless of what type of education and flexibility they include.[61] Though the effect is more dramatic on poor women and women of color, even upper-class women earn less money than their male counterparts because of occupational segregation. A quarter of *all* employed women are concentrated in the following jobs: health care supporter, domestic worker, early childhood caregiver, beauty worker, and cashier.[62] Allen's mother started and ended her paid career in the last one of these occupations, in spite of being overeducated for it. No matter what she thought she was *for*, there were only certain places people like her belonged.

There is a deep relationship between the symbolic inequalities embodied in denial of abortion rights and material inequalities. A society that expresses in its law that women are *for* caregiving—so *for* it that they shouldn't even have a say about whether they want to reproduce—doesn't just arise from a sexist status quo. It legitimizes it. Abortion law also affects social norms beyond those about carrying a pregnancy to term. To the extent that it creates and reinforces general views about women's servile role, restrictive abortion laws also treat women who cannot reproduce, or have not reproduced, as inferior. This, too, is something we won't see if we only think of abortion restrictions as restrictions on freedom. Abortion restrictions slot women into service and caregiving roles—and not just the women they prevent from having abortions. A sad irony of Allen's mom's experience was that she ended up in the job she did long after her gestating years were over.

BUT ISN'T EQUALITY CANCELED?

Sometime in the mid-2010s, I founded myself being handed a clipboard in the New York offices of a major national reproductive rights organization. It was a heady time, in the pre-Trump years, when it was still within our power to prevent *Roe* from being overturned. I had spent my post-college years working in similar organizations, giving similar trainings, and the feel of the clipboard in my hands was eerily familiar.

So, I was pleased to learn that something important *had* changed in the years since I had been the one passing them out. The organization was intent that everyone would leave this training aware that women of color have criticized the choice framing of abortion. It was only people with privilege whose activism could stop at the legality of abortion, the trainer said, since accessing abortion required all kinds of resources, financial and otherwise. To talk about "choice" was also to trivialize abortion for those who experienced circumstances like poverty and racism as making their decisions for them. Sometimes, support for having children was as important as support for the right not to have them, a pink slide deck reminded us.

Since this was all so sympatico with my thoughts about the restriction myth, I was nodding along supportively. But all of that changed when we shifted from talking about choice to talking about something else. A new slide appeared, featuring a bunch of people and a fence.[63]

In the graphic, which many of you will likely have seen somewhere in a training or on the internet, there were two frames. They were set up almost like a before and after photo, but here the contrast was supposed to be between bad and good. On the left, "bad" side stood three people of unequal heights. They were all standing on blocks of the same size on one side of a fence. The result was that the tallest person, who could have stepped over with no assistance, was on a block they didn't need. Meanwhile the shortest person still couldn't get over the fence because the one-size-fits all block was too small to be helpful.

In block letters sat a simple, one-word description of this scenario: EQUALITY.[64]

Was this what equality meant, I wondered that day? Did equality mean giving everyone the same thing, irrespective of what they had to begin with? Did it mean ignoring the needs of the least advantaged people? Was canceling equality the lesson to draw from women of color's criticism of the restriction myth applied to abortion?

I believed then, and believe now, that the answer to all these questions was no. But the idea that equality was the enemy was rooted in something undeniably real. Equality has not historically been a very radical value in mainstream US political discourse. This is because of two related facts. First, the idea that people have equal worth—or, to use the language of the Declaration of Independence, are "created equal"—is, paradoxical as it might seem, often used *against* critics of historically embedded inequalities. This is the bread and butter of conservative arguments against affirmative action or the teaching of so-called "critical race theory."[65] Repairing longstanding inequalities sometimes means treating people who are victims of injustice differently. Conservatives like to claim that treating people differently means treating them unequally. Their claim, though, is based on an assumption that is straightforwardly false. Achieving equality does not have to mean treating people the same. Treating people differently, especially if they have not been treated equally up to this point, is sometimes exactly what is required to achieve equality.

Second, the concept of equality is often reduced to equality of opportunity, which, in the United States, translates to the right to compete for a place at the top. Feminists across generations have noted that this type of equality will primarily benefit women who are only oppressed due to gender. Alexandra Kollontai, the early twentieth-century socialist feminist I mentioned in chapter 1, argued that a feminism that left the system of class inequality intact would only benefit women of the upper classes.[66] Historian Sue Cobble argues that women in the labor movement in the early twentieth century were skeptical of equality because it might mean an equal "right to be exploited."[67]

In the tradition of the Black feminism I've been discussing in this chapter, bell hooks famously argued that white elite women can weaponize feminism for their self-interest—and against women facing multiple oppressions—because they want to be equal to white men.[68] They, hooks argued, think feminism is about needing to be equal *to someone*. This is a win-win for them; they can move "up" while keeping capitalism and white supremacy chugging along, continuing to reap the benefits of both.

If equality means giving everyone an equal right to compete in a system that is already rigged, then the graphic I saw at the training that day was right. But there's a simple reason we shouldn't be so quick to cancel equality. It's the reason that Taylor gestured at when she argued that Black women understood abortion as about equality, and a reason that is implicit in hooks's argument that seeking to be the equals of white men is not a very transformative agenda. The problem with these superficial forms of equality is that they leave too much inequality intact. To dismantle systems of oppression is to ask for *more equality*, not less.

A TALE OF TWO EQUALITIES

To see another understanding of inequality, we can look to the life of another twentieth-century Black feminist activist. In the 1970s, Johnnie Tillmon introduced herself to mainstream feminists in a way that made no qualms about the place she occupied in America's pecking order. "I'm a woman. I'm a Black woman. I'm a poor woman. I'm a fat woman. I'm a middle-aged woman. And I'm on welfare," she wrote in an article in *Ms*. She continued, "In this country, if you're any of those things you count less as a human being. If you're all of those things, you don't count at all."[69]

The truth Tillmon dropped in that piece was supposed to be a wakeup call for middle- and upper-class white women who had no idea what it was like to have the government literally knocking on their doors, checking to see if there was a man in their closet or if they secretly had a fridge full of bonbons. They might not know what it was like, but they were not as far removed from it as they might think. As Tillmon saw it, every woman was just "one man away from welfare." Women on welfare were just the canaries in the mine. Welfare was a form of punishment that served a social function; "society needs women on welfare as 'examples' to let every woman . . . know what will happen if she lets up, if she's laid off, if she tries to go it alone without a man. So these ladies stay on their feet or on their knees all their lives instead of asking why they're only getting 90-some cents an hour, instead of daring to fight and complain."[70]

In other words, welfare was a way of keeping women down; it was patriarchy distilled to its most basic logic. The tools it used to keep women down were the ones used to keep all women down, just in their most severe, most direct forms. "Welfare is like a super-sexist marriage," she wrote. "You trade in a man for *the* man." Upper- and middle-class white women were living lives of dependency too. Upper- and middle-class and white women also had their sexualities restricted. Black women on welfare just had the added bonus of the government literally telling them who they could sleep with and what they could eat.

Tillmon was the president of the National Welfare Rights Organization (NWRO), an organization that counted members in the tens of thousands. At the organization's height, 85 percent of its membership was Black.[71] NWRO was an explicitly feminist organization, but it was at odds with more mainstream feminist organizations like NOW about what gender and economic equality would look like.[72]

It wasn't that NOW didn't care about the economic face of gender inequality. The vast majority of NOW's membership in the 1970s believed women's poverty was *the* issue[73] the organization should prioritize. Merrillee Dolan, who would become the head of NOW's anti-poverty taskforce, had started a newsletter called *Sisters in Poverty*. She had even authored a scathing critique of the Moynihan report, the famous government document blaming women-headed households for Black Americans' alleged "culture of poverty."[74]

NOW was not always great at putting money (or concern about women's lack of it) where its mouth was. There was no anti-poverty workshop at the 1970 national NOW conference, and when Dolan tried to make one up on the spot, only two people raised their hands to participate.[75] NOW members seemed to care about poverty and yet to think that the path to reducing it was . . . increased freedom from social expectations. They thought that the way to end women's poverty was to make and enforce antidiscrimination law.[76] In their view, women were poor because they were housewives, or because they were excluded from the more lucrative professions. They just needed society to let go of the assumption that they didn't belong in the world of work.

This strategy made perfect sense for a group of people invested in freedom feminism. Privilege no doubt helped lay the groundwork for this investment. Employment discrimination, coupled with gender socialization, were likely the actual major causes of many NOW members' economic difficulties. Expectations around housewifery extended to the workplace such that women, even when employed, were expected to make the coffee and straighten their bosses' ties. For them, the main obstacle to their reaching the place they saw for themselves in the system—the place occupied by men of their race and class—seemed to be social expectations that antidiscrimination law would punish and erode.

NOW's favored strategy included other trappings of freedom feminism, too, like posing tradition as the enemy and paid work as liberation. Tradition told women like them to be housewives; participating in the workforce would loosen the hold of that tradition. In fact, the idea that "investing in women" in the Global South will liberate them from sexism, which I talked about in chapter 3, probably stems from the idea that it "worked" in the United States.

Except that it didn't. As I discussed in chapter 2, much of the effect of middle-class women's entry into the workforce has been to shift domestic labor onto less privileged women. NOW would eventually recognize that their membership was not well-equipped to tackle this issue. Perhaps ironically, NOW would eventually decide to "outsource" anti-poverty work to NWRO.

Just because NOW couldn't see that mass entry into the workforce wasn't going to liberate all women doesn't mean that no one could see it. The women who had been cleaning other people's houses and other people's children for centuries had already been living the downsides of middle- and upper-class women's freedom from housewifery. Poor Black women had been caring for other people's children and doing their laundry for as long as they could remember. It had begun in slavery and continues to this day. Tillmon herself had worked in a laundry service in Compton. She was aware enough of the precariousness of that job to have become a union leader there.

Poor Black women, the women who formed the core of the NWRO, were not under the illusion that being allowed to work for pay would lead to equality—gender or otherwise. They could see through that ruse, partly because, as Toni Morrison argued at the time, they already had freedom that white women did not have, freedom that white women likely envied.[77] Poor Black women had not been expected to be house-wives, or—though this was a double-edged sword—been seen as beacons of sexual purity. The flipside of this freedom from the expectations of white womanhood was being expected to work, to be useful in ways that were, to say the very least, not very pleasant or gratifying. Tillmon and women like her knew that there was "shit work" out there, and that it wasn't just discrimination or socialization that led to it. The jobs that they—and the men they knew, for that matter—were doing were mostly . . . not great.

But they also knew something special about the "shit work" they had been socially assigned to do—especially the work of caring for children, people who were sick, and disabled people who needed care: There was nothing *inherently* shit about it. NWRO's social experience of care had not just been about caring for other people's children. It had been about being actively prevented from, and not supported in, caring for *their* children. For generations, Black women had been the "mammies" of white children while their own children were literally sold away from them, or paid nannies and maids, or, as I discussed earlier in this chapter, literally prevented from reproducing. Black women's political priorities in this country have always involved a quest for what political theorist Shatema Threadcraft calls "intimate justice."[78]

This was why the NWRO's core political demand had nothing to do with getting jobs. They wanted society to pay them for being moth-ers. They called themselves "mother-recipients." "Work for welfare" was flawed because women on welfare *were already working.*

As NWRO activist Cassie Downer put it at the time, "I think the most valuable thing a woman can do is raise her own children, and our society should recognize it as a job. A person should be guaranteed an income to do that."[79] If caring for children really was the "full-time job" people often declare it to be when celebrating the lives of upper- and middle-class housewives, why shouldn't it be paid?

NWRO members' experiences of caring for, and cleaning up after, other people's families didn't just make them insist that caring was a job. It made them deeply invested in what would happen to those women who would inevitably end up caring for other people's families. NOW and other mainstream feminist organizations were not nearly as immersed in freedom feminism—especially the individualism myth— as the girlbosses of today. They lived in a much less neoliberal time, and feminists of all stripes would show up and pack Fifth Avenue demanding twenty-four-hour daycare centers.[80]

NWRO dreamed of this, too, but more skeptically. They knew that the only way this was going to work for all women was for there to be careful attention to the status of these daycare workers. Paying them the market wage—when the market wage for this work was so low, for both gender and racial reasons—threatened to create an army of "institutionalized, partly self-employed mammies."[81] Universal childcare needed to be implemented in a way that didn't create a "reservoir of cheap female labor." NWRO could see that freedom feminism needed a plan and that it kind of didn't have one.

NWRO was keenly aware of two hierarchies that structure women's involvement in the paid workforce. One was a gender hierarchy that ensured that care work would be a source of vulnerability. "Women's work" would be poorly paid or unpaid, and this was what made every woman "one man away from welfare."

The other was a racial hierarchy among women. Why was it that even though society refused to pay affluent white women for care work, it at least showered them with praise? As NWRO member Juliet Greenlaw, asked, why were white homemakers encouraged to treat themselves while Black women doing the same work were treated as drains on society? Women on welfare deserved "what every other woman had." That included the same right to joy, pleasure, the occasional luxury. "Why shouldn't we be able to buy perfume once in a while, or a ring, or even a watch?" Greenlaw wanted to know.[82]

The NWRO could see that NOW's vision of equality would leave plenty of *inequalities* untouched, and perhaps even exacerbate some of them. The mass entry of women into the workforce would not guarantee the humanization of care workers, nor would it ensure a fair wage. The NWRO's activism is an indictment of the view that equality for privileged women with privileged men will "trickle down" to everyone; the way our society treats care work makes that structurally impossible.

It is also an indictment of the view that we can achieve gender equality without changing deep features of our culture and economic systems. In a feminist world, care work, and the people who do it, will need to be seen as worth more. To borrow language from Cobble, elite feminists have criticized the "feminine mystique" for stifling them. But it is "the masculine mystique" that degrades care that keeps all women down, and this is why nonelite women have often prioritized fighting it.[83]

The path to this more feminist world can only be one that dismantles hierarchies. The NWRO's activism just doesn't make sense without the larger context that it is wrong for some work to "count" and other work not to, for some people to be seen as worthy of love and pleasure when others are not. We can quibble about the term *equality*, reject it to the point of presenting it as the source of feminism's problems in a slide-show. But we cannot escape the fact that, to borrow Crenshaw's image, intersectional feminist activism has always been in response to some people being on top of others in the social hierarchies that shape our lives. We need to stop pretending that the house of our society doesn't have an attic and a basement. We also need to stop pretending that people aren't sometimes standing on top of one another within the basement.

A hallmark of Black feminism has always been the idea that there is an antidote to this situation—the situation where attempts to liberate women cause or perpetuate hierarchies *among* women. The antidote is to fight for what the most vulnerable within a group need. The NWRO knew this. What would liberate poor Black women was a revaluation of care work, and a public investment in it. This also happened to be what would liberate all women. Benita Roth names this idea, which is so deeply threaded through generations of Black feminism, the theory of the "vanguard center." In the late 1970s, the Combahee River Collective would state the reasoning behind it explicitly: "If Black women were free, it would mean that everyone else would have to be free since our freedom would necessitate the destruction of all the systems of oppression."

THIS IS WHAT EQUALITY LOOKS LIKE

When abortion became illegal in thirteen states after *Dobbs*, New Mexico was not one of them. The story of why has everything to do with a feminism that prioritized fighting inequality. The women and gender-expansive people of color who had been organizing for reproductive justice there in the 2010s were assumed to be fighting a major uphill battle. New Mexico is a majority-minority state, whose population is 15 percent Indigenous and almost 50 percent Latinx. National political strategists, who were in the habit of writing off the Latinx community as conservative, thought this spelled danger for abortion rights.[84]

Instead, the young activists who fought to save abortion rights in New Mexico in the 2010s found themselves laying the groundwork for one reproductive rights victory after another. It helped that they had deep roots in the communities being written off. They were inheritors of the theory of the vanguard center and had built organizations like Young Women United (now Bold Futures), whose mission was to center "the lived experiences and expertise of those most impacted by an issue, engaging with people at the intersection of their identities."[85] Unsurprisingly, at least given who its members were and the history I've described in this chapter, choice was not core to Young Women United's agenda. The organization had instead swept onto the scene introducing and passing a bill for comprehensive sex education. To those in more traditional positions of power, they seemed to accomplish this out of nowhere. The cutting-edge organization would also later become famous for blowing up the shame-based narrative surrounding teen pregnancy.

One of the activists who laid the groundwork to protect abortion rights in New Mexico had once been a pregnant teen herself. Her name was Adriann Barboa, and she had not been spared the "shame-based" messaging our society doles out to young parents.[86] "Girls who look like me were routinely warned against what would happen to us and to our kids if we became parents too soon. From low birth-weight babies to high drop-out rates, our kids were likely to be on the losing end of every childhood measure."[87] She knew firsthand that the hierarchy of moms Beal and Tillmon talked about, like all old habits, would die hard. Single moms of color were still our country's favored scapegoat when social services like welfare were on the chopping block.

So, when Barboa became the leader of the statewide "Coalition for Choice," even she was surprised.[88] She had always been skeptical of choice language. As she put it, New Mexico "was one of the poorest states in the country, and people don't have a lot of options in many parts of their life, so 'my body, my choice' doesn't resonate."[89] But when a twenty-week abortion ban was on the ballot, it was clear that it was time for communities of color to lead the fight to protect abortion rights in the state.[90] And even though there were lots of "hard conversations," it became clear that choice wasn't the language that would mobilize people to come out to the polls to keep abortion rights intact.[91]

Instead, Barboa and the women of color activists who have fought to keep abortion legal in New Mexico over the last fifteen years have used an arsenal of values that would surprise freedom feminists—respect for the disrespected, an end to divides between the haves and the have-nots, culture and community care. These values had been threaded through the activism of many intersectional feminist activists before them, values oriented toward opposing the form of group-based inequality they had referred to as "oppression." Barboa and her colleagues in Albuquerque crafted a simple message: #RespectABQwomen. And it coupled that message with lovingly depicted images of local women and families, often ones who were clearly not living the life of the '50s housewife with the white picket fence.[92]

Just as one rarely has to declare that one's life matters if one is already treated that way, the demand for respect is almost always a response to having been *dis*respected. The campaign posters spoke at the first level to the fact that the proposed abortion ban, written by out-of-state organizations, disrespected locals. But the imagery invited reflection on deeper forms of disrespect. The local families depicted were families of color, sometimes queer, sometimes young, sometimes single-parent-headed. The subtle result was to recast abortion rights denial as a form of sexist, racist, and homophobic degradation; to not respect these people would be to dare to say that some people deserved this decision-making power, but not *these* people.

To disrespect local women, the campaign imagery suggested, was also to deny them the tools to fight the violence inflicted by racial and economic inequality. In a different poster, a woman in a Central American skirt stands with her three children. One is in her arms. She is flanked by two others, one looking forward, one looking back, as though haunted by the violence of the US–Mexico border. Another poster, held by young people in full Day of the Dead makeup in a newspaper photo from the time, mentions the border explicitly and calls us to reject what it stands for.

"We dream of bodies without borders," the sign reads. The border between the US and Mexico is not just a border in the sense of a barrier to physical movement. It is a restriction heavy with violence, a restriction that divides the haves and have-nots. In New Mexico that divide literally cuts through families, where some have the advantages of being documented and some do not.

The border is also a divide that speaks to historical and ongoing racist and imperialist violence. As the popular American Southwest quip "We didn't cross the border; the border crossed us" declares, the 1848 treaty of Guadalupe-Hidalgo imposed a new map on people with a very different conception of their roots and their homeland. The sign includes language that does more than reject the border. It also calls for more active support for the families whose lives straddle it. It reads, "All families deserve access to the healthcare they need."

The idea of abortion as healthcare, and a means of community care for communities that had been disrespected for too long, continued to be a mainstay of the fight to protect abortion rights in New Mexico even after the campaign Barboa led in the 2010s achieved the seemingly impossible: getting voters to reject a late-term abortion ban. The seemingly impossible win was still not enough to keep abortion legal in New Mexico in a post-*Dobbs* world. Abortion was still a fourth-degree felony in New Mexico according to the law that had remained on the books since the 1960s. *Roe* had made it unenforceable. But by 2021, it became clear that this was not something pregnant people should bank on.

By then, the pandemic was raging, and legislative hearings were all online. This introduced an unexpected twist. The "room" was full of Indigenous people who were ready to force the legislators who sat cozy in their living rooms "to sit with" something else: their "personal, vulnerable stories"[93] of being denied reproductive justice. These stories were not about choice, or about freedom from the government or social expectations. They were partly about lack of access to abortion. In a state where one in five Native Americans reports lacking access to reproductive health care, Indigenous pregnant people were among those most likely to be affected by the illegalization of abortion in New Mexico.[94]

They also knew what it was like for abortion to be de facto unavailable, because the Hyde Amendment's prohibition of abortions on reservations meant many of them had been living it. And because they were living it, they had insights into the importance of abortion rights and access that all women needed to know about. As Krystal Curley, the Diné executive director of Indigenous Lifeways put it at the time, "We're kind of used to these types of policies being passed and implemented." It was just that now "it's the whole US that's going to have to experience what we've been experiencing . . . and it's traumatic."[95]

The Indigenous women framed the denial of abortion rights as being about another form of inequality in addition to gender inequality: settler colonialism. As many Indigenous activists went to great pains to explain, restrictions on abortion were just one part of a series of games settlers had been playing with Indigenous people's reproductive lives for hundreds of years. In the same era when Beal was writing about la operacion in Puerto Rico, some 25 percent of Native women in the United States were sterilized.[96] For generations, Native women had been experimented on, and their children taken from them. Denial of abortion rights would be another chapter in this legacy of the colonizer treating them as inferior in the most brutal of ways.

This meant that abortion rights were a tool for resisting colonial subjugation, but also that restoring gender equality was part of the struggle to restore what was taken from Indigenous people, to fight against all that had been done to them in the name of white superiority. Indigenous activists insisted that—contra freedom feminism's tendency to paint culture as an engine of sexism—gender equality *was* their culture. Abortion was a form of culturally sanctioned care. Curley testified that day that abortion was "a natural decision, available to us in the natural world." She continued, "For indigenous women, reproductive rights are a way of life."[97]

To take abortion rights from them would be to violently enforce colonialism and patriarchy at once. After all, as Indigenous feminists often argue,[98] a favorite tactic of colonizers had always been to enforce a type of patriarchy that hadn't been there before.[99] Many Indigenous communities were matriarchal, Curley told the legislators that day, and a society where abortion was illegal was one that undermined traditions of respecting their mothers and grandmothers. Restoring reproductive control was a way of restoring to women a status that settler colonialism had violently diminished. Undermining women's health was a way of undermining the community as a whole. Others testified that Indigenous worldviews required thinking about future generations, about the type of care they wanted for their children. And what they wanted for their children happened to include abortion access.

These victories in New Mexico were at once huge and tiny. Huge because they would undoubtedly save pregnant people's lives. Because they demonstrated the power of moral languages besides choice and freedom. And because they showcased the potency of feminist organizing led by women of color.

But they were also tiny because they basically brought reproductive rights back to 1973. Not even to 1973, actually, since that was before the Hyde Amendment removed abortion access from millions of poor women and women of color. But perhaps now is the moment where we can rewrite the future of reproductive rights, and the future of feminism, the way Taylor suggests it should have been written the first time.

Black women, she argued, thought of abortion, and reproductive justice more generally, as central to women's equality. They have developed a feminism that challenges "the totality of American society, not just one's place in it."[100] Perhaps the second time around we can imagine a feminism that gets that hierarchy is the problem—not just restriction or lack of individual bodily autonomy. Perhaps we can talk about inequality in a way that makes clear that its sources often lie deep in our understandings of what and who is valuable, and in who does what work for whom—and that inequality doesn't just come in the form we call "sexism." Perhaps we can see that fighting for what will lift up those facing multiple oppressions is the antidote. Another equality is possible, and a vision of it has been with us all along.

THE SOUL OF FEMINISM

In the late 2010s, in the same cultural moment as when the US media started branding startup culture's cool girls as the new face of feminism, two Zimbabwean activists had a different idea.

Rudo Chigudu and Hope Chigudu's conversation about how to sustain feminist change began with a simple greeting, one that was a far cry from the exhortations to hustle that had become the trademark of the #girlboss. They are also a far cry from the injunctions to buy adaptogens and take a #hotgirlsabbatical so you can work harder next time that remain with us today. *Makadini*, Rudo Chigudu asked in Shona. "What is your state of being?"[1] *Ndiripo*, Hope Chigudu replied. "I am present. Thank you for your interest in my well-being."[2]

Chigudu and Chigudu talked about how feminism meant committing to nurturing each other and committing to reminding one another about the vision we stand for. Their vision of what that looked like came from a longstanding practice in their Beinika clan. When a Beinika woman wants to conceive, she ventures into the forest alone and composes a song. On her return, she teaches it to her sisters and peers, so that they continue to sing the song back to her. The song is the first song her child hears when it enters the world. It becomes the child's compass whenever their life needs reorienting. The song is the child's soul; it calls them back to their self.[3]

The Zimbabwean feminists were responding to the same care trap that has been churning out neoliberal and white feminists for the last fifteen years, but they saw a different way out. One attraction of freedom feminism is that it responds to the reality that women all over the world are genuinely overwhelmed by others' expectations of care. Being the world's caregivers and emotional laborers can leave even the most privileged women very, very depleted. One way we can respond to this fact is by railing against others' expectations. We can vow to say "No" or buy crystals or IDGAF T-shirts.

Or, as Chigudu and Chigudu suggest, we can do something else. We can fight for a world where everyone has a flourishing self because everyone is taken care of. We can fight for a world where giving care is not a liability, where the groups of people our society has deemed the "natural" care*givers* are seen as equally worthy of receiving care.

Which of these fights any of us chooses will have to do with a lot of things—ranging from how much privilege we have, to how much energy we have, to which battles it seems important to pick on a given day. But our actions will also reflect our values and deeply held ideas. I began this book by claiming that the song we choose to sing ourselves about what feminism is will become its soul. I have argued that if we tell ourselves that feminism is about liberating individual women from social expectations, feminism risks dissolving into a tool of power. One future for feminism, the one offered by freedom feminism, is a world in which feminist ideas increasingly serve as justifications for policies that harm or exclude nonelite women.

But there is another possible future, one we can make possible by thinking differently about feminism's core commitments. We can think of the soul of feminism as opposition to oppressive hierarchies or inequalities. If this is the political moment where feminism threatens to become a tool of power, it is also one where reclaiming feminism's radical soul is possible. Feminism is so popular partly because elite women have unprecedented power. But it is also popular partly because we, as a society, are finally reckoning with deep questions about justice. We are having important conversations about how deeply inequality is woven into the structure of our society.

To put it differently, the popularity of feminism is not just a reason to worry; it is a reason to hope. We are in an age of unprecedented concern for social justice, ranging from widespread support for the movement for Black lives to burgeoning union activism and the fact that the majority of Americans now believe that there is too much economic inequality.[4] Yes, the phrase "My feminism will be intersectional or it will be bullshit" has made its way onto a T-shirt. On the other hand, people want to wear that shirt.

I began this book with a meditation on how difficult it can be to understand our principles and put them into practice. Freedom feminism emerges partly from a failure to fully think through the implications of the very intuitive idea that feminism is about releasing women from expectations that prevent us from doing what we want. If we want to conceive the soul of feminism differently, we need to get clearer about the core ideas of feminism for the many and how they translate into action.

Our concrete political goals look different once we put opposition to hierarchy at the center of our feminism. Feminism for the many tells us that feminism, rather than being a fight for freedom, is a fight against a certain type of inequality. That inequality, as bell hooks famously put it, is sexist oppression.[5] Oppression exists when a society's ideas, practices, and institutions—its systems—work to ensure that some people will get less and count less than others.

To get to feminism for the many, we have to see that oppression is not the same thing as unfreedom. As we have seen in this book, there are all kinds of ways we can be restricted without being oppressed. There are also forms of oppression that do not take the form of restrictions, ranging from the orgasm gap and the hierarchy of "fit" mothers to the devaluation of caring and emotional labor. To borrow Crenshaw's house metaphor, oppression is not about the fact that the house of society has walls. It is about the house being built in ways that ensure some groups of people will be relegated to the basement.

If oppression is about social structures keeping entire groups of people down, it will not be eliminated by individual women being freer—especially not in a world where individual women often stand to benefit from harming or excluding other women. Some women have privilege over other women, and, as I argued in chapter 4, the best way to get by within our existing social structures often means reinforcing sexism. The antidote is no more for individual women to purify themselves of patriarchal choices than it is for individual women to be left alone. It is to create new, less hierarchical structures, ones that benefit all women as a group. Movements large and small around the world are making that a reality.

FEMINISM IS A MOVEMENT FOR AN *US*

The contents of the girls' backpack stashes had evolved over time.[6] Lemons and vinegar for the tear gas. Glitter and paint for joy. A green bandana for both. It could cover your face and show the world why you were there.

These seas of green kerchief–clad revelers have become the face of abortion rights in Latin America.[7] But the movement that felled abortion bans in Argentina, Mexico, and Colombia in quick succession in the early 2020s hadn't begun as a movement about reproductive rights. It had begun with the brutal murder of a fourteen-year-old girl. Two hundred thousand protestors in Buenos Aires chanted the name of Chiara Paez, and, over the years, the names of many, many others—Maria Eugenia Lanzetti, Lucia Perez, Dayana Sacayán—determined that none of these women would become just another statistic.

They chanted the names (a tactic consciously shared with Black Lives Matter)[8]—because the statistics were mind-boggling. A woman in Argentina is murdered every thirty-two hours.[9] The murderers might have told women that this was about their individual behavior, that they had stepped out of line in some way, but the numbers told another story. It was a story, the protestors came to understand, about a world where some groups of people counted more than others. To be precise, it was a world where women counted so little as to be reduced to *nothing*. A world where a boy's family would help kill his pregnant girlfriend, where a teacher could be killed in front of her pupils, where feminized bodies were literally found in garbage bags.

Freedom feminism might be telling us that we can get out of sexism one by one, but femicide makes it clear that there is no individual escape. The only way out is together. The only way out, for the Argentine protestors, was together because femicide targeted all women. Murder was the "bloodiest"[10] step in what anthropologist Rita Segato famously calls a "pedagogy of cruelty."[11] One femicide teaches all the women, all the feminized bodies, to be afraid, to know what will happen if they step out of their subordinate role.

The movement even took its name from the idea that the goal was liberation for *all* women. A harm to one of them was a harm to all of them. "Ni Una Menos!" they chanted, and this became the name of the movement. "Not one [woman] less!" "They are killing us," they chanted. "Aren't we going to do anything about it?"

What it means for feminism to be a movement for an *us*, for Ni Una Menos, is to think about whose liberation we need to fight for, starting with who is being subordinated. When we look at victims of gender-based violence, two things are clear: people are being targeted to preserve the hypervaluation of masculinity, and victims are not only people who were assigned female at birth. "Women cis and trans" appears in the movement's earliest manifestos.[12] Today, organizers also often talk about "feminized bodies" and have coined terms like *transfemicide* and *travesticido*.[13]

Ni Una Menos sees gender policing as a tool of gender-based subordination. They want to fight what they call "la violencia machista" (masculinist violence; *machista* has the same root as the word *macho*). For these activists, it makes sense for a society that values "real" men above everyone else to punish anyone who threatens the hierarchy of men and women, including the gender binary that makes that hierarchy easy to enforce. In one social media post, activists wrote that femicides represent the "disciplinarisation of women and all the roles this society sustains at full speed; you will be what is supposed to be normal or you will be nothing."[14]

Part of the beauty of Ni Una Menos is how it shows that fights for greater freedom of gender and sexual expression do not have to be tethered to freedom feminism. Feminists can criticize gender norms, and the concrete violence they make manifest, without falling into the view that social expectations are always harmful, or that when they are, it's only because they stifle individuality. Fighting for groups and communities doesn't have to mean accepting longstanding patriarchal traditions, or capitulating to endless demands that women's unacknowledged labor be the thing that holds those communities together. Instead, fighting for the interests of a group can be about recognizing a shared fate and working to reshape that fate. Ni Una Menos is at once a fight against gender subordination and a fight for gender joy. This is why, in a nod to queer marches all over the world, the activists carry glitter.[15]

As for the green bandanas, they speak to another way that emphasizing the fate of a group lets us improve on freedom feminism. Freedom feminism inadvertently trivializes all kinds of gender injustices. Since restriction is just a part of life, railing against restriction on its own opens feminists to the criticism that the things we are fighting for don't really matter. As we have seen at a number of points in this book, restriction talk trivializes the abortion decision. Putting abortion in the context of the overall devaluation of women, on the other hand, does the opposite. Latin American activists talk about illegal abortion as a form of femicide. Once Ni Una Menos started talking about a society that devalued women to the point of seeming to want to annihilate them, the things that feminism needed to care about started snowballing (to include things like the valuation of care work and political representation for people of all genders).[16] The stakes of these things became undeniable.

Feminist activists in Latin America have been winning by framing illegal abortion as a form of gender-based violence.[17] Illegal abortion doesn't just threaten a pregnant person's privacy, or their career. Instead, keeping abortion illegal is yet another of society's ways of killing women, of wanting women to be nothing—especially if they are poor. As Mariana Alvarez, a feminist lawyer in northern Argentina, puts it, "Subordination requires violence. That is, you can't keep an entire group, an entire population, subordinated if you don't exercise violence on this group. It's a basic form of domination. This violence translates into many methods and many forms, but basically, what you have to understand is that it's the violence of a system that needs you reproducing—a mother, docile, subordinated to another gender, heterosexualized, exploited in every way."[18]

The movement manages at once to talk about the violence that all feminized bodies face and the unique forms of violence against those facing other oppressions, like poverty. Part of the point is that the less privileged among those bodies unmask the logic that renders all inferior. A recent news photo shows a woman who has turned her green bandana into a tube top, leaving room for a macabre message on her back. There, she has scrawled, the black smoldering through the glitter: "the rich abort; the poor die."[19] Elite women might have an escape hatch, but that doesn't mean there is nothing to escape *from*, or that elite women are not on the hook for fighting for those who lack their privileges. It is *because* the poor die that all those subordinated by machista violence have to fight for abortion rights.

In other words, for Ni Una Menos, concern about vulnerable members of the group enacts something like the theory of the vanguard center developed by Black feminists in the US. The situations of poor women, and of trans and gender nonconforming people, lay bare how the systems of oppression really work. Wins for elite women won't trickle down, but fights for the most marginalized might chance to trickle up—and even transform our social world.

FEMINISM IS ABOUT CHANGING NORMS, NOT (JUST OR ALWAYS) DEFYING THEM

There is another reason feminists have to keep groups at the center of our thinking, and it's that norms change through collective action. Freedom feminism might keep telling us that change happens through individual defiance. Sometimes it does. But this is the exception and not the rule. As I explained in my discussion of the judgment myth, women often stand to lose a lot from individual resistance. And when we resist as individuals, the norms often keep trucking on.

Essence Kendall, a high school student in Washington, DC, might have thought she was resisting the hypersexualization of Black women. She was showing that you could (imagine!) be a Black girl wearing the pants style that was currently trending *and* be in school and learn. She certainly thought she had covered all her bases by covering her thighs.

Her decision to wear shorts under her ripped jeans to school that day was nothing if not strategic; she was trying to be what society said she couldn't be. She was also hedging her bets. She hoped a little extra fabric would help her not get in trouble for violating the school's "no ripped jeans" rule. But apparently, none of this was enough to stave off the sexualizing commentary. "You know what I don't like about holes above the knee?" a teacher told her. "A boy can put his finger in there."[20]

Freedom feminism has been telling us we should celebrate the agency of girls like Kendall, that we shouldn't criticize her wardrobe choices. Freedom feminism is right about that. But stopping there would do nothing about the social norms that won't let a Black girl study in peace. And to be clear, these norms matter in ways that are not obvious if we think that dress codes are bad just because they are restricting. (After all, a common refrain is that dress codes affect boys too.) One in five girls between the ages of fourteen and eighteen has been touched or kissed without their consent.[21] Kendall's teacher's remark about boys' fingers makes crystal clear that dress codes communicate different things to boys and girls, and that they create a hierarchy of needs in education. Apparently, schools should bend over backwards to make sure boys can learn without "distraction." Policing girls' clothing choices to this end is more important than keeping girls in school.

Because that is the real, though not obvious to most, harm of school dress codes. They keep girls out of the classroom, especially girls of color. Sixteen-year-old Ceon Dubose, another teen from Washington, DC, gets it: "If you want us to have good grades, why would you all not allow us at school?"[22] In 2017, more than 70 percent of public schools in Washington, DC, allowed punishments for violating school dress codes that entailed being kept out of class.[23] These punishments can translate into lower educational performance and lower graduation rates, which can haunt a girl for the rest of her life. Poor educational performance, for example, is known to depress long-term earning potential.[24] School dress codes communicate that keeping boys "undistracted" is more important than having girls in school at all.

Dress-code discipline can, for Black, Latinx, and Indigenous girls in particular, become a step in the school-to-prison pipeline. Being dress-coded can be the beginning of a disciplinary interaction that ends with the police being called. When the exclusion from class takes the form of suspension (or suspension-like removal from school by any other name to avoid the legal ramifications), it's not like girls always end up in safe places.[25] They can end up at increased risk for contact with the criminal justice system because they are on the streets, or vulnerable to sexual abuse, or using drugs (often to cope with such sexual abuse).[26] In other words, dress-coding can become a tool of racial and gender hierarchy, and set up girls and people of color to receive less over a lifetime.[27] The rewards of educational attainment are flowing away from girls of color, and dress codes are part of the reason.

Girls like Essence and Ceon have been smart enough to see that they don't have less of a right to be in school than anyone else. And they have also seen that the only way to get that right respected is to change the rules that have been treating them as less deserving of an education. They are among the thousands of teens across the country revolting against dress codes.

Girls are organizing school walkouts. They aren't just individually wearing jeans with holes and showing their midriffs; they are doing it all at once and daring schools to punish all of them. They are demanding that *social interpretation* of their bodies change, painting "distraction" and "skinny pass" on their abdomens to call out the race and body type privilege that allows only some of them to show their bellies.[28] One Black girl in Washington, DC, made a documentary. Another group of Black girls organized "headwrap clapbacks." And it's working; a walkout in a Washington, DC, school caused the administration to rewrite the dress code.[29]

Of course, the social practices that keep women down aren't always as explicit as dress codes. It's also not always obvious how to change them, since there isn't always an "administration" that can change norms that perpetuate inequality. But feminism for the many asks us to take an important page from these girls' book. Being free to make choices isn't enough if all the available choices harm us or perpetuate our subordination.[30] And being restricted is often not the most important way that sexism harms us. We have to dismantle a world where some groups get and count less, and to do this, we have to find the norms that sustain inequality and work together to change them. Celebrating whatever clever tactics we may have developed for navigating the basement is not the same thing as getting out of it, or rebuilding the house entirely.

TRADITION IS NOT THE ENEMY (AND SOMETIMES "PROGRESS" IS)

If I had searched the words "Indigenous women Guatemala," I would have gotten the wrong impression about Elena Choc Quib's Mayan skirt. When I plugged those terms into Google while writing this chapter, I got a Reuters article offering up the standard fare about third-world women. Women like her were "sick, illiterate, poor and overwhelmed by too many unplanned children."[31] The reporter had interviewed a forty-something mother of eleven. She noted in print that one of the woman's many grandchildren hid in the folds of just the same type of skirt.

I would also have misunderstood the face of patriarchy that defined Choc Quib's life. She couldn't bear to talk about it herself, but her co-plaintiff Margarita Caal recounted to the *New York Times* her own experience of the episode of gender-based violence that had transformed their lives. It began on what seemed like just another day in the kitchen. Caal was preparing a meal for her children while her husband was away in the fields. Half a dozen men appeared suddenly in her home. They took turns raping her. They set her home on fire as they left.[32]

The men were representatives of the Canadian mining company, Hudbay Minerals. They were claiming land in the El Estor region of Guatemala through any means possible, including raping women and killing their husbands for speaking out against the mine, enforcing a perpetual reign of terror. Alongside the literal violence, Caal, Choc Quib, and other women faced increased gendered work burdens. They were constantly working to heal and sustain a community that was literally under attack. The effluents from the mine were, they claimed, polluting their water source. The women were devoting more time to caring for their children, who suffered from mysterious hair loss, rashes, and gastrointestinal disease.[33]

So, Choc Quib, Caal, and a number of other plaintiffs stood up to patriarchy in a way that is difficult to imagine from the perspective of freedom feminism. They are suing Hudbay Minerals. They are trying to bring a corporation from the Global North to justice in a Canadian court. In doing so, they represent one of the most important feminist struggles of our time, but one you likely haven't heard of within the context of feminism: the struggle for transnational corporate accountability.

The case against Hudbay is ongoing, but the company has sold the mine to the Swiss company Fenix, against whom the women have similar complaints about environmental degradation and human rights violations. In countries all over the Global South, mining companies, factories, and agribusiness companies are promoting sexual violence and harassment, destroying women's livelihoods, and shifting more care work onto them.[34] In 2022, the NGO ActionAid launched a groundbreaking campaign aimed at acknowledging the persistent, global scale of these gender injustices and demanding that an international legal framework be created to hold multinational corporations accountable.[35]

This movement shows just how radically global feminist strategies might change if we put inequality, rather than freedom, at the center of our thinking. Once we start asking about the sources of gender hierarchy and subordination, we can stop assuming that what women need is freedom from culture. We can start seeing how gender violence is not just locally grown, and how the exacerbation of gendered labor burdens are a major cause of sexist oppression. Freedom feminism has been telling us for a long time that sexism comes mostly from tradition and community, that it takes the form of roles that have been imposed on women since time immemorial.

Feminism for the many acknowledges that inequality can come from anywhere, and doesn't only take the form of dictating individual women's destinies. Where freedom feminism sustains imperialism and white supremacy by encouraging us to direct pretty much all of our attention to local men and local practices, feminism for the many challenges the colonial narrative that moral progress means movement away from culture.[36] If feminism is about freedom from culture, it is difficult to distinguish women's attachment to their cultures from an endorsement of sexism. If feminism is about reducing inequality, we can begin to see that culture can support feminist change, and that women's enemies often come from without.

Choc Quib died without seeing justice, but the women's case continues to wind its way through Canadian courts. She wanted people to know why she was brave enough to stand up against her rapists and the Western corporation that supported them. She wiped her eyes with the blue cardigan she wore over her woven skirt as she told a reporter she could no longer speak of the crime. But she could speak about her roots. "I have a voice. I am an indigenous woman, and I am strong, and I am worthy of this," she said, sighing deeply. "I am a woman and I am worthy of this."[37]

In calling her Indigenous roots a source of strength, she was in company with Indigenous women activists all over Latin America. Many of them cite their cultures as the source of their belief in women's power. Many also cite their indigeneity as a source of their value for the earth. Other Latin American Indigenous activists speak of being driven to defend the land out of responsibility to the Pachamama, the earth mother,[38] or out of the deep sense that their bodies are made of the same stuff as the earth.[39] Sometimes women's sense of the urgency of environmental change originates in culturally embedded gendered responsibilities. The responsibility of caregiver and culture bearer is also a responsibility to think about future generations. Women in El Estor say that it is women who think about children and grandchildren and what the mine will do to them.[40]

Feminism for the many does not just ask us to acknowledge that culture can be a feminist resource. It makes it clear why the destruction of tradition, culture, and community should not be understood as merely the collateral damage of feminism.[41] The forces of the Global North and West are deeply associated with moral progress in the Western imaginary, but feminism for the many asks us to break that deep association. We need to see that these agents who are so often assumed to be agents of freedom are sometimes themselves purveyors of gender hierarchy—especially when it comes to women's work and environmental degradation. This is a reality that freedom feminism makes it very difficult for us to see, but it is a reality for many women of the global majority.

EQUALITY IS A RELATIONSHIP

Calls for women to be more assertive are everywhere. We are told that women are behind professionally because of a "dream gap" or a "confidence gap," that our lack of self-assurance is a "force holding [us] back," that "the power centers of this nation are zones of female self-doubt."[42] If you're like me, somebody older than you has probably told you that you need to stop saying "like" and making everything you say sound like a question. If practicing saying "No" in front of the mirror isn't working for you, you can literally download an email extension that forces you to stop apologizing.

With advice like this all around us, it's no wonder that it's become easy to think that the path to feminist change is for individual women to change ourselves. We are constantly told that gender socialization has made us too timid or other-directed, and that the way to throw off this socialization is to care a little bit less about what other people think. We are assigned plenty of work on ourselves that is supposed to help us fix this problem. This combination of ideas has had different faces over the last half-century, ranging from the "career women" and supermoms of the late twentieth century, to the #girlbosses and work-life balance enthusiasts of the 2010s, to the more woo iterations of the 2020s that tell us we will realize we are "powerful beyond measure" if we just stop trying to pour from an empty cup.

In the bustling city of Lucknow, India, a boy named Tarun is living the alternative to assertiveness culture.[43] He is starting a revolution by filling someone else's cup, literally. His mother's, to be precise. She, like most mothers around him, rises each day before sunrise to make bread and tea for the family. But Tarun has started telling her she can sleep in on cold mornings. He can be the one to make the tea. Tarun has realized he wants to be a different kind of man, one whose masculinity is oriented around caring.

Tarun's realization didn't come about accidentally. It came about as the result of grassroots feminist activism, including the work of the educational innovator Urvashi Sahni. Like most feminist educators, Sahni began her work with a strategy focused on girls. In 2003, she founded Prerna Girls School, which sought to empower girls to fight practices like child marriage and dowry. The idea that educating girls is a catalyst for feminist change has become a truism, but Sahni noticed early on that traditional academics alone were not going to cause a revolution. Sahni knew educated women who accepted practices like dowry, and so she was not under the illusion that teaching girls to add and subtract was going to help them dismantle patriarchy.[44]

So, Sahni's school developed a "critical feminist pedagogy." Infused through the years of students' education were dialogues, student-led dramas, and collective actions that centered feminist critical thought and practice. Girls developed a greater sense of what they deserved, but, at a certain point, Sahni realized something was missing. The families of the girls, who lived in the same economic poverty as their brothers, started asking what the school could do for boys. And a lightbulb went off for Sahni. The boys needed economic and educational opportunities, and this was also an opportunity to figure out the "other half" of gender equality.

It was only because equality was at the center of Sahni's thinking that she was able to have this realization. The concept of equality is relational; the concept of freedom is not.[45] To know whether an inequality is present, whether it's gotten better or worse, we have to look at a relationship between at least two entities—who has more, who has less, who is expected to serve the other, and so on. This just isn't true about freedom. We can tell whether a person is free to throw a basketball by looking at whether their body can do it, whether they have a ball or a hoop. We might have to look at whether someone else is preventing them from throwing the basketball, but that's where the relational analysis ends.

In contrast, feminism for the many reminds us that feminist change can't only focus on women. And this is especially true when it comes to work. One of the dangers of freedom feminism is that it turns our eyes away from the fact that work inequalities—even ones that increase women's freedom—can become engines of oppression. There are usually good reasons for women to want to work more. Many of us live under conditions of poverty and insecurity, and many of us find good in our jobs that we cannot find elsewhere, such as the opportunity to interact with other adults.

This means that women often have their sense of freedom enhanced by working. The metaphors of liberating once-restricted potential that often accompany freedom feminism do not help us acknowledge the problem of women's overwork either.[46] Is it *fair* for women to have to work more? Does feminism always have to change women? What about changing men? These are the questions that we can only ask from the perspective of interest in equality. They are questions that feminism for the many forces us to ask.

The Prerna Boys School was born from the realization that feminism meant changing men. Tarun, and boys like him, get asked—just like they get asked what seven plus eight is, or what the capital of Japan is—"Where are your sisters when you go out to play in the evening?" "Is this fair?" when the girls are washing up after dinner while the boys are out playing. And the teachers probe. They ask questions freedom feminists are afraid to ask, including about whether girls' and women's choices are the final say about whether gender equality is acceptable. For example, if the boys say the girls like being at home, teachers respond, "You say they like it, but have you asked them?"[47]

The school demonstrates that changing men does not have to come from a place of scorn for men. The "men are trash" narrative is having a decade-long moment in our discussions of work and dating, and there is probably a social place for it. We live in a world where care mostly flows from women to men, especially when those men are elite. But the boys at Prerna are also very, very socioeconomically disadvantaged, and feminism for the many does not pretend that gender is the only unjust social hierarchy. The educators at the Prerna School have realized that changing masculinity can help boys too.

The school aims to create a transformed masculinity that allows boys like Tarun to see their role as being "nurturers and caregivers of their families."[48] This view doesn't just transform their sisters' and mothers' and future wives' lives. It helps them fight caste, class, and race degradation that assigns them a masculine role that is difficult to fulfill. If being a nurturer and caregiver is part of what it means to be a man, demonstrating love for their families doesn't have to be financial. This is a love they can, and do, demonstrate today. Tarun helps his mom get a little extra sleep; Shivpoojan has started watching his three-year-old brother; Ambrendra shares housework with his sister.[49]

These stories are living proof of two key points of feminism for the many: that feminist change shouldn't mean increased work for women, and that feminist change often means changing men. In the Global North, maybe it's time to stop focusing so heavily on encouraging women to be more assertive, and instead focus on encouraging men to be more caring. The Zimbabwean activists I discussed at the beginning of this chapter thought the way of the future was to build systems that provide care for those who give it. US author Ruth Whippman tells a story about walking into the boys' section of Target and feeling shocked to discover that the shirt that said "Be Kind" was actually supposed to be there.[50] Feminism for the many is the hope for a world where things like that are no longer shocking—where we expect men to change too.

WE ALL DEPEND ON "WOMEN'S WORK"

The moment in 2020 when the term *essential worker* entered the American vocabulary was an opportunity. At the height of the pandemic, it was difficult to ignore our interdependence. It was difficult to ignore how deeply we relied on the labor of others. It even seemed we might start to notice how inequitably our society values labor and distributes risk.

Even in the moment, we seized this opportunity very imperfectly. The US government did provide unexpected social supports, ranging from increases in food stamps to paid sick and caregiving leave to a nearly universal childcare allowance. By now, most of this support has evaporated. Much of our public attention, even at the time, focused on declaring health workers "heroes," and letting them learn the hard way that this accolade was supposed to serve as a substitute for hazard pay or trauma counseling.

I have referred several times in this book to my own dependency on another kind of essential worker, one rarely discussed in the pandemic news, and even more rarely since then—even in the content bemoaning the condition of "working moms" I continue to devour. I mean daycare workers, nannies, house cleaners, home health aides. These workers, especially those in childcare and house cleaning, were terminated in droves during the pandemic. Most work in a shadow area of the economy that is poorly paid and unregulated. Most lack access to unemployment insurance. Undocumented workers, who are dramatically overrepresented in these industries, could not even access the $1,200 stimulus checks the federal government was cutting in the first months of the 2020 emergency.[51]

But the working-class women of color and immigrant women who bear the brunt of this work have never seen their precarity as part of some momentary crisis. Domestic worker organizations like We Dream in Black have been playing the long game since before the pandemic. They see that the work they do has never been valued appropriately. Before 2020, We Dream in Black members began fighting for, and winning, basic labor protections. In New York City, they fought for, and won, paid sick and safe leave.[52] They helped workers recover over $500,000 of stolen wages. In Philadelphia, We Dream in Black members won a Domestic Workers Bill of Rights,[53] requiring written agreements outlining hours and rates of pay, and advance notice of termination.

These protections are a just a floor, and a very low one at that. Diane Heller, a member of the Atlanta chapter, knows that making deeper change on the issue of care work means changing how people think about the work. She wants the world to know she sees the work she does as a calling.[54] She remembers always looking out for the senior citizens in her community, stopping to chat on porches, taking time from her day to run errands for them.[55]

Caring "has always been embedded in me," she says. "We love what we do." And why shouldn't they be proud? The work they do, the members' refrain says, is "the work that makes all other work possible." Heller is one of many members speaking publicly about what domestic work is and why it's important, who sees that bigger policy change is going to happen alongside a revolution in our system of value.

For this revolution to happen, we have to think of the soul of feminism as something other than freedom. If we think feminist change will come about through improving the lives of individual women—or even if we hold the adjacent view that one woman getting to the status of an elite man breaks barriers for all of us—we are in denial of a basic fact.

I don't mean the (also important) fact that women can get ahead at the expense of other women. I mean the fact that there is *no way* all of us can get to the status of elite men. If all of us engaged in the type of labor elite white men do, we literally could not sustain life. If nobody cared for us in the periods of dependency typical of our species, most notably childhood, old age, illness, and disability, we simply could not survive.[56]

Freeing ourselves from the expectation of caring for others is no feminist solution. This is partly because it is not a *human* solution. The idea that we can, or should, want to be free from the needs and expectations of others is deeply woven into the Western imaginary. Freedom feminism is evidence of just how deeply. Even attempts at radical social change, like feminism, struggle to imagine justice as something other than a world of independent, mutually noninterfering individuals. But our attachment to this ideal cannot change the basic truth. We can individually try to free ourselves from the expectation that we care for others, but we cannot free human beings from the need for care.

Even freedom feminism lite, the view that we need to free women from the expectation that we be caregivers (rather than the problematic suggestion that we can free human beings from care), will not give us the change we need. This view is what has led us to see women's workforce participation as an indicator of progress.[57] It has also sidelined conversations about how private households cannot bear the sole responsibility for caregiving.[58] It's just not true that most households with dependent children and elders can easily afford to provide the care their family members need—care that ultimately supports the economy that all of us benefit from, whether we have children or not.[59]

More importantly, freedom feminism misses the reason that caregiving has become something one would want to be liberated from in the first place. Care work and housework are invisible, low status, not seen as work. To say that women shouldn't be expected to do this work is to leave untouched the system that makes this work low-status in the first place. To think about the form of inequality called oppression, as feminism for the many does, is to ask about its deep sources, about how the fundamental design of society is shot through with unjust hierarchy.

For care work to have been gendered does not just mean that women have been expected to do it. If gender is a system of hierarchy, we have to see that the work done by those on the lower end of the hierarchy carries the stamp of inferiority—and that we have to erase that stamp. This is doubly true when the work is also racialized, as much of the care work not done by biological family members has always been, at least in the United States.

Joi Roberts, a We Dream in Black member in Atlanta, speaks against the idea that there is something inherently inferiorizing about care work: "We love what we do; we just want to make it work for you and us."[60] If freedom feminism ignores care and domestic work or treats it as something women should transcend, feminism for the many asks us to revalue and redistribute it. It also asks us to envision the future of the care worker differently. It's not just that we need to stop degrading the work itself; it's that we need to stop degrading the worker. At the end of the day, to be a care worker has to mean not being more controlled than other workers and not counting less than them.

We Dream in Black has a single-word name for their agenda, one that articulates this vision perfectly. They want to be "unbossed."[61] They borrow this word from the presidential campaign of Shirley Chisolm, a proud Black feminist who was also the first African American woman in Congress. In 2023, members of We Dream in Black, and its parent organization, the National Domestic Workers Alliance, rallied in Philadelphia's Rittenhouse Square. They chose the location for a reason. The wealthy neighborhood was a site of multiple violations of the Domestic Worker Bill of Rights they had won in 2020. But it was 2023, and workers were getting fired when they tried to claim the rights written down in the law. One member had asked for a break at some point in a nine-hour day, only to end up fired at day's end.[62] Others had found themselves blacklisted on social media when they asked for basic accommodations like sick days.[63]

This was the road ahead. It was one thing to get minimal protections on the books. It was another to get those protections enforced, and to get to a world where those protections were so incorporated into our culture that they were seen as the floor and not the ceiling. To get there, women of the middle and upper classes have to get that we are dependent on the labor of paid care workers, that feminism for the many can only be achieved by acknowledging this—that the fight to revalue care work is our fight too. The history of domestic worker organizing is full of attempts to get women of *all* classes to see how our fate is tied to our society's value of care work. Since at least the 1960s, feminist activists of various stripes, ranging from labor movement to civil rights leaders,[64] have insisted that this is a critical path away from feminism for the few.

The twentieth-century activist Carolyn Reed realized the support of middle- and upper-class women was crucial to making the Fair Labor Standards Act apply to domestic workers. Reed's organization, the National Committee on Household Employment (NCHE) fought to get women who employed domestic workers to take a stance with a simple act. They would put stickers on their houses that said, "This is a Fair Labor Standards Household."[65]

And there is an important (and complicated) history of middle- and upper-class feminists showing up in other ways, ways that we might take a page from today, reminding us that freedom feminism needn't be the only position available to women with race or class privilege. Gloria Steinem famously hired members of Reed's Household Technicians of America to cater her events. Later, Reed would say that Steinem was the first name that came to mind when thinking of feminists you could count on.[66]

Part of the damage of freedom feminism is that it has undermined cross-class solidarity among women. One of the main expectations we have tried to free women from is one that none of us can be freed from, and one whose costs are borne predominantly by working-class women and women of color. Feminism for the many tells us to dismantle the hierarchy that devalues the work and to come up with a solution that works for *all* women. This is why We Dream in Black fights for public investment in care that they themselves, and not just elite women, will be able to access.

After all, it's not like domestic workers don't have their own family care responsibilities. Yet, infant daycare costs more than college tuition at most state universities—roughly $10,000 a year across the country, and more like $20,000 a year in my own New York City.[67] This is why We Dream in Black members in North Carolina are fighting for state funds to support daycare infrastructure. It is also why the National Domestic Workers Alliance has crafted a proposal for Universal Family Care, a type of public care insurance that would support people caring for young, aging, or ill loved ones, or paying for someone else to care for them.

If Crenshaw was right that a society is like a house, the house we have built is one where the people living in the attic and on the main floors literally cannot survive without the work being done by the people in the basement. The natural question to ask is why that work destines the people who do it for the basement and what can be done about it. Feminism for the many allows us to ask this question, because it begins from an understanding of our politics as opposition to group-based hierarchy or inequality. It imagines feminism as a movement not to reshape women, or to leave women to pursue their individual potential, but to reshape the world.

If oppression consists in structures that give some groups higher places in the social hierarchy than others, and a world without structures is not an option, the path forward can only be to build new structures. We have to change our social architecture. This is not the same thing as just acknowledging that we are interdependent; it is demanding *terms* of interdependence that do not push people into the basement. We cannot stop living together, but we can build another house.

Or, as Congresswoman Alexandria Ocasio-Cortez recently Instagrammed, women and gender-expansive people "cannot knock on anyone else's door. We need to build our own house." She followed it with a dig on individualism. "Let's build this house together."[68]

The idea that we need to change the shape of society, that the structures that produce inequality need to be dismantled, is possibly *the* idea of our political time. The extent of economic and racial inequality has become undeniable. We are developing a widespread understanding that inequalities can be structural, that they are embedded deeply in our society, and that we need to fight against a world where some people matter less and a tiny minority of people hold vast wealth and influence. We are also starting to see and talk about how accountability and mutual concern, rather than freedom from one another, are part of the solution.

In a moment of increasing awareness of social inequality, feminism has been threatening on many occasions to go out and do its own thing, to become a tool for privileged women to advance their interests at the expense of others. Sometimes we do this on purpose—and I am including myself in the "we" on purpose, because I have many forms of privilege in spite of being a woman of color—and sometimes we do this with little awareness of what we are doing. Much of my aim in this book has been to help us see what we are doing so that we can stop, to see the trap of freedom feminism before we have already fallen in, to reclaim or reinvent the soul of feminism before it is too late.

Once we can recognize freedom feminism for what it is, we can begin to see the downsides of perpetuating arguments and images that tout freeing individual women from social expectations. We can also see the way that bad and faux feminisms that keep popping up like a game of whack-a-mole are part of a single gestalt. There are important similarities, for example, among the problems with what is called "white feminism" and what is called "neoliberal," "lean in," or "girlboss" feminism. All are able to paint racist and capitalist policies as beneficial to women because of our background willingness to reduce women's subjection to social expectations. Once we accept freedom feminism, it is easy to buy the idea that more work is a positive break from a past of domesticity, or that feminist change means freeing women of color from their cultures and communities.

I have spent much of this book dragging the idea of individual women *dreaming* big. But feminism for the many is also a call for feminism to *go* big. We need to work for a world without unjust hierarchy, and doing that has to mean fighting for women as a group, especially the most vulnerable among us. The ideal of opposition to gender-based oppression, and the other oppressions that intersect with it, makes clear what feminism needs to fight against. The ideal of freedom is, in contrast, inherently ambivalent. Being free does not mean supporting social justice or the liberation of other women. In a world where women's options are structured by sexism and other inequalities, and where women often stand to benefit from harming other women, encouraging women to do "whatever the fuck they want" could end up with any number of results.

Still, the impulse to confuse pursuit of our individual goals with feminism comes from an important place—a place most feminists can identify with. Yes, it sometimes comes from people cynically using feminism to get what they want. But it is also often a response to the fact that being expected to care about everyone else is a very real, and very common, face of women's oppression. The "thank you for your interest in my well-being" vision offered by the Zimbabwean activists at the beginning of this chapter is only a feminist vision if someone is actually interested in women's well-being. A future where women do all the giving is not a feminist one. To put unjust hierarchy at the center of our thinking is at once to see what is wrong with many unfreedoms foisted on women (Why does Tarun get to go out at night when his sister doesn't? Why are girls the ones who are supposed to change how they dress?) and to see that sometimes what we need is something other than freedom. Sometimes we need care and support.

If you are a feminist, somebody has probably given you the advice not to settle. At this moment when feminism is incredibly popular, we have a choice about what to do with that advice. Feminism can focus on allowing elite women to face fewer social restrictions while still being exhausted—and, more importantly, while leaving the majority of women behind. We can, as a member of Ni Una Menos put it "settle for the individual autonomy of women, now with freedom to lead, govern, and enjoy pleasure."[69] Or, we can "hope and aim for more."[70] Now is a great time not to settle.

ACKNOWLEDGMENTS

It seems fitting, in retrospect, to have written a book critical of independence during one of the least independent seasons of my life.

I could not have produced the pages here without having basically been retaught how to write. I thank my agent, Markus Hoffman, for taking on this formidable task—likely more than he bargained for. I also needed to be convinced to go get an agent to begin with in a moment where all of life's forces seemed to be conspiring to keep me on the familiar path. I am grateful to Linda Martín Alcoff, Myisha Cherry, Jean Hannah Edelstein, Carol Hay, Kate Manne, and Olúfẹ́mi Táíwò for encouraging me to do the new thing instead.

I am grateful to my editor at Beacon, Rachael Marks, for helping me find my voice, and for saving me from the feeling that I was writing into the void. Thank you for "getting" this book and for helping me feel seen throughout this process. A number of research assistants also helped keep this project moving forward when life got in the way, including Emily Crandall, Maggie Fife, and Jodell Ulerie.

I wrote the proposal for this book in the throes of the pandemic, with a toddler at home full time. I wrote the book itself in a haze of sleep deprivation with a newborn still often attached to my body. If this book makes sense at all—and even if it doesn't—I owe a huge debt to those who have cared for my children. I am grateful to all of my children's professional caregivers and daycare providers. Special thanks to Grey for his kindness to my children, and his supererogatory willingness to eat salad and chat about ideas while the little one was asleep.

Thanks also to innumerable friends, colleagues, students, and other interlocutors who have kept my thoughts alive and who have supported me in moments of deep uncertainty. My parents and my siblings are also present in everything I write. With each passing day, I realize more what a gift it has been to have a family of origin who taught me to love knowledge.

I am grateful to my children for making it so easy for me to find joy and meaning every single day, and for keeping me honest about what this book was for.

Finally, thank you to my love, Matt Lindauer. My research and experience could have easily left me believing that trying to have a gender-equal relationship was tilting at windmills, especially if kids were involved. You care for me every day in ways that demonstrate the opposite. And I am so lucky to write and live alongside someone who keeps me intellectually and morally brave.

NOTES

INTRODUCTION

1. Heritage Reporting Corporation, "Transcript of Supreme Court Oral Arguments in *Dobbs v. Jackson Women's Health*," Dec. 1, 2021, 56–57, https://www.cnn.com/2021/12/01/politics/read-transcript-dobbs-jackson-womens-health/index.html.

2. Isabelle Chapman and Daniel A. Medina, "Conservatives Have Pushed Infant Safe Haven Laws as an Alternative to Abortion. But Few American Women Use Them," CNN, Aug. 9, 2022, https://www.cnn.com/2022/08/09/us/infant-safe-haven-law-abortion-invs/index.html.

3. Barrett was citing the reasoning in *Roe* and *Casey* rather than endorsing the view that pregnancy was a burden. But the argument she was making—the only argument she made during the oral arguments of *Dobbs*—had been put forward by an amicus brief that claimed that safe haven laws gave women "total freedom" (see Chapman and Medina, "Conservatives Have Pushed Infant Safe Haven Laws as an Alternative to Abortion"). Barrett also explicitly affirmed the idea that forced pregnancy was an infringement on bodily autonomy, though she compared it to "the vaccine" (Transcript of Supreme Court Oral Arguments in *Dobbs v. Jackson Women's Health Organization*, 2022, 56–57).

4. Moira Donegan, "White Nationalists Are Flocking to the US Anti-Abortion Movement," *The Guardian*, Jan. 24, 2022, https://www.theguardian.com/commentisfree/2022/jan/24/white-nationalists-are-flocking-to-the-us-anti-abortion-movement.

5. Barrett was a member of People of Praise, an organization that holds that men are divinely appointed heads of household and whose members say it teaches that wives should be submissive to their husbands. https://apnews.com/article/new-orleans-donald-trump-amy-coney-barrett-us-supreme-court-courts-307b039f041e22448c98a3397353dfd4.

6. Mary Alice Royce, "'Mutilating bodies of children'; Sen. Blackburn calls for FDA investigation into hormone blockers," WSMV4, September 22, 2022, https://www.wsmv.com/2022/09/23/mutilating-bodies-children-sen-blackburn-calls-fda-investigation-into-hormone-blockers/; John Partiplo and Holly McCall, "US Senator Marsha Blackburn Heads Anti-Transgender Rally in Nashville," *Tennessee*

Lookout, October 27, 2022, https://tennesseelookout.com/2022/10/21/u-s
-sen-marsha-blackburn-headlines-anti-transgender-rally-in-nashville/.

7. Emma Green, "The Irony at the Heart of the Amy Coney Barrett Fight," *The Atlantic*, Oct. 12, 2020, https://www.theatlantic.com/politics/archive/2020/10
/amy-coney-barrett-conservative-feminism/616696.

8. Christina Cauterucci, "The Insidious Sexism on Display at Amy Coney Barrett's Hearing," *Slate*, Oct. 12, 2020, https://slate.com/news-and-politics/2020/10
/amy-coney-barrett-feminism-sexism.html.

9. "Tillis Discusses Role of Supreme Court in Opening Remarks of Judge Amy Coney Barrett's Confirmation Hearing," Thom Tillis, US Senator for North Carolina, Oct. 12, 2020, https://www.tillis.senate.gov/2020/10/tillis-discusses
-role-of-upreme-court-in-opening-remarks-of-judge-amy-coney-barrett-s
-confirmation-hearing.

10. Kylie Cheung, "Amy Coney Barrett Is the Final Dystopian Girlboss," *Jezebel*, Dec. 1, 2021, https://jezebel.com/amy-coney-barrett-could-be-the-final-dystopian
-girlbos-1848144829.

11. The history of the relationship of feminists to the term *pro-choice* is complicated. However, the term *choice* has undoubtedly become the popular understanding of the feminist side in the abortion debate. The term was in fact coined by a feminist who was looking for a response with the catchiness of the term *pro-life*, but feminists had long been advocating for abortion as an issue of equality and domination. See Linda Greenhouse and Reva B. Siegel, *Before Roe v. Wade: Voices that Shaped the Abortion Debate Before the Supreme Court's Ruling* (New York: Kaplan, 2010) for a discussion of this history. The large reproductive rights organizations advocated for choice and abortion access, and have increasingly adopted a reproductive justice agenda, but many of them have continued to use choice language throughout the 2000s. I was an employee of one of these organizations when they organized the 2004 March for Women's Lives. This march had originally been called the March for Choice until women of color objected (see Kimala Price, "What Is Reproductive Justice?" *Meridians* 10, no. 4 [2010]). NARAL, another of these organizations, changed its name to Naral Pro-Choice America in the early 2000s and is now called Reproductive Freedom for All.

12. Dorothy Roberts, *Killing the Black Body: Race, Reproduction, and the Meaning of Liberty* (New York: Vintage, 1997).

13. See Loretta Ross and Rickie Solinger, *Reproductive Justice: An Introduction* (Berkeley: University of California Press, 2017).

14. See Melissa V. Harris-Perry, *Sister Citizen: Shame, Stereotypes, and Black Women in America* (New Haven, CT: Yale University Press, 2011).

15. "After Dobbs: Does 'Big Tent' Feminism Exist? Should It?," *New York Times*, Sept. 14, 2022, https://www.nytimes.com/2022/09/14/opinion/roe-v-wade
-future-of-feminism.html.

16. For a discussion of how the values expressed in mainstream therapy can be alienating to people from less individualistic cultural backgrounds, see #browngirltherapy and Sahaj Kohli, "How to Do Therapy with Founder of

Brown Girl Therapy," *Truth Be Told* podcast, KQED, Dec. 17, 2020, https://www.kqed.org/podcasts/778/how-to-do-therapy-with-sahaj-kohli.

17. See Serene J. Khader, *Decolonizing Universalism: A Transnational Feminist Ethic*, Studies in Feminist Philosophy (Oxford: Oxford University Press, 2019), 50–76, for a more academic discussion of this issue.

18. Mikki Kendall, *Hood Feminism: Notes from the Women That a Movement Forgot* (New York: Penguin, 2020), 138.

19. Saba Mahmood, *Politics of Piety: The Islamic Revival and the Feminist Subject* (Princeton, NJ: Princeton University Press, 2005).

20. See Serene J. Khader, "Do Muslim Women Need Freedom?," *Politics and Gender* 12, no. 4 (2016): 727–53, for a philosophical argument that distinguishes sexism from tradition and explains how culturally embedded feminisms are possible.

21. Sara Farris, *In the Name of Women's Rights: The Rise of Femonationalism* (Durham, NC: Duke University Press, 2017).

22. Olúfẹ́mi O. Táíwò, "Identity Politics and Elite Capture," *Boston Review*, May 7, 2020, http://bostonreview.net/race/olufemi-o-taiwo-identity-politics-and-elite-capture.

23. See Kyla Schuller, *The Trouble with White Women: A Counterhistory of Feminism* (New York: Bold Type Books, 2021), chapter 4.

24. See Jennifer Nelson, *Women of Color and the Reproductive Rights Movement* (New York: New York University Press, 2023); Ross and Solinger, *Reproductive Justice*.

25. See Dorothy Sue Cobble, Linda Gordon, and Astrid Henry, *Feminism Unfinished: A Short, Surprising History of American Women's Movements* (New York: W. W. Norton, 2014).

26. Shani Orgad and Rosalind Gill, *Confidence Culture* (Durham, NC: Duke University Press, 2022); Catherine Rottenberg, *The Rise of Neoliberal Feminism* (New York: Oxford University Press, 2018).

27. Stanton said, two decades after Seneca Falls and after the abolition of slavery, "I do not believe in allowing ignorant Negroes or ignorant and debased Chinamen to make laws for me to obey" (see Schuller, *The Trouble with White Women*, 20). Catt wrote that "white supremacy would be strengthened, not weakened by women's suffrage."

28. Schuller, *The Trouble with White Women*, 163.

CHAPTER 1: THE RESTRICTION MYTH

1. *Humans of CIA*, 2021, https://www.youtube.com/watch?v=X55JPbAMc9g.

2. For an extended discussion of the problem with thinking of oppression as identical with restriction, see Marilyn Frye, "Oppression," in *The Politics of Reality: Essays in Feminist Theory* (Trumansburg, NY: Crossing Press, 1983).

3. Sonya Renee Taylor, *The Body Is Not an Apology: The Power of Radical Self-Love* (Oakland, CA: Berrett-Koehler, 2018), 75.

4. Frye, "Oppression," argues that the practice of men opening doors for women mocks women's labor, making it seem like men are serving women rather than the converse.

5. Michaele L. Ferguson, "Choice Feminism and the Fear of Politics," *Perspectives on Politics* 8, no. 1 (2010): 247–53.

6. Tressie McMillan Cottom, "When Your (Brown) Body Is a (White) Wonderland," Tressie McMillan Cottom, Aug. 27, 2013, https://tressiemc.com/uncategorized /when-your-brown-body-is-a-white-wonderland.

7. Liz Truss, "Destiny [sic] Child had it right when they celebrated All the Honey's Making Money. Grab your independence, women! #freedomfeminism," Twitter, Mar. 8, 2018, https://twitter.com/trussliz/status/971824701889794051.

8. On *Fox and Friends*, Lahren decried the direction the "modern feminist" movement had taken seemingly in order to hold space for the idea that a true feminism would be compatible with her views. She also affirmed the importance of "lifting up women" and empowering women. Tomi Lahren, "The 'Pendulum' Is Swinging on the Feminist Movement," *Fox and Friends*, Oct. 29, 2022, https:// www.foxnews.com/video/6314580733112.

9. Mikki Kendall, *Hood Feminism: Notes from the Women That a Movement Forgot* (New York: Penguin, 2020).

10. Tressie McMillan Cottom, *Thick: And Other Essays* (New York: The New Press, 2018), 64.

11. Cottom, "When Your (Brown) Body Is a (White) Wonderland."

12. Cottom, *Thick*, 59.

13. Cottom, *Thick*, 71.

14. Or by changing their behavior and buying the right products. Cottom argues that white and Black women have different investments in the idea that our ideal of beauty is too restrictive, where the former are particularly invested in showing that anyone can make themselves beautiful, because the idea of beauty as a meritocracy works to hide its function in upholding white supremacy.

15. Cottom, *Thick*, 44.

16. Robert D. Mare, "Educational Homogamy in Two Gilded Ages," *Annals of the American Academy of Political Science* 663, no. 1 (2015).

17. Gustaf Bruze, "Male and Female Returns to Schooling," *International Economic Review* 56, no. 1 (2015): 207–34.

18. See Raj Chetty et al., "Race and Economic Opportunity in the United States: An Intergenerational Perspective," *Quarterly Journal of Economics* 135, no. 2 (May 1, 2020): 711–83, https://doi.org/10.1093/qje/qjz042.

19. Cottom, *Thick*, 60.

20. A Miss Black America pageant was happening at the same time as the Miss America pageant and New York Radical Women's protest. For a discussion of the politics of the two events and the relationship between them, see Paige Welch, "Miss America 1968: When Civil Rights and Feminist Activists Converged on Atlantic City," *The Conversation*, Sept. 9, 2016, http://theconversation.com/miss-america-1968-when -civil-rights-and-feminist-activists-converged-on-atlantic-city-64850.

21. Cottom, *Thick*, 67.

22. Heather Widdows, *Perfect Me: Beauty as an Ethical Ideal* (Princeton, NJ: Princeton University Press, 2018).

23. The book became Widdows, *Perfect Me*.

24. Widdows, *Perfect Me*, 116.

25. Widdows, *Perfect Me*, 149.

26. Deborah Rhode, *The Beauty Bias: The Injustice of Appearance in Life and Law* (New York: Oxford University Press, 2010).

27. "How Much Is Your Face Worth? Woman's Daily Worth Value 2017 Survey—SkinStore," Skinstore US, Mar. 8, 2017, https://www.skinstore.com/blog/skincare/womens-face-worth-survey-2017.

28. Maurie Backman, "Here's How Much the Average Woman Has Saved for Retirement," CNN Money, Mar. 13, 2018, https://money.cnn.com/2018/03/13/retirement/women-saved-for-retirement/index.html.

29. Amia Srinivasan, "Does Anyone Have the Right to Sex?," *London Review of Books*, Mar. 22, 2018, https://www.lrb.co.uk/the-paper/v40/n06/amia-srinivasan/does-anyone-have-the-right-to-sex.

30. "Elliot Rodger's Manifesto Shows Self-Hate Fueled Anti-Asian Violence That Kicked off Isla Vista Rampage," AALDEF, May 25, 2014, https://www.aaldef.org/blog/elliot-rodgers-manifesto-shows-self-hate-fueled-anti-asian-violence-that-kicked-off-isla-vista-rampa.

31. There is definitely a racial dimension to the practice of looksmaxing, in the sense that the "alpha" aesthetic is mostly white. The idea of the superiority of white men is explicit in many incel communities. There is something to be said for the idea that men of color who are incels are subject to racist beauty standards, but the function of these standards is to create a hierarchy among men, not a hierarchy between men and women.

32. There are important conceptual questions to be raised about the notion of "fuckability" Srinivasan develops, both because being sexually desired can be a pathway to victimization rather than advantage, and because women's oppression consists partly in needing to be sexually desired in order to have access to other goods in the first place. Srinivasan starts to address the former when she notes that Black women are victimized by their excess of "fuckability." Amia Srinivasan, *The Right to Sex: Feminism in the Twenty-First Century* (New York: Farrar, Straus, and Giroux, 2021), 103.

33. Srinivasan, *The Right to Sex*, 94.

34. Srinivasan, "Does Anyone Have the Right to Sex?"

35. Katie Notopoulos, "Tinder Says It Is Really Into Interracial Love," *BuzzFeed News*, Feb. 27, 2018, https://www.buzzfeednews.com/article/katienotopoulos/tinder-users-are-most-open-to-interracial.

36. Lester Fabian Brathwaite, "Why Dating Apps Are Racist AF—With or Without Ethnicity Filters," *Rolling Stone* (blog), Aug. 21, 2020, https://www.rollingstone.com/culture/culture-features/dating-apps-grindr-ethnicity-filters-1047047.

37. Patricia Hill Collins, "Mammies, Matriarchs, and Other Controlling Images," in *Black Feminist Thought: Knowledge, Consciousness, and the Politics of Empowerment* (New York: Routledge, 1990), 69–96.

38. Srinivasan, *The Right to Sex*, 103.

39. Ana Cristina Santos and Ana Lúcia Santos, "Yes, We Fuck! Challenging the Misfit Sexual Body Through Disabled Women's Narratives," *Sexualities* 21, no. 3 (Mar. 2018): 303–18, https://doi.org/10.1177/1363460716688680.

40. See Ellen Willis, "Lust Horizons," *Village Voice*, Oct. 18, 2005, https://www .villagevoice.com/lust-horizons; Lorna Norman Bracewell, "Beyond Barnard: Liberalism, Antipornography Feminism, and the Sex Wars," *Signs: Journal of Women in Culture & Society* 42, no. 1 (Oct. 2016): 23–48, https://doi.org/10 .1086/686752.

41. For more on the limits of defining sex around consent, see Manon Garcia, *The Joy of Consent: A Philosophy of Good Sex* (Cambridge, MA: Harvard University Press, 2023).

42. David A. Frederick, H. Kate St. John, et al., "Differences in Orgasm Frequency Among Gay, Lesbian, Bisexual, and Heterosexual Men and Women in a U.S. National Sample," *Archives of Sexual Behavior* 47, no. 1 (Jan. 2018): 273–88, doi.org/10.1007/s10508-017-0939-z.

43. Nicole Andrejek, Tina Fetner, and Melanie Heath, "Climax as Work: Heteronormativity, Gender Labor, and the Gender Gap in Orgasm," *Gender and Society* 36, no. 2 (Jan. 31, 2022): 189–213, https://doi.org/10.1177/08912432211073062.

44. Andrejek, Fetner, and Heath, "Climax as Work."

45. Andrejek, Fetner, and Heath, "Climax as Work."

46. Breanne Fahs, "Coming to Power: Women's Fake Orgasms and Best Orgasm Experiences Illuminate the Failures of (Hetero)Sex and the Pleasures of Connection," *Culture, Health, and Sexuality* 16, no. 8 (June 18, 2014): 974–88, https:// doi.org/10.1080/13691058.2014.924557.

47. Sara McClelland, "Intimate Justice," *Social and Personality Psychology Compass* 4, no. 9 (2010): 663–80.

48. Aysha Tabassum, "Sexual Liberation While Racialized," *The Journal*, Jan. 22, 2021, https://www.queensjournal.ca/story/2021-01-21/features/sexual-liberation -while-racialized.

49. Kristen Ghodsee, *Why Women Have Better Sex Under Socialism: And Other Arguments for Economic Independence* (New York: Bold Type Books, 2018), 118.

50. Ghodsee, *Why Women Have Better Sex Under Socialism*, 118.

51. Ghodsee, *Why Women Have Better Sex Under Socialism*, 118.

52. Ghodsee, *Why Women Have Better Sex Under Socialism*, 113.

53. Ghodsee, *Why Women Have Better Sex Under Socialism*, 58.

54. Ghodsee, *Why Women Have Better Sex Under Socialism*, 58.

55. Ghodsee, *Why Women Have Better Sex Under Socialism*, 116.

56. Daniel L. Carlson et al., "The Gendered Division of Housework and Couples' Sexual Relationships: A Reexamination," *Journal of Marriage and Family* 78, no. 4 (2016): 975–95, https://doi.org/10.1111/jomf.12313.

57. Eva Johansen et al., "Fairer Sex: The Role of Relationship Equity in Female Sexual Desire," *Journal of Sex Research* (May 27, 2022): 1–10, https://doi.org/10 .1080/00224499.2022.2079111.

58. Claire Cain Miller, "How Society Pays When Women's Work Is Unpaid," The Up-shot, *New York Times*, Feb. 23, 2016, https://www.nytimes.com/2016/02/23 /upshot/how-society-pays-when-womens-work-is-unpaid.html.

59. The political philosopher Iris Marion Young (1990) argued that an important problem with models of equality that focus only on distributions of goods was that they ignore inequalities in the process that determine what counts as a good to begin with. See "Displacing the Distributive Paradigm" in *Justice and the Politics of Difference* (Princeton, NJ: Princeton University Press, 2022).

60. Andrejek, Fetner, and Heath, "Climax as Work," 189–213.

61. Fahs, "Coming to Power."

62. Frederick, St. John, et al., "Differences in Orgasm Frequency Among Gay, Lesbian, Bisexual, and Heterosexual Men and Women in a U.S. National Sample," 273–88.

63. Taylor, *The Body Is Not an Apology*; Rebecca Traister, *Good and Mad: The Revolutionary Power of Women's Anger* (New York: Simon & Schuster, 2018), 62.

64. Joni Sweet, "10 Wellness Trends You Have to Try in 2023," *Forbes*, Dec. 30, 2022, https://www.forbes.com/sites/jonisweet/2022/12/30/10-wellness-trends -you-have-to-try-in-2023.

65. Katherine Rowland, *The Pleasure Gap: American Women & the Unfinished Sexual Revolution* (New York: Seal Press, 2020), 324.

66. Serene Khader, "Passive Empowerment: How Women's Agency Became Women Doing It All," *Philosophical Topics* 46, no. 2 (2018): 141–63.

67. Serene J. Khader, *Adaptive Preferences and Women's Empowerment* (New York: Oxford University Press, 2011).

68. Kendall, *Hood Feminism*, 142.

69. Kollontai would not have used this term to describe herself, since she associated feminism with bourgeois women's movements that sought access to the profession that bourgeois men had access to and that did not prioritize things like support for childcare. See her 1909 pamphlet *The Social Basis of the Woman Question*, where she criticizes elite women's pursuit of equality in a way similar to how bell hooks would in 1990.

70. Kristen Ghodsee, *Red Valkyries: Feminist Lessons from Five Revolutionary Women* (New York: Verso, 2022), 59.

71. We should not conclude from Kollontai's exile that she was critical of the extreme repressive violence of the Russian regime. She continued to work for Stalin, and though she was a critic, it would be a stretch to describe her as a critic of most of what the Russian Revolution had become. For more details of her role within the party and her views about Stalin, see Barbara Evans Clements, *Bolshevik Feminist: The Life of Aleksandra Kollontai* (Bloomington: University of Indiana Press, 1979). As Kristen Ghodsee (2018) argues, today's feminists need to learn from Kollontai's ideas about love without endorsing the brutal form of government that came into being in her lifetime.

72. There are some important reasons not to adopt Kollontai's particular view of sexual liberation, since she was against sex work and, like most able-bodied feminists of her generation, seemed to advocate for eugenics.

73. Alexandra Kollontai, *Selected Writings*, with introduction and commentaries by Alix Holt (New York: W. W. Norton, 1977).

74. Ghodsee, *Why Women Have Better Sex Under Socialism*, 96.

75. Kollontai, *Selected Writings*.

CHAPTER 2: THE INDIVIDUALISM MYTH

1. Nikkya Hargrove, "Miss Potkin Got Fed Up and Refused to Clean Her House—We Love Her for It," *Scary Mommy*, Apr. 16, 2021, https://www.scarymommy.com/miss-potkin-refused-clean-house-twitter; Lily Potkin, "Lily Potkin on Twitter," Twitter, Mar. 18, 2021, https://twitter.com/MissPotkin/status/1372484962688057345.

2. Ruchika Tulshyan, "How to Say No to Office Housework," *The Muse*, Jan. 18, 2022, https://www.themuse.com/advice/how-to-say-no-office-housework.

3. Jess Zimmerman, "'Where's My Cut?': On Unpaid Emotional Labor," *The Toast*, July 13, 2015, https://the-toast.net/2015/07/13/emotional-labor.

4. Rose Hackman, "'Women Are Just Better at This Stuff': Is Emotional Labor Feminism's Next Frontier?," *The Guardian*, Nov. 8, 2015, https://www.theguardian.com/world/2015/nov/08/women-gender-roles-sexism-emotional-labor-feminism.

5. Allard Dembe and Xiaoxi Yao, "Chronic Disease Risks from Exposure to Long-Hour Work Schedules over a 32-Year Period," *Journal of Occupational and Environmental Medicine* 58 (June 1, 2016): 1, https://doi.org/10.1097/JOM.0000000000000810.

6. Hackman, "'Women Are Just Better at This Stuff.'"

7. Premilla Nadasen, *Household Workers Unite: The Untold Story of African American Women Who Built a Movement* (Boston: Beacon Press, 2016).

8. Sarah Jaffe, "The Women of Wages for Housework," *The Nation*, Mar. 14, 2018, https://www.thenation.com/article/archive/wages-for-houseworks-radical-vision.

9. Arlie Hochschild, *The Second Shift: Working Families and the Revolution at Home* (New York: Penguin, 2012).

10. Polaris Project, "Human Trafficking at Home," July 1, 2019, https://polarisproject.org/wp-content/uploads/2019/09/Human_Trafficking_at_Home_Labor_Trafficking_of_Domestic_Workers.pdf.

11. Cynthia Hess, Tanima Ahmed, and Jeff Hayes, "Providing Unpaid Household and Care Work in the United States: Uncovering Inequality," Institute for Women's Policy Research, Briefing Paper, Jan. 2020, 26.

12. Yes, as a whole genre of recent viral content reminds us, *emotional labor* was a technical term invented by the sociologist Arlie Hochschild in *The Managed Heart: Commercialization of Human Feeling* (1983) to describe the labor of suppressing one's emotions on the job, as flight attendants have to do. I think our social conversations have shifted so that it now means something broader, so I'm following suit.

13. I first heard this one in the early 2000s when a conservative commentator said on CNN that feminists protesting the exclusion of women from an elite club (where many business deals were made) should instead focus on women in

Afghanistan. For a more contemporary version see "Tomi Lahren: Afghan Women and Girls Are 'Truly Oppressed,' Unlike US Olympic Athletes," Fox News, Aug. 17, 2021, https://www.foxnews.com/media/afghanistan-women-oppressed-olympics-tomi-lahren.

14. Ali Rosen, "Want to Have It All? Then Do More of This in Your 20s," *Refinery 29*, Mar. 3, 2020, https://www.refinery29.com/en-us/having-it-all-advice.

15. Ella Alexander, "Michelle Obama Says No, Actually, Women Can't Have It All," *Harper's Bazaar*, Dec. 3, 2018, https://www.harpersbazaar.com/uk/culture/culture-news/a25374999/michelle-obama-says-women-cant-have-it-all.

16. Alexis Krivkovich et al., "The State of Burnout for Women in the Workplace," McKinsey & Company, Jan. 4, 2022, https://www.mckinsey.com/featured-insights/diversity-and-inclusion/the-state-of-burnout-for-women-in-the-workplace.

17. Krivkovich et al., "The State of Burnout for Women in the Workplace."

18. Jessica Grose, "The Primal Scream," *New York Times*, February 4, 2021.

19. National Partnership for Women and Families, "Did the Economy Deliver for Women in 2023? Will It in 2024?" https://nationalpartnership.org/did-economy-deliver-for-women-jobs-day-january-2024.

20. Ad Council, "She Can STEM Campaign & Media Assets," https://www.adcouncil.org/campaign/empowering-girls-in-stem, accessed Mar. 4, 2022. See also Ad Council, "Champion for Good: Alpha's Linda Gramsch," https://www.adcouncil.org/champion-for-good-alphas-linda-gramsch, accessed Dec. 13, 2023.

21. Rheanna O'Neil Bellomo, "Here's Why Toll House Chocolate Chips Don't Taste the Same Anymore," *Delish*, Apr. 21, 2016, https://www.delish.com/food-news/a46880/did-nestle-change-its-chocolate-chip-recipe.

22. Darcy Lockman, *All the Rage* (New York: Harper Collins, 2019), 30.

23. Lockman, *All the Rage*, 30.

24. "Men Enjoy Five Hours More Leisure Time per Week Than Women," Office for National Statistics UK, Jan. 9, 2018, https://www.ons.gov.uk/peoplepopulationandcommunity/wellbeing/articles/menenjoyfivehoursmoreleisuretimeperweekthanwomen/2018-01-09.

25. A. Roeters, T. van der Lippe, and E. S. Kluwer, "Parental Demands and the Frequency of Child-Related Activities," *Journal of Marriage and Family* 71, no. 5 (2009): 1193–1204.

26. Lockman, *All the Rage*, 239.

27. Lockman, *All the Rage*, 154.

28. Lockman, *All the Rage*, 51.

29. Gabby Hinsliff, "I was Puzzled by Young Women's Reaction to Barbie," *The Guardian*, February 2, 2024, https://www.theguardian.com/commentisfree/2024/feb/02/younger-women-barbie-gen-z-men-feminism.

30. Deborah Rhode notes that men may feel satisfied by less than equal household labor participation because they compare themselves to other men, instead of measuring their progress relative to actual equality. Deborah Rhode, *Speaking of Sex: The Denial of Gender Inequality* (Cambridge, MA: Harvard University Press, 1999).

31. Darcy Lockman, "Don't Be Grateful that Dad Does His Share," *The Atlantic*, April 2019.

32. Ian Bannon and Maria C. Correia, *The Other Half of Gender: Men's Issues in Development*, Woodrow Wilson Center, 2006.

33. Angela Davis, "The Approaching Obsolescence of Housework," in *Women, Race, and Class* (New York: Vintage Books, 1981).

34. To be clear, the effects of mass incarceration on Black women are not only indirect. Black women are incarcerated at alarming rates and subject to particular forms of carceral violence. See Kimberlé Crenshaw, "From Private Violence to Mass Incarceration," *UCLA Law Review*, no. 1418 (2012): 1419–71.

35. Ella Baker Center for Human Rights, Forward Together, and Research Action Design, "Who Pays? The True Cost of Incarceration on Families," Sept. 2015, https://ellabakercenter.org/wp-content/uploads/2022/09/Who-Pays-FINAL.pdf.

36. Margaret Goff, "Three Ways Mass Incarceration Affects Women of Color," Urban Institute, Mar. 30, 2018, https://www.urban.org/urban-wire/three-ways-mass -incarceration-affects-women-color.

37. Melissa V. Harris-Perry, *Sister Citizen: Shame, Stereotypes, and Black Women in America* (New Haven, CT: Yale University Press, 2011).

38. Sylvia Chant, "The 'Feminisation of Poverty' and the 'Feminisation' of Anti-Poverty Programmes: Room for Revision?," *Journal of Development Studies* 44, no. 2 (Feb. 1, 2008): 177, https://doi.org/10.1080/00220380701789810.

39. Serene Khader and Matthew Lindauer, "The Daddy Dividend," *APA Newsletter on Feminism and Philosophy* 19, no. 2 (2020).

40. Daisy Dwyer and Judith Bruce, *A Home Divided: Women and Income in the Third World* (Palo Alto, CA: Stanford University Press, 1988); Naila Kabeer, "Money Can't Buy Me Love," IDS Development Studies Brooklyn, 1998; Linda Mayoux, "Questioning Virtuous Spirals," *Journal of International Development* 11 (Dec. 13, 1999): 957–84; Janakee Chavda, "In a Growing Share of U.S. Marriages, Husbands and Wives Earn About the Same," *Pew Research Center's Social & Demographic Trends Project* (blog), Apr. 13, 2023, https://www.pew research.org/social-trends/2023/04/13/in-a-growing-share-of-u-s-marriages -husbands-and-wives-earn-about-the-same.

41. Leslie C. Gates, "The Strategic Uses of Gender in Household Negotiations: Women Workers on Mexico's Northern Border," *Bulletin of Latin American Research* 21, no. 4 (Oct. 2002): 507–26, https://doi.org/10.1111/1470–9856 .00057.

42. Aliya Hamid Rao, "Even Breadwinning Wives Don't Get Equality at Home," *The Atlantic*, May 12, 2019, https://www.theatlantic.com/family/archive/2019/05 /breadwinning-wives-gender-inequality/589237.

43. Australian Associated Press, "Stay-at-Home Fathers Do Less Childcare than Working Mothers, Research Shows," *The Guardian*, May 15, 2017, https://www .theguardian.com/lifeandstyle/2017/may/16/stay-at-home-fathers-childcare -working-mothers-research-finds.

44. Lockman, *All the Rage*, 33.

45. Gemma Hartley, "Women Aren't Nags—We're Just Fed Up," *Harper's Bazaar*, Sept. 27, 2017, https://www.harpersbazaar.com/culture/features/a12063822 /emotional-labor-gender-equality.

46. Julia Wolfe et al., "Domestic Workers Chartbook," Economic Policy Institute, May 14, 2020, https://files.epi.org/pdf/194214.pdf.

47. Jennifer Schaffer, "We Spoke to Lauren Chief Elk, the Woman Behind #GiveYourMoneytoWomen, About the Power of Cold Hard Cash," *Vice* (blog), Aug. 2, 2015, https://www.vice.com/en/article/8gkxd5/give-your-money-to -women-its-simple-284.

48. See Davis, "The Approaching Obsolescence of Housework," for an argument that much housework is a product of capitalism and not actually necessary. This is clearly true about pressures like having a spotless home, but I am less sure about the extent to which her critique of housework applies to care work.

49. Audre Lorde, *Burst of Light* (Minneola: Ixia Press, 1988), 130.

50. Jeff Nelson, "The Reign of Taylor Swift! The Pop Superstar Tops *People*'s 2023 Most Intriguing People of the Year List," *People*, https://people.com/taylor -swift-tops-people-2023-most-intriguing-people-list-8410695.

51. Andrew Flanagan, "Taylor Swift Wins Sexual Assault Lawsuit Against Former Radio Host," *The Record*, NPR, Aug. 14, 2017, https://www.npr.org/sections /therecord/2017/08/14/543473684/taylor-swift-wins-sexual-assault-lawsuit -against-former-radio-host.

52. Isabella O'Malley, "Why Taylor Swift's Globe-Trotting in Private Jets Is Getting Scrutinized," Associated Press, https://apnews.com/article/taylor-swift-climate -jet-carbon-emissions-kelce-chiefs-02ac425d24281bd26d73bfdf4590bc82.

53. Oxfam International, "Richest 1% Bag Nearly Twice as Much Wealth as the Rest of the World Put Together over the Past Two Years," press release, January 16, 2023, https://www.oxfam.org/en/press-releases/richest-1-bag-nearly-twice -much-wealth-rest-world-put-together-over-past-two-years.

54. Time Staff, "700,000 Female Farmworkers Stand Up Against Sexual Assault," *Time*, Nov. 10, 2017, https://time.com/5018813/farmworkers-solidarity-hollywood -sexual-assault.

55. Sheree Atcheson, "Having a Glass Ceiling to Break Through Is Privilege. Here's Why," *Forbes*, May 13, 2021, https://www.forbes.com/sites/shereeatcheson /2021/05/13/having-a-glass-ceiling-to-break-through-is-privilege-heres-why.

56. Anne Crittenden, *Price of Motherhood: Why the Most Important Job in the World Is Still the Least Valued* (New York: Metropolitan Books, 2001).

57. Pew Research Center, *The American Middle Class Is Losing Ground: No Longer the Majority and Falling Behind Financially*, Pew Research Center, Dec. 9, 2015, https://www.pewresearch.org/social-trends/2015/12/09/the-american -middle-class-is-losing-ground.

58. Lauren Chief Elk-Young Bear, Yeoshin Lourdes, and Bardot Smith, "Give Your Money to Women: The End Game of Capitalism," *Model View Culture* (blog), Aug. 10, 2015, https://modelviewculture.com/pieces/giveyourmoneytowomen -the-end-game-of-capitalism.

59. In transactional sex, gifts are an important part of the relationship, as with "sugar babies," for example.

60. See Molly Smith and Juno Mac, *Revolting Prostitutes: The Fight for Sex Workers' Rights* (New York: Verso, 2018).

61. Zoe Williams, "Turned Off by Tart-Lit," *The Guardian*, Nov. 13, 2008, https://www.theguardian.com/commentisfree/2008/nov/13/prostitution-belle-de-jour-novel.

62. See Serene J. Khader, "Can Women's Compliance with Oppressive Norms Be Self-Interested?," in *Phenomenology of the Political*, ed. S. West Gurley and Geoff Pfeifer (Lanham, MD: Rowman & Littlefield, 2016), 165–81; Serene Khader, "Self-Respect Under Conditions of Oppression," in *Respect: Philosophical Essays*, ed. Richard Dean and Oliver Sensen (New York: Oxford University Press, 2021).

63. Rasheed Malik, Katie Hamm, and Won F. Lee, "The Coronavirus Will Make Child Care Deserts Worse and Exacerbate Inequality," *Center for American Progress* (blog), June 22, 2022, https://www.americanprogress.org/article/coronavirus-will-make-child-care-deserts-worse-exacerbate-inequality.

CHAPTER 3: THE CULTURE MYTH

1. Jasbir Authi, "Park View Banned Girls from Mixed Sports Because It Made 'Male Staff Uncomfortable,' Hearing Told," *BirminghamLive*, Oct. 26, 2015, http://www.birminghammail.co.uk/news/midlands-news/park-view-banned-girls-mixed-10334889.

2. Lauren Jackson, "The Inside Story of How a 'Bogus' Letter Roiled Britain," *New York Times*, Mar. 11, 2022, https://www.nytimes.com/2022/03/11/podcasts/trojan-horse-podcast-takeaways.html.

3. Jackson, "The Inside Story of How a 'Bogus' Letter Roiled Britain."

4. Jonathan Montpetit, "Religious Symbols Ban Pits Quebec Feminists against Each Other," CBC, May 16, 2019, https://www.cbc.ca/news/canada/montreal/bill-21-quebec-feminists-on-opposite-sides-of-religious-symbols-ban-1.5139422.

5. Kimberley Molina, "Quebec Teacher Removed from Classroom for Wearing Hijab Under Law Banning Religious Symbols," CBC, Dec. 9, 2021, https://www.cbc.ca/news/canada/ottawa/fatemeh-anvari-removed-from-grade-three-classroom-1.6278381.

6. Alma Garcia, "The Development of Chicana Feminist Discourse," *Gender and Society* 3, no. 2 (1989): 217–38.

7. In spite of similar rapes occurring in the United States by people of all races, Britt framed the rape she discussed as a new phenomenon in the United States, brought by immigrants. The rape she described had in fact occurred in Mexico through the activities of drug cartels. See Alexandra Marquez, "Senator Britt Attempts to Clear Up Her Misleading State of the Union Response," NBC News, https://www.nbcnews.com/politics/immigration/sen-katie-britt-attempts-clean-misleading-state-union-response-rcna142650. Britt also failed to discuss the role of the North American Free Trade agreement in empowering drug cartels in Mexico.

8. In 2019, the (false) claim that the majority of violence against Indigenous women in Canada was committed by Indigenous men went viral. See Emma

McIntosh, "We Fact-Checked a Viral Claim about Who's Killing MMIWG. It Was Wrong," *National Observer*, June 7, 2019, https://www.national observer.com/2019/06/07/analysis/we-fact-checked-viral-claim-about-whos -killing-mmiwg-it-was-wrong.

9. Marie Quasius, "Note: Native American Rape Victims: Desperately Seeking an Oliphant-Fix," *Minnesota Law Review De Novo Blog* (blog), Jan. 24, 2012, https://minnesotalawreview.org/article/note-native-american-rape-victims -desperately-seeking-oliphant-fix/.

10. Ann Coulter, "Where do you think all that spicy stuff about Mexican rape culture came from?," July 2, 2015, Twitter, https://twitter.com/anncoulter/status /616504525508100096.

11. Alanna Nunez, "Ann Coulter Says Latinos Have a 'Cultural Acceptance of Child Rape,'" *Cosmopolitan*, Aug. 7, 2015, https://www.cosmopolitan.com/politics /news/a44428/ann-coulter-latinos-child-rape-comments.

12. Ann Coulter, "Who's Doing the Raping? Don't Ask 'Law & Order: SVU,'" *Cleburne Times-Review*, Dec. 14, 2019, https://www.cleburnetimesreview.com /opinion/ann-coulter-who-s-doing-the-raping-don-t-ask-law-order-svu/article _50f7f0da-1dec-11ea-88be-d720aa9f9d55.html.

13. Laurence Rossignol, "Interdiction du burkini: pour Rossignol, 'procéder par amalgame n'est jamais utile,'" *Le Parisien*, Aug. 16, 2016, https://www.leparisien .fr/politique/proceder-par-amalgame-n-est-jamais-utile-16–08–2016–6043833.php.

14. "US Records Show Physical, Sexual Abuse at Border," Human Rights Watch, Oct. 21, 2021, https://www.hrw.org/news/2021/10/21/us-records-show-physical -sexual-abuse-border.

15. Muslim Advocates, "'Honor Killings' and the Muslim Ban: How President Trump's Executive Orders Are Premised on Animus and Negative Stereotypes Against Muslims," Issue Briefs, Sept. 2017, https://muslimadvocates.org/files /IssueBrief_HonorKillingsandMuslimBan.pdf.

16. Uma Narayan, "Minds of Their Own: Choices, Autonomy, Cultural Practices, and Other Women," in *A Mind of One's Own: Feminist Essays on Reason and Objectivity*, ed. Louise M. Antony and Witt Charlotte (Boulder, CO: Westview, 2002), 418–32.

17. Coulter, "Who's Doing the Raping?"

18. Sherene Razakh, *Casting Out: The Eviction of Muslims from Western Law and Politics* (Toronto: University of Toronto Press, 2008).

19. Melinda Gates, *The Moment of Lift: How Empowering Women Changes the World* (New York: Flatiron Books, 2019), 109.

20. Chandra Talpade Mohanty, "Under Western Eyes: Feminist Scholarship and Colonial Discourses," *Boundary* 2, nos. 12/13 (1984): 333–58, https://doi.org/10 .2307/302821.

21. Saba Mahmood, *Politics of Piety: The Islamic Revival and the Feminist Subject* (Princeton, NJ: Princeton University Press, 2005).

22. See Chris Bobel, *The Managed Body: Developing Girls and Menstrual Health in the Global South* (Cham, Switzerland: Palgrave Macmillan, 2019), https://doi .org/10.1007/978-3-319-89414-0.

23. Belinda Archibong and Francis Annan, "Climate Change, Disease, and Gender Gaps in Human Capital Investment," in *Women and Sustainable Human Development: Empowering Women in Africa*, ed. Maty Konte and Nyasha Tirivayi (Cham, Switzerland: Palgrave Macmillan, 2020).

24. Girls Not Brides, *Child Marriage in Humanitarian Contexts*, Thematic Brief, Aug. 2020, https://www.girlsnotbrides.org/documents/959/Child-marriage-in -humanitarian-contexts_August-2020.pdf.

25. Elisabeth Bumiller, *May You Be the Mother of a Hundred Sons: A Journey Among the Women of India* (New York: Ballantine Books, 1991), 145.

26. National Crime Records Bureau, "Crime in India 2019," Sept. 3, 2021, https:// data.gov.in/catalog/crime-india-2019.

27. Uma Narayan, *Dislocating Cultures: Identities, Traditions, and Third-World Feminism* (New York: Routledge, 1997).

28. Veena Oldenberg, *Dowry Murder: Imperial Origins of a Cultural Crime* (New York: Oxford University Press, 2002).

29. Narayan, *Dislocating*, 66.

30. Narayan, *Dislocating*, 60.

31. See Narayan, *Dislocating Cultures*; Serene J. Khader, *Decolonizing Universalism: A Transnational Feminist Ethic*, Studies in Feminist Philosophy (Oxford: Oxford University Press, 2019).

32. Poulami Roychowdhury, "The Delhi Gang Rape: The Making of International Causes," *Feminist Studies* 39, no. 1 (2013): 282.

33. Tithi Bhattacharya, "In the Streets against Rape," SocialistWorker.org, Jan. 10, 2013, http://socialistworker.org/2013/01/10/in-the-streets-against-rape.

34. Roychowdhury, "The Delhi Gang Rape."

35. Tithi Bhattacharya, "Explaining Gender Violence in the Neoliberal Era," *International Socialist Review*, no. 91 (Winter 2013), https://isreview.org/issue/91 /explaining-gender-violence-neoliberal-era/index.html.

36. Bhattacharya, "Explaining Gender Violence in the Neoliberal Era."

37. See Alison Jaggar, "Saving Amina: Global Justice for Women and Intercultural Dialogue," *Ethics and International Affairs* 19, no. 3 (2005): 55–75.

38. Miriam Bruhn, "Did Yesterday's Pattern of Colonial Exploitation Determine Today's Patterns of Poverty?," *World Bank Blogs: All About Finance*, Nov. 23, 2010, https://blogs.worldbank.org/allaboutfinance/did-yesterday-s-patterns-of-colonial -exploitation-determine-today-s-patterns-of-poverty.

39. "Why the Majority of the World's Poor Are Women," Oxfam International, May 25, 2022, https://www.oxfam.org/en/why-majority-worlds-poor-are-women.

40. Martha Alter Chen and Rachel Moussié, *Turning a Blind Eye to Women in the Informal Economy* (London: The Bretton Woods Project, 2017).

41. Rafia Zakaria, *Against White Feminism: Notes on Disruption* (New York: W. W. Norton, 2021).

42. Rich coined the term *compulsory heterosexuality* in 1980 to refer to the system that coerces people into heterosexual relationships by naturalizing and rewarding them and by privileging the man/woman relationship over other relationships.

43. This term was coined by the philosopher Elizabeth Brake. See *Minimizing Marriage: Marriage, Morality, and the Law* (Oxford: Oxford University Press, 2012).

44. I use the term *Islamic feminism* to mean a feminism that grounds its fight against sexism at least partly in reference to ideas found in Muslim texts and practices. However, the term is sometimes used more narrowly to refer to Muslim feminisms that promote Islamism, a school of thought according to which the state should be founded on Islamic principles, and according to which the state should not be secular. One can be an Islamic feminist in the sense I am using the term here without being an Islamist. I use the term *Islamic feminism* with some hesitation, since it is also the topic of significant debate, especially from women in majority-Muslim countries who see it as possibly eclipsing other approaches to feminism in their societies. See Amal Grami, "Islamic Feminism: A New Feminist Movement or a Strategy by Women for Gaining Rights?" *Contemporary Arab Affairs* 6, no. 1 (2013).

45. I borrow this phrase from Lila Abu-Lughod's *Do Muslim Women Need Saving?* (Cambridge, MA: Harvard University Press, 2013).

46. Kim TallBear, "Couple-Centricity, Polyamory and Colonialism," Aug. 14, 2021, originally published July 27, 2014, on *The Critical Polyamorist*, https://kim tallbear.substack.com/p/couple-centricity-polyamory-and-colonialism#details.

47. Kim TallBear, "Making Love and Relations Beyond Settler Sex and Family," in *Making Kin Not Population*, ed. Adele E. Clarke and Donna Haraway (Chicago: Prickly Paradigm Press, 2018).

48. Kim Anderson, "Affirmations of an Indigenous Feminism," in *Indigenous Women and Feminism: Politics, Activism, Culture* (Vancouver: University of British Columbia Press, 2011).

49. Kim TallBear, "Identity Is a Poor Substitute for Relating," in *Routledge Handbook of Critical Indigenous Studies*, ed. Brendan Hokowhitu et al. (London: Routledge, 2021).

50. Kim TallBear, "Disrupting Settlement, Sex, and Nature," lecture, Future Imaginary Lecture Series, Concordia University, Oct. 14, 2016, 7–8, https://indigenousfutures.net/wp-content/uploads/2016/10/Kim_TallBear.pdf.

51. TallBear, "Making Love and Relations Beyond Settler Sex and Family," 154.

52. TallBear, "Making Love and Relations Beyond Settler Sex and Family," 154.

CHAPTER 4: THE JUDGMENT MYTH

1. Lorde was a major twentieth-century feminist thinker, author of second-wave classic essays such as "The Master's Tools Will Never Dismantle the Master's House" and "The Uses of Anger." She was a Black lesbian, and she theorized extensively about how feminists should live with, and learn from, differences among women. She coined the term *self-care* in her writings about her second battle with cancer. Much of her point there was that caring for herself was critical to her continuing to function as an activist, and to setting an example of how to resist a society that devalued people like her.

2. Audre Lorde, *Burst of Light* (Minneola: Ixia Press, 1988), 130.

3. Brianna Wiens and Shana McDonald, "Living Whose Best Life? An Intersectional Feminist Interrogation of Postfeminist #solidarity in #selfcare," *NECSUS*, Spring 2021, https://necsus-ejms.org/living-whose-best-life-an-intersectional -feminist-interrogation-of-postfeminist-solidarity-in-selfcare.

4. Jordan Kisner, "The Politics of Conspicuous Displays of Self-Care," *New Yorker*, Mar. 14, 2017, https://www.newyorker.com/culture/culture-desk/the-politics -of-selfcare.

5. This lyric is from Ariana Grande, "Yes, And?" *Eternal Sunshine*, 2024. See Shaad D'Souza, "Ariana Grande's 'Yes, And' Strikes a Familiar-Sounding Pose," *New York Times*, Jan. 18, 2024, https://www.nytimes.com/2024/01/18/arts/music /ariana-grande-yes-and-madonna-vogue.html, for a discussion of how Grande's song slides between uncritical self-affirmation and nods to queer cultures of self-determination.

6. Kisner, "The Politics of Conspicuous Displays of Self-Care."

7. Daphne Merkin, "Publicly We Say Me Too, Privately We Have Misgivings," *New York Times*, Jan. 5, 2018, https://www.nytimes.com/2018/01/05/opinion /golden-globes-metoo.html.

8. These are Garrison Keillor's own words about his conduct. Merkin mentioned his case and Jonathan Schwartz's in her anti-#MeToo piece, though the details of the accusations I mention here were likely unavailable to Merkin at the time. Associated Press, "Garrison Keillor Says Sexually Suggestive Emails Were 'Romantic Writing,'" NBC News, Feb. 26, 2018, https://www.nbcnews.com/storyline /sexual-misconduct/garrison-keillor-says-sexually-suggestive-emails-were -romantic-writing-n851141.

9. Once again, Keillor's own description of what happened. Jamie Ducharme, "Garrison Keillor Releases Statement After Termination," *Time*, Nov. 29, 2017, https://time.com/5041869/garrison-keillor-statement-prairie-home-companion -allegations.

10. Ilya Marritz and Jessica Gould, "New York Public Radio Fires Hosts Lopate and Schwartz," WNYC, Dec. 21, 2017, https://www.wnyc.org/story/new-york-public -radio-fires-hosts-lopate-schwartz.

11. Merkin, "Publicly We Say Me Too, Privately We Have Misgivings."

12. Roche Darragh, "GOP Rep. Says Women Can Control 'Intake of Semen' as Utah Outlaws Abortion," *Newsweek*, June 25, 2022, https://www.newsweek.com/utah -gop-rep-karianne-lisonbee-women-control-intake-semen-outlaw-abortion -roe-v-wade-1719152.

13. My colleague Linda Alcoff pointed this out in a professional development workshop for women in philosophy.

14. Emily St. James, "The Assimilationist, or: On the Unexpected Cost of Passing as a Trans Woman," *Vox*, Feb. 19, 2020, https://www.vox.com/the-highlight/2020 /2/12/21075683/trans-coming-out-cost-of-womanhood-pink-tax.

15. Susan Faludi, *Backlash: The Undeclared War Against American Women* (New York: Crown, 1991).

16. Faludi, *Backlash*, 4.

17. Faludi, *Backlash*.

18. Fox Butterfield, "At Wellesley, a Furor over Barbara Bush," *New York Times*, May 4, 1990, https://www.nytimes.com/1990/05/04/us/at-wellesley-a-furor-over -barbara-bush.html.

19. Lily News, "Wellesley Seniors Were Wary of Having Barbara Bush as Their Commencement Speaker. She Wowed Them Anyway," *The Lily*, Apr. 18, 2018, https://www.thelily.com/wellesley-seniors-were-wary-of-having-barbara-bush -as-their-commencement-speaker-she-wowed-them-anyway.

20. Stephanie H. Murray, "How the Pandemic Could Finally End the Mommy Wars," *Time*, Dec. 29, 2021, https://time.com/6130336/mommy-wars-pandemic.

21. Kirsten Swinth, *Feminism's Forgotten Fight: The Unfinished Struggle for Work and Family* (Cambridge, MA: Harvard University Press, 2018).

22. Premilla Nadasen, "Expanding the Boundaries of the Women's Movement: Black Feminism and the Struggle for Welfare Rights," *Feminist Studies* 28, no. 2 (June 22, 2002): 271–303.

23. Annie Kelly, "The Housewives of White Supremacy," *New York Times*, June 1, 2018, sec. Opinion, https://www.nytimes.com/2018/06/01/opinion/sunday /tradwives-women-alt-right.html.

24. Sian Norris, "Frilly Dresses and White Supremacy: Welcome to the Weird, Frightening World of 'Trad Wives,'" *The Guardian*, May 31, 2023, https://www .theguardian.com/commentisfree/2023/may/31/white-supremacy-trad-wives -far-right-feminist-politics.

25. See Swinth, *Feminism's Forgotten Fight*.

26. See Isaiah Berlin, "Two Concepts of Liberty," in *Four Essays on Liberty* (Oxford: Oxford University Press, 1969), 118–72.

27. Radicals usually understand freedom in one (or both) of two other ways: a) as the end of domination, i.e., rule by another who declares themselves superior, or b) the ability to flourish, or have access to conditions that would enable human flourishing. The first view has been very important in Black politics because slavery embodied domination par excellence. See Frederick Douglass, *My Bondage and My Freedom* (New York: Orton, Miller and Mulligan, 1866), for a development of this view of freedom, and Richard King, *Civil Rights and the Issue of Freedom* (Athens: University of Georgia Press, 1996), for an argument for why freedom rather than equality (conceived as the idea that human beings are "born equal") was central to civil rights struggles. I think the end of domination is necessary for the kind of equality I advocate for in this book, since domination is the manifestation of unjust hierarchy. However, I believe that oppression does not have to involve reduced freedom, as I argue in Serene J. Khader, "Why Is Oppression Wrong?" *Philosophical Studies* (Feb. 22, 2024), https://doi.org/10.1007/s11098-023-02084-5. I am also somewhat skeptical of the value of retaining the idea of freedom as access to conditions for flourishing (b), since, as I have argued at length in my academic writings (see *Adaptive Preferences and Women's Empowerment* [New York: Oxford University Press, 2011], and "The Feminist Case Against Relational Autonomy," *Journal of Moral Philosophy* 17, no. 5 [2020]), it obscures the fact that we should respect the choices of oppressed and deprived people. My basic worry is that

equating freedom (or agency) with the ability to choose flourishing undermines the case for respecting the choices of people who live under conditions in which they cannot flourish. I think it's a lot less messy to keep freedom and flourishing separate and hold that both are important.

28. Martha Fineman, Gwendolyn Mink, and Anna Marie Smith, "No Promotion of Marriage in TANF!," *Social Justice* 30, no. 4 (94) (2003): 126–34.

29. See Catharine A. MacKinnon, *Toward a Feminist Theory of the State* (Cambridge, MA: Harvard University Press, 1989).

30. Rosa is the name I have assigned to an anonymous redditor. https://www
.reddit.com/r/TalesFromYourServer/comments/46zmhv/i_make_more_tips
_when_i_look_pretty/.

31. Restaurant Opportunities Center United, *Take Us off the Menu: The Impact of Sexual Harassment in the Restaurant Industry*, May 2018, https://rocunited
.org/wp-content/uploads/sites/7/2020/02/TakeUsOffTheMenuReport.pdf.

32. Restaurant Opportunities Center United, *Take Us off the Menu*, 5.

33. Restaurant Opportunities Center United, *Take Us off the Menu*, 17.

34. Jen Agg, "Sexism in the Kitchen," *New York Times*, Oct. 19, 2015, https://www
.nytimes.com/2015/10/20/opinion/sexism-in-the-kitchen.html.

35. *Waging Change*, Women Make Movies, 2019.

36. Restaurant Opportunities Center United, *Take Us off the Menu*, 14.

37. Restaurant Opportunities Center United, *Take Us off the Menu*, 7.

38. Ruby Lott-Lavigna and Liz Seabrook, "Perfect Is Boring: What It's Like to Be Trans in the Restaurant Industry," *Vice* (blog), Oct. 9, 2018, https://www.vice
.com/en/article/qv9xnb/perfect-is-boring-what-its-like-to-be-trans-in-the
-restaurant-industry.

39. Restaurant Opportunities Center United, *Take Us off the Menu*, 2.

40. Restaurant Opportunities Center United, *Take Us off the Menu*.

41. Matthew Parrett, "Customer Discrimination in Restaurants: Dining Frequency Matters," *Journal of Labor Research* (Jan. 1, 2011), https://vc.bridgew.edu/econ
_fac/3.

42. Matt Parrett, "Beauty and the Feast: Examining the Effect of Beauty on Earnings Using Restaurant Tipping Data," *Journal of Economic Psychology* 49 (Aug. 1, 2015): 34–46, https://doi.org/10.1016/j.joep.2015.04.002.

43. Laura Guillén, Margarita Mayo, and Natalia Karelaia, "Appearing Self-Confident and Getting Credit for It: Why It May Be Easier for Men Than Women to Gain Influence at Work," *Human Resource Management* 57, no. 4 (2018): 839–54, https://doi.org/10.1002/hrm.21857; Timothy A. Judge, Beth A. Livingston, and Charlice Hurst, "Do Nice Guys—and Gals—Really Finish Last? The Joint Effects of Sex and Agreeableness on Income," *Journal of Personality and Social Psychology* 102, no. 2 (2012): 390–407, https://doi.org/10.1037/a0026021; Alicia A. Grandey and Gordon Sayre, "Emotional Labor: Regulating Emotions for a Wage," *Current Directions in Psychological Science* 28, no. 2 (Jan. 2019).

44. Timothy G. Kundro et al., "A Perfect Storm: Customer Sexual Harassment as a Joint Function of Financial Dependence and Emotional Labor," *Journal of Applied Psychology* 107, no. 8 (2022): 1385–96, https://doi.org/10.1037/apl0000895.

45. Jespersen v. Harrah's Operating Co., No. 03–15045 (US Court of Appeals, Ninth Circuit, Apr. 14, 2006).

46. Talia Bettcher, "Trapped in the Wrong Theory: Rethinking Trans Oppression and Resistance," *Signs* 39, no. 2 (Winter 2014): 383–406, argues that the logic of transphobia involves expecting people's outward appearances to reveal their genitalia, and reality enforcement is the set of social practices that attempt to force trans people to present themselves in ways consistent with this logic.

47. See Mindy E. Bergman et al., "The (Un)Reasonableness of Reporting: Antecedents and Consequences of Reporting Sexual Harassment," *Journal of Applied Psychology* 87, no. 2 (Apr. 2002): 230–42, https://doi.org/10.1037/0021–9010.87.2.230; Lilia M. Cortina and Vicki J. Magley, "Raising Voice, Risking Retaliation: Events Following Interpersonal Mistreatment in the Workplace," *Journal of Occupational Health Psychology* 8, no. 4 (Oct. 2003): 247–65, https://doi.org/10.1037/1076–8998.8.4.247.

48. Céline Jacob et al., "Waitresses' Facial Cosmetics and Tipping: A Field Experiment," *International Journal of Hospitality Management* 29, no. 1 (Mar. 1, 2010): 188–90, https://doi.org/10.1016/j.ijhm.2009.04.003; Parrett, "Beauty and the Feast"; Michael Lynn, "Determinants and Consequences of Female Attractiveness and Sexiness: Realistic Tests with Restaurant Waitresses," *Archives of Sexual Behavior* 38, no. 5 (Oct. 2009): 737–45, https://doi.org/10.1007/s10508–008–9379–0.

49. Helen Rosner, "One Year of #MeToo: A Modest Proposal to Help Combat Sexual Harassment in the Restaurant Industry," *New Yorker*, Oct. 10, 2018, https://www.newyorker.com/culture/annals-of-gastronomy/one-year-of-metoo-a-modest-proposal-to-help-dismantle-the-restaurant-industrys-culture-of-sexual-harassment.

50. Rax Will, "When 'Sir' and 'Ma'am' Miss the Mark: Restaurants Rethink Gender's Role in Service," *New York Times*, Mar. 28, 2022, https://www.nytimes.com/2022/03/28/dining/restaurant-service-gender.html.

51. Restaurant Opportunities Center United, *Take Us off the Menu*.

52. Stefanie K. Johnson and Juan M. Madera, "Sexual Harassment Is Pervasive in the Restaurant Industry. Here's What Needs to Change," *Harvard Business Review*, Jan. 18, 2018, https://hbr.org/2018/01/sexual-harassment-is-pervasive-in-the-restaurant-industry-heres-what-needs-to-change.

53. Michelle Alexander, "Tipping Is a Legacy of Slavery," *New York Times*, Feb. 5, 2021, https://www.nytimes.com/2021/02/05/opinion/minimum-wage-racism.html.

54. Lily Roberts and Galen Hendricks, "Short-Changed: How Tipped Work Exacerbates the Pay Gap for Latinas," *Center for American Progress* (blog), Nov. 20, 2019, https://www.americanprogress.org/article/short-changed-tipped-work-exacerbates-pay-gap-latinas.

55. "Restaurant Workers Rally for Fair Wage," *Albany Times-Union*, 2020.

56. One Fair Wage, "Our Work," https://onefairwage.site/our-work, accessed Dec. 13, 2023.

57. Catherine Deneuve, "Nous défendons une liberté d'importuner, indispensable à la liberté sexuelle," *Le Monde*, Sept. 1, 2018.

58. Katie Way, "I Went on a Date with Aziz Ansari. It Turned into the Worst Night of My Life," *babe*, Jan. 13, 2018, https://babe.net/2018/01/13/aziz-ansari-28355.

59. "Perspectives On The 'MeToo' Movement," *All Things Considered*, NPR, Sept. 1, 2019, https://www.npr.org/2019/09/01/756564705/perspectives-on-the-metoo-movement.

60. Michaele L. Ferguson, "Choice Feminism and the Fear of Politics," *Perspectives on Politics* 8, no. 1 (2010).

61. Ferguson, "Choice Feminism and the Fear of Politics," 249.

62. Frye, "Oppression," calls these situations double-binds. For philosophical discussions of whether these double-binds make all options equally bad, and how they harm agents, see Serene Khader, "Self-Respect Under Conditions of Oppression," in *Respect: Philosophical Essays*, ed. Richard Dean and Oliver Sensen (New York: Oxford University Press, 2021); "Empowerment Through Self-Subordination," in *Poverty, Agency, and Human Rights*, ed. Diana Tietjens Meyers (New York: Oxford University Press, 2014); "Can Women's Compliance with Oppressive Norms Be Self-Interested" in *Phenomenology of the Political* (Latham, MD: Rowman & Littlefield, 2016); and Sukaina Hirji, "Oppressive Double Binds," *Ethics* 131, no. 4 (July 2021): 643–69.

63. Ferguson, "Choice Feminism and the Fear of Politics," 49.

64. Allie Fasanella, "Alexandria Ocasio-Cortez Reveals Her Remedy for Walking in Heels for 12 Hours," *Yahoo Finance*, Mar. 21, 2019, https://finance.yahoo.com/news/alexandria-ocasio-cortez-reveals-her-143657882.html.

65. Zoe Ruffner, "Congresswoman Alexandria Ocasio-Cortez on Self-Love, Fighting the Power, and Her Signature Red Lip," *Vogue*, Aug. 21, 2020, https://www.vogue.com/article/alexandria-ocasio-cortez-beauty-secrets.

66. Naomi Pomeroy, "As a Chef and a Woman, I Regret Joining the Boys' Club," *Eater*, June 21, 2018, https://www.eater.com/2018/6/21/17468790/boys-club-kitchen-culture-gabrielle-hamilton-ken-friedman-naomi-pomeroy.

67. Christina Cauterucci, "The Insidious Sexism on Display at Amy Coney Barrett's Hearing," *Slate*, Oct. 12, 2020, https://slate.com/news-and-politics/2020/10/amy-coney-barrett-feminism-sexism.html.

68. Elizabeth Segran, "High Heels, Invented for the Male Gaze, Get a Feminist Makeover," *Fast Company*, Apr. 13, 2018, https://www.fastcompany.com/40556015/meet-the-women-reinventing-the-high-heel-without-the-sexism.

69. Segran, "High Heels, Invented for the Male Gaze, Get a Feminist Makeover."

70. See Shani Orgad and Rosalind Gill, *Confidence Culture* (Durham, NC: Duke University Press, 2022); Catherine Rottenberg, *The Rise of Neoliberal Feminism* (New York: Oxford University Press, 2018).

71. Nancy Fraser, *Fortunes of Feminism: From State-Managed Capitalism to Neoliberal Crisis* (New York: Verso, 2013).

72. Laura Bliss, "Irregular Work Schedules Have the Biggest Impact on Women," Bloomberg.com, May 20, 2015, https://www.bloomberg.com/news/articles/2015-05-20/a-center-for-popular-democracy-reports-women-suffer-most-from-instability-of-hourly-work.

73. Dawn Foster, "Sheryl Sandberg's Trickle-Down Feminism Stands Exposed," Dec. 11, 2018, https://jacobin.com/2018/12/sheryl-sandberg-lean-in-feminism-class.

74. bell hooks, *Feminist Theory: From Margin to Center* (Boston: South End Press, 2000), 117.

75. Sophie Haigney, "Meet the Self-Described 'Bimbos' of TikTok," Opinion, *New York Times*, June 15, 2022, https://www.nytimes.com/2022/06/15/opinion/bimbo-tiktok-feminism.html; and hooks, *Feminist Theory*.

76. Chrissy Chlapecka, "Who Is the Gen-Z Bimbo?" TikTok, Nov. 26, 2020, https://www.tiktok.com/@chrissychlapecka/video/6899540522721922310.

77. Terry Nguyen, "Gen Z Does Not Dream of Labor," *Vox*, Apr. 11, 2022, https://www.vox.com/the-highlight/22977663/gen-z-antiwork-capitalism.

78. Emily Alford, "The Wing's Merchandise Sure Looks a Lot Like Popular Feminist Instagram Content," *Jezebel*, Sept. 17, 2019, https://jezebel.com/the-wings-merchandise-sure-looks-a-lot-like-popular-fem-1838168169.

79. Amanda Hess, "The Wing Is a Women's Utopia. Unless You Work There," *New York Times Magazine*, Mar. 17, 2020, https://www.nytimes.com/2020/03/17/magazine/the-wing.html.

80. Hess, "The Wing Is a Women's Utopia. Unless You Work There."

81. Hess, "The Wing Is a Women's Utopia. Unless You Work There."

82. Katherine Rosman, "Audrey Gelman, the Wing's Co-Founder, Resigns," *New York Times*, June 12, 2020, https://www.nytimes.com/2020/06/11/style/the-wing-ceo-audrey-gelman-resigns.html.

83. Hess, "The Wing Is a Women's Utopia. Unless You Work There."

84. Hess, "The Wing Is a Women's Utopia. Unless You Work There."

85. Alex Abad-Santos, "Girlboss Ended Not with a Bang, but a Meme," *Vox*, June 7, 2021, https://www.vox.com/22466574/gaslight-gatekeep-girlboss-meaning.

86. Elyse Dupre, "Rachel Hollis Backtracks After Declaring She's 'Freaking Privileged,'" E Online, Apr. 6, 2021, https://www.eonline.com/news/1255994/author-rachel-hollis-apologizes-for-controversial-comments-on-privilege.

87. Abad-Santos, "Girlboss Ended Not with a Bang, but a Meme."

88. Matt Stevens, "Firm Behind 'Fearless Girl' Statue Underpaid Women, U.S. Says," *New York Times*, Oct. 6, 2017, https://www.nytimes.com/2017/10/06/business/fearless-girl-settlement.html.

CHAPTER 5: EQUALITY AND INTERSECTIONALITY

1. Keeanga-Yamahtta Taylor, "How Black Feminists Defined Abortion Rights," *New Yorker*, Feb. 22, 2022, https://www.newyorker.com/news/essay/how-black-feminists-defined-abortion-rights.

2. bell hooks, *Feminist Theory: From Margin to Center* (London: Pluto Press, 2000).

3. The term *liberal feminism* is sometimes used to mean feminism that accepts the core values of liberalism, such as individual rights, and sometimes to mean feminism that proceeds from the assumption that extending existing legal and political protections to women will be sufficient to achieve gender equality.

The latter is the dominant use of the term, even if it is not the most common one in academic philosophy.

4. The anti-racist philosopher Charles Mills argued that there was an important difference between the value of opposing inequality and the value of equality. See Charles Mills, "Retrieving Rawls for Racial Justice?" *Critical Philosophy of Race* 1, no. 1 (2013), and Anne Phillips, *Unconditional Equals* (Princeton, NJ: Princeton University Press 2021).

5. Patricia Romney, *We Were There: The Third World Women's Alliance and the Second Wave* (New York: Feminist Press, 2021).

6. Jade Lawson, "Abortion Rights Activists Vow to Continue Decadeslong *Roe v. Wade* Fight: 'They're Not Going to Win,'" ABC News, June 24, 2022, https://abcnews.go.com/US/abortion-rights-activists-vow-continue-decadeslong-roe-wade/story?id=85414310.

7. Lawson, "Abortion Rights Activists Vow to Continue Decadeslong *Roe v. Wade* Fight."

8. Lawson, "Abortion Rights Activists Vow to Continue Decadeslong *Roe v. Wade* Fight."

9. Frances Beale, "Double Jeopardy: To Be Black and Female on JSTOR," *Meridians* 8, no. 2 (2008): 172.

10. Iris Lopez, *Matters of Choice: Puerto Rican Women's Struggle for Reproductive Freedom* (New Brunswick, NJ: Rutgers University Press, 2008).

11. Harriett Besser, "The Role of Sterilization in Controlling Puerto Rican Fertility," *Population Studies* 23, no. 3 (1969): 343–61.

12. *La Operacion*, Latin American Film Project, 1982.

13. Beale, "Double Jeopardy," 172.

14. Beale, "Double Jeopardy," 172.

15. Laura Meyer, Ife Floyd, and Ladonna Pavetti, *Ending Behavioral Requirements and Reproductive Control Measures Would Move TANF in an Antiracist Direction*, Center on Budget and Policy Priorities, Feb. 23, 2022, https://www.cbpp.org/research/income-security/ending-behavioral-requirements-and-reproductive-control-measures-would.

16. Beale, "Double Jeopardy," 172.

17. Maria Figueroa, one of the plaintiffs in *Madrigal v. Quilligan*, was under anesthesia and in surgery when her husband "consented" to her sterilization on her behalf. See Antonia Hernandez, "Chicanas and the Issue of Involuntary Sterilization," *Chicana/o Latina/o Law Review* 3, no. 3 (1976).

18. Camilo Montoya-Galvez, "Investigation Finds Women Detained by ICE Underwent 'Unnecessary Gynecological Procedures' at Georgia Facility," CBS News, Nov. 15, 2022, https://www.cbsnews.com/news/women-detained-ice-unnecessary-gynecological-procedures-georgia-facility-investigation.

19. Beale, "Double Jeopardy," 171.

20. Beale, "Double Jeopardy," 171.

21. Rebecca Kluchin, *Fit to Be Tied: Sterilization and Reproductive Rights in America: 1950–1980* (New Brunswick, NJ: Rutgers University Press, 2011).

22. Only one of the two sisters, Mary Alice, was diagnosed with a medical condition that qualified as a disability.

23. CDC Office of Health Equity, "Working Together to Reduce Black Maternal Mortality," Health Equity Features, CDC, Apr. 3, 2023, https://www.cdc.gov /healthequity/features/maternal-mortality/index.html.

24. Donna L. Hoyert, "Maternal Mortality Rates in the United States, 2020," National Center for Health Statistics, CDC, Feb. 22, 2022, https://www.cdc.gov/nchs /data/hestat/maternal-mortality/2020/maternal-mortality-rates-2020.htm.

25. Lucia Cheng, "Stories from the Black Maternal Mortality Crisis," *Smithsonian*, July 25, 2022, https://www.smithsonianmag.com/smart-news/aftershock -documentary-black-maternal-mortality-crisis-180980452.

26. Kimberlé Crenshaw, "Demarginalizing the Intersection of Race and Sex: A Black Feminist Critique of Antidiscrimination Doctrine, Feminist Theory and Antiracist Politics," *University of Chicago Legal Forum* 1989, no. 1 (1989): 139–67.

27. Men have sometimes been preferred targets of coercive sterilization. A well-known case was the mass sterilization of men in India in the 1970s in the name of population control, but since this era, it has been predominantly women who have been—and continue to be—targeted for sterilization.

28. Crenshaw, "Demarginalizing the Intersection of Race and Sex," 152.

29. In her discussion of safe haven laws during the oral arguments of *Dobbs*, Barrett referred to both autonomy and equal opportunity, claiming that the reduction in equality of opportunity caused by a forced pregnancy was dramatically reduced by the ability to abandon one's child soon after birth. As some feminists of color have pointed out, she did not discuss issues like differential adoption rates for children of color, or the historical use of adoption as a tool for tearing Indigenous families apart (see Lauren van Schilfgaarde, "Native Reproductive Justice: Practices and Policies from Relinquishment to Family Preservation," *Bill of Health*, May 12, 2022, https://blog.petrieflom.law.harvard.edu/2022/05/12/native -reproductive-justice-adoption-relinquishment-family-preservation.

30. Elena Gutiérrez, *Fertile Matters: The Politics of Mexican-Origin Women's Reproduction* (Austin: University of Texas Press, 2008), 105.

31. Gutiérrez, *Fertile Matters*, 105.

32. For an argument that freedom from restriction, when imposed on an unequal background context, perpetuates reproductive inequality, see Dorothy Roberts, *Killing the Black Body: Race, Reproduction, and the Meaning of Liberty* (New York: Vintage, 1997), ch. 7.

33. Roberts, *Killing the Black Body*, 371.

34. Arwa Mahdawi, "The Chinese Government Is Trying to Rebrand Forced Sterilization as Feminism," *The Guardian*, Jan. 9, 2021, https://www.theguardian.com /commentisfree/2021/jan/09/china-forced-sterilizations-feminist-rebrand.

35. Romney, *We Were There*, 23.

36. Romney, *We Were There*, 29.

37. Romney, *We Were There*, 31.

38. Romney, *We Were There*, 31.

39. The philosopher Marilyn Frye defines oppression as a set of social relations where social structures disadvantage entire groups.

40. See also Serene J. Khader, "The Wrong of Oppression," *Philosophical Studies* (Feb. 22, 2024), https://doi.org/10.1007/s11098-023-02084-5.

41. See Charles V. Hamilton and Kwame Ture, *Black Power: Politics of Liberation in America* (New York: Knopf Doubleday, 1967), for a discussion of why the term *institutional racism* was coined.

42. Quoted in Benita Roth, *Separate Roads to Feminism: Black, Chicana, and White Feminist Movements in America's Second Wave* (New York: Cambridge University Press, 2003), 54.

43. Roth, *Separate Roads to Feminism*.

44. Marge Piercy, "The Grand Coolie Damn," *The Feminist eZine*, 1969, http://www.feministezine.com/feminist/modern/The-Grand-Coolie-Damn.html. Quoted in Roth, *Separate Roads to Feminism*, 54.

45. Beale, "Double Jeopardy," 168.

46. White radical feminists shared with feminists involved in racial and economic liberation movements a sense that oppression was a form of unjust hierarchy. But they often believed that sexism was more fundamental than other oppressions, and historian Benita Roth (*Separate Roads to Feminism*) links this view to their race and class privilege. I also believe that these groups still sometimes lapsed into something like freedom feminism, because privileged people were more likely to see "culture" and symbols as the engine of oppression and less likely to be attuned to the more insidious and material structures of racial and economic inequality.

47. Third World Women's Alliance, "Equal to What?," 1969, https://www-personal.umd.umich.edu/~ppennock/doc-third%20world%20women.htm.

48. Anita Allen, "The Proposed Equal Protection Fix for Abortion Law: Reflections on Citizenship, Gender, and the Constitution," *Harvard Journal of Law & Public Policy* (Jan. 1, 1995): 430.

49. Allen, "The Proposed Equal Protection Fix for Abortion Law," 431.

50. Allen, "The Proposed Equal Protection Fix for Abortion Law," 431.

51. Audre Lorde, *Sister Outsider: Essays and Speeches* (New York: Crossing Press, 2007).

52. See the Combahee River Collective, *A Black Feminist Statement. This Bridge Called My Back: Writings by Radical Women of Color*, ed. Gloria Anzaldúa and Cherríe Moraga (Albany: SUNY Press, 2015), and bell hooks, *Feminist Theory from Margin to Center* (Boston: South End Press, 1984) for explicit articulation. See Roth, *Separate Roads to Feminism*, for a discussion of how this view emerged in historical activism.

53. Keeanga-Yamahtta Taylor, "Abortion Is About Freedom, Not Just Privacy," *New Yorker*, July 6, 2022, https://www.newyorker.com/news/our-columnists/abortion-is-about-freedom-not-just-privacy.

54. Allen's mother was a homemaker and did experience some important class advantages.

55. Allen, "The Proposed Equal Protection Fix for Abortion Law," 431.

56. Allen, "The Proposed Equal Protection Fix for Abortion Law," 431.

57. Beale, "Double Jeopardy," 174; Taylor, "Abortion Is About Freedom, Not Just Privacy."

58. Frye argued that women were consigned to a sector of personal, sexual, and ego service. See Marilyn Frye, "Oppression," in *The Politics of Reality: Essays in Feminist Theory* (Trumansburg, NY: Crossing Press, 1983). See Kate Manne, *Entitled: How Male Privilege Hurts Women* (New York: Penguin Random House, 2020), for a more contemporary discussion of this phenomenon.

59. Allen's mother was economically dependent on her husband, Allen's father. Allen also recounts that her father dictated her mother's contraceptive choices.

60. Ariane Hegewisch and Heidi Hartmann, *Occupational Segregation and the Gender Wage Gap: A Job Half Done*, Institute for Women's Policy Research, Jan. 2014, 15, https://iwpr.org/wp-content/uploads/2020/08/C419.pdf.

61. The devaluation seems to "stick" to these jobs even as they become less gendered; many of them are less women-dominated now than they were twenty years ago, as they are now largely entered by men of color.

62. Elyse M. Shaw et al., *Undervalued and Underpaid in America: Women in Low-Wage, Female Dominated Jobs*, Institute for Women's Policy Research, 2016, 15, https://iwpr.org/wp-content/uploads/2020/09/D508-Undervalued -and-Underpaid.pdf.

63. The image can be found here: IISC, "Illustrating Equality vs. Equity," Interaction Institute for Social Change, Jan. 14, 2016, https://interactioninstitute.org /illustrating-equality-vs-equity.

64. The real purpose of this graphic is to distinguish equality, which is understood as giving the same thing to everyone or treating everyone the same, from equity, which is supposed to permit giving different forms of support and attention to people in different situations. However, this contrast gets off the ground by starting with a really narrow understanding of equality. We might, for example, understand equality as the ability for every person to achieve certain valued functionings, like accessing education or living free of violence. If this is what equality is, equity is a version of it (after all, the aim for everyone is the same, even in the image: to get over the fence). It is absolutely right that different people need different things in order for us to get to a society that treats people as equals, but we shouldn't forget that the goal is still to get to a society that treats people as equals.

65. In academia, the term *critical race theory* refers to a specific school of thought in legal studies, one that sees racial inequality partly as a product of the law and legal institutions. Right-wing opponents of feminism and anti-racism are now weaponizing the term to claim that almost any mention of race and racism in school curricula and diversity and inclusion initiatives is part of a broader agenda.

66. Alexandra Kollontai, "The Social Basis of the Woman Question," 1909, https:// www.marxists.org/archive/kollonta/1909/social-basis.htm.

67. Dorothy Sue Cobble, Linda Gordon, and Astrid Henry, *Feminism Unfinished: A Short, Surprising History of American Women's Movements* (New York: W. W. Norton, 2014), 42.

68. bell hooks, *Feminist Theory: From Margin to Center* (Boston: South End Press, 2000), 18–34.

69. Johnnie Tillmon, "From the Vault: 'Welfare Is a Women's Issue' (Spring 1972)," *Ms.*, Mar. 25, 2021, https://msmagazine.com/2021/03/25/welfare-is-a-womens -issue-ms-magazine-spring-1972.

70. Tillmon, "From the Vault: 'Welfare Is a Women's Issue.'"

71. Premilla Nadasen, "From Widow to Welfare Queen," *Black Women, Gender, and Families* 1, no. 2 (2007): 52–77.

72. Historian Premilla Nadasen, author of a significant body of scholarship about the NWRO, occasionally suggests that their activism was against equality (see "Expanding the Boundaries of the Women's Movement," *Feminist Studies* 2, no. 28 [2002]: 271–30). However, she only refers to equality under the law. The arguments I make later in this chapter should also hold against the critique of equality she makes on behalf of the NWRO.

73. Martha Davis, "Welfare Rights and Women's Rights in the 1960s," *Journal of Policy History* 8, no. 1 (1996): 156.

74. The Moynihan Report was a study released by then assistant secretary of labor Daniel Patrick Moynihan. It claimed that woman-headed households were a significant cause of African American poverty and is widely credited with creating the idea of a "culture of poverty," even if it did not coin the term.

75. Davis, "Welfare Rights and Women's Rights in the 1960s."

76. Davis, "Welfare Rights and Women's Rights in the 1960s."

77. Toni Morrison, "What the Black Woman Thinks About Women's Lib," *New York Times*, Aug. 22, 1971, https://www.nytimes.com/1971/08/22/archives/what-the -black-woman-thinks-about-womens-lib-the-black-woman-and.html.

78. See Serene J. Khader, *Decolonizing Universalism: A Transnational Feminist Ethic*, Studies in Feminist Philosophy (Oxford: Oxford University Press, 2019), 50–76.

79. Nadasen, "Expanding the Boundaries of the Women's Movement."

80. Kirsten Swinth, *Feminism's Forgotten Fight: The Unfinished Struggle for Work and Family* (Cambridge, MA: Harvard University Press, 2018).

81. Nadasen, "Expanding the Boundaries of the Women's Movement."

82. Felicia Kornbluh, "The Goals of the National Welfare Rights Movement: Why We Need Them Thirty Years Later," *Feminist Studies* 24, no. 1 (1998): 72, https://doi.org/10.2307/3178619.

83. Cobble, Gordon, and Henry, *Feminism Unfinished*, 31.

84. Frances Kunreuther, "The Respect ABQ Women Campaign," Building Movement Project, 2015.

85. Bold Futures NM, "Who We Are," https://www.boldfuturesnm.org/who-we-are, accessed Dec. 13, 2023.

86. Micaela Cadena et al., *Dismantling Teen Pregnancy Prevention 2016*, Young Women United, May 2016, https://static1.squarespace.com/static/60de56b2 ee6ab037e6ef9219/t/60f2e155b84a576e6cfa88a3/1626530139405/ywu -dismantlingtpp-DEC2016-digital-interactive.pdf.

87. Miriam Perez, "Teen Moms Look for Support, but Find Only Shame," *Truthout*, May 8, 2011, https://truthout.org/articles/teen-moms-look-for-support-but-find-only-shame.

88. Kunreuther, "The Respect ABQ Women Campaign," 4.

89. Susan Buttenwieser, "The Reproductive Justice and Rights Movement Is Fighting Back," Women's Media Center, Dec. 16, 2020, https://womensmediacenter.com/news-features/the-reproductive-justice-movement-is-fighting-back.

90. Kunreuther, "The Respect ABQ Women Campaign," 4.

91. Kunreuther, "The Respect ABQ Women Campaign."

92. Strong Families, another New Mexico organization involved in reproductive justice organizing, conceives itself as fighting for the four out of five families that live "beyond the picket fence."

93. Jennifer Gerson, "How Indigenous Women Repealed New Mexico's Longstanding Abortion Ban," *Bustle*, Mar. 8, 2021, https://www.bustle.com/politics/new-mexico-abortion-ban-trigger-law-indigenous-women.

94. Southwest Women's Law Center and Forward Together, "Road to Reproductive Justice: Native Americans in New Mexico," Southwest Women's Law Center, 2020, https://swwomenslaw.org/wp-content/uploads/2020/12/Road-to-RJ-2020_Slideck-for-SFN-Webinar.pdf.

95. Emily Hofstaedter, "Abortion Was Already Inaccessible on Reservation Land. Dobbs Made Things Worse," *Mother Jones* (blog), Aug. 12, 2022, https://www.motherjones.com/politics/2022/08/abortion-dobbs-tribal-land.

96. Brianna Theobald, "A 1970 Law Led to the Mass Sterilization of Native American Women. That History Still Matters," *Time*, Nov. 28, 2019, https://time.com/5737080/native-american-sterilization-history.

97. Gerson, "How Indigenous Women Repealed New Mexico's Longstanding Abortion Ban."

98. See Lorena Cabnal, "El Relato de las violencias desde me territorio cuerpo-tierra," *En Tiempos de Muerte: Cuerpos, Rebeldias, Resistencias*, ed. Xochitl Leyva Solano and Rosalba Icaza (San Cristobal de Las Casas, Chiapas, Mexico: Cooperativa Editorial Retos, 2019); Bonita Lawrence, "Gender, Race, and the Regulation of Native Identity in Canada and the United States: An Overview," *Hypatia* 18, no. 2 (2003): 3–31; Cyndy Baskin, "Contemporary Indigenous Women's Roles: Traditional Teachings or Internalized Colonialism?," *Violence Against Women* 26, nos. 15–16 (Dec. 2020): 2083–2101.

99. Rita Segato and Pedro Monque, "Gender and Coloniality," *Hypatia* 36, no. 4 (2021).

100. Keeanga-Yamahtta Taylor, "How Black Feminists Defined Abortion Rights," *New Yorker*, Feb. 22, 2022, https://www.newyorker.com/news/essay/how-black-feminists-defined-abortion-rights.

CONCLUSION

1. Hope Chigudu and Rudo Chigudu, "An Organisation with a Soul," African Institute for Integrated Responses to VAWG and HIV/AIDS, 2015.

2. Chigudu and Chigudu, "An Organisation with a Soul," 17.

3. Chigudu and Chigudu, "An Organisation with a Soul," 24.

4. Katherine Schaeffer, "6 Facts about Economic Inequality in the U.S.," *Pew Research Center* (blog), Feb. 7, 2020, https://www.pewresearch.org/short-reads /2020/02/07/6-facts-about-economic-inequality-in-the-u-s.

5. It's not clear that hooks would have called it an inequality, since she associated equality with attempts to achieve the status of some existing group of men. I'm calling it one, since oppression involves a dynamic of one group mattering more than, getting more than, or being in a position to control another. hooks would later go on to argue that feminism was a fight against all intersection oppressions. See hooks, *Feminist Theory: From Margin to Center* (Boston: South End Press, 2000).

6. Maria Pia Lopez, *Not One Less: Mourning, Disobedience and Desire* (London: Polity, 2020), 131.

7. The green scarves originated, not with Ni Una Menos, but with the organization Campana por el Aborto Legal. See Paulina Cohen, "Not One Less," *UCLA Journal of Gender and Law* 29, no. 1 (2022).

8. Lopez, *Not One Less*, likens the chanting of names by Ni Una Menos to that by Black Lives Matter, but she does not claim that Ni Una Menos adopted the tactic because of Black Lives Matter, and tactics like it have been used in a variety of protests across time and space. The Mothers of the Plaza de Mayo, for example, painted silhouettes of the disappeared accompanied by names all over Buenos Aires and displayed their pictures while wearing headscarves embroidered with the names of their children.

9. Roberto Valent, "Tackling Femicide in Argentina: A UN Resident Coordinator Blog," Spotlight Initiative, Jan. 20, 2020, https://www.spotlightinitiative.org/fr /node/17578.

10. Vir Cano and Marta Dillon, "Que La Rabia Nos Valga," Facebook, Mar. 27, 2015, https://www.facebook.com/virginia.cano.547/posts/10155609107635508.

11. Absalón Opazo, "Rita Segato: 'Una falla del pensamiento feminista es creer que la violencia de género es un problema de hombres y mujeres,'" *El Ciudadano*, Sept. 2, 2017, https://www.elciudadano.com/entrevistas/rita-segato-una-falla -del-pensamiento-feminista-es-creer-que-la-violencia-de-genero-es-un-problema -de-hombres-y-mujeres/09/02.

12. The expression "women, cis and trans" has been part of Ni Una Menos's rhetoric more or less since the movement began. See Lopez, "Not One Less."

13. The term *travesti* in Latin America refers to people with various feminine gender identities who were assigned male at birth.

14. Quoted in Natália Maria Félix de Souza, "When the Body Speaks (to) the Political: Feminist Activism in Latin America and the Quest for Alternative Democratic Futures," *Contexto Internacional* 41, no. 1 (Apr. 2019): 97, https://doi.org /10.1590/s0102–8529.2019410100005.

15. Lopez, "Not One Less."

16. Argentina is a world leader in legal protections for trans people and in 2021 adopted a law reserving 1 percent of public sector jobs for trans people.

17. Paulina Cohen, "Not One Woman Less: An Analysis of the Advocacy and Activism of Argentina's Ni Una Menos Movement," *UCLA Journal of Gender and Law* 29, no. 1 (2022): 136, https://doi.org/10.5070/L329158298.

18. Zoe Sullivan, "Latin American Feminists Are Fighting for Intersectional Gender Justice," *Ms.*, Mar. 28, 2022, https://msmagazine.com/2022/03/28/latin-america-feminist-abortion-gender-women.

19. Jordana Timerman, "Misogyny, Femicide and an Unexpected Abortion Debate," *New York Times*, May 15, 2018, https://www.nytimes.com/2018/05/15/opinion/argentina-abortion-ni-una-menos.html.

20. National Women's Law Center, *Dress Coded*, National Women's Law Center, 2018, https://nwlc.org/wp-content/uploads/2018/04/5.1web_Final_nwlc_DressCodeReport.pdf.

21. National Women's Law Center, *Dress Coded*, 17.

22. National Women's Law Center, *Dress Coded*, 17.

23. National Women's Law Center, *Dress Coded*, 24.

24. National Women's Law Center, *Dress Coded*, 26.

25. Kathryn C. Monahan et al., "From the School Yard to the Squad Car: School Discipline, Truancy, and Arrest," *Journal of Youth and Adolescence* 43, no. 7 (July 1, 2014): 1110–22, https://doi.org/10.1007/s10964-014-0103-1.

26. Sandra B. Simkins et al., "School to Prison Pipeline for Girls: The Role of Physical and Sexual Abuse," *Children's Legal Rights Journal* 24, no. 4 (2016): 56–72.

27. In fact, dress codes are a step in the school to prison pipeline for some boys, whose haircuts and durags are assumed to be gang symbols.

28. Courtne Brogle, "High School Student Sparks Debate After Protesting School's 'Sexist' Dress Code," *Newsweek*, June 9, 2021, https://www.newsweek.com/high-school-student-sparks-debate-after-protesting-schools-sexist-dress-code-1599157.

29. National Women's Law Center, *Dress Coded*, 21.

30. For more on the idea that being oppressed means having all available choices perpetuate the subordination of one's group, see Marilyn Frye, "Oppression," in *The Politics of Reality: Essays in Feminist Theory* (Trumansburg, NY: Crossing Press, 1983); Khader, "Why Is Oppression Wrong," 2024; Serene J. Khader, "Can Women's Compliance with Oppressive Norms Be Self-Interested?," in *Phenomenology of the Political*, ed. S. West Gurley and Geoff Pfeifer (Lanham, MD: Rowman & Littlefield, 2016), 165–81; Screne Khader, "Empowerment Through Self-Subordination? Microcredit and Women's Agency," in *Poverty, Agency, and Human Rights*, ed. Diana Tietjens Meyers (New York: Oxford University Press, 2014); and "Oppression and Self-Respect" (2021); and Sukaina Hirji, "Oppressive Double Binds," *Ethics* 131, no. 4 (July 2021): 643–69.

31. Ellen Wulfhorst, "Indigenous and Female: Life at the Bottom in Guatemala," Reuters, May 3, 2017, https://www.reuters.com/article/us-guatemala-women-indigenous-idUSKBN17Z07N.

32. Suzanne Daley, "Guatemalan Women's Claims Put Focus on Canadian Firms' Conduct Abroad," *New York Times*, Apr. 2, 2016, https://www.nytimes.com/2016/04/03/world/americas/guatemalan-womens-claims-put-focus-on-canadian-firms-conduct-abroad.html.

33. Kalowatie Deonandan, Rebecca Tatham, and Brennan Field, "Indigenous Women's Anti-Mining Activism: A Gendered Analysis of the El Estor Struggle in Guatemala," *Gender & Development* 25, no. 3 (Sept. 2, 2017): 405–19, https://doi.org/10.1080/13552074.2017.1379779.

34. See Elliaa Jutte, "Pathway to a Feminist International Corporate Accountability Framework," ActionAid Nederland, Oct. 23, 2022, https://actionaid.nl/2022/10/24/pathway-to-a-feminist-international-corporate-accountability-framework.

35. Jutte, "Pathway to a Feminist International Corporate Accountability Framework."

36. I call this idea "the Enlightenment Teleological Narrative" (see Khader, *Decolonizing Universalism*).

37. Ben Dangl, "Demanding Justice: Indigenous Women from Guatemala Battle Canadian Mining Giant," *Upside Down World* (blog), Jan. 26, 2018, https://upsidedownworld.org/archives/guatemala/demanding-justice-indigenous-women-guatemala-battle-canadian-mining-giant.

38. Deonandan, Tatham, and Field, "Indigenous Women's Anti-Mining Activism."

39. This is one idea at the heart of the notion of *cuerpo territorio* coined by Lorena Cabnal and used by anti-extractivist feminist activists in Latin America (see also Khader and Monque, "Decolonizing Women's Human Rights: Insights from Latin American Ecoterritorial Feminist Movements," in *The Routledge Companion to the Philosophy of Human Rights*, ed. Kerri Woods and Jesse Tomalty, forthcoming).

40. Deonandan, Tatham, and Field, "Indigenous Women's Anti-Mining Activism," 409.

41. For more on this idea, see Serene J. Khader, *Decolonizing Universalism: A Transnational Feminist Ethic*, Studies in Feminist Philosophy (Oxford: Oxford University Press, 2019), 50–75.

42. Katty Kay and Claire Shipman, "The Confidence Gap," *The Atlantic*, Apr. 15, 2014, https://www.theatlantic.com/magazine/archive/2014/05/the-confidence-gap/359815.

43. This term was coined by Ruth Whippman. See Ruth Whippman, "Enough Leaning In. Let's Tell Men to Lean Out," *New York Times*, Oct. 10, 2019, https://www.nytimes.com/2019/10/10/opinion/sunday/feminism-lean-in.html.

44. Urvashi Sahni, "A Life Knowledge Approach to Life Skills: Empowering Boys with New Conceptions of Masculinity," in *Life Skills Education for Youth: Critical Perspectives*, ed. Erin Murphy-Graham and Joan DeJaeghere (New York: Springer Cham, 2022), 193–213.

45. Philosophers and political theorists might object that there is, in fact, a relational concept of freedom, namely the concept of freedom as nondomination. However, nondomination is not relational in the relevant way for my discussion here; it tells us that freedom consists in a relation between two agents, but it does not tell us that we have to compare distributive shares to assess the justice of a situation. My point here is that we cannot determine whether an inequality is present without at least comparing the distributive shares of the relevant parties.

46. For more on how value for women's agency leads to women's overwork, see Serene Khader, "Passive Empowerment: How Women's Agency Became Women Doing It All," *Philosophical Topics* 46, no. 2 (2018).

47. "We Can Change Beliefs About Gender Norms," Dr. Urvashi Sahni, *Inside Global Girls' Education*, podcast, ep. 3, Apr. 12, 2021.

48. Sahni, "A Life Knowledge Approach to Life Skills," 198.

49. Sahni, "A Life Knowledge Approach to Life Skills," 209.

50. Lauren Schiller, "More Than Power Poses: Why Self-Empowerment Is a Myth and What We Can Do Instead—Ruth Whippman, Author," *Inflection Point* podcast, Nov. 21, 2018, https://www.inflectionpointradio.org/episodes/2018/11/20/more-than-power-poses-why-self-empowerment-is-a-myth-and-what-we-can-do-instead-ruth-whippman-author.

51. Anna Orso, "Law Protecting Philadelphia Domestic Workers Takes Effect as They're Losing Jobs in Droves," *Philadelphia Inquirer*, May 1, 2020, https://www.inquirer.com/news/philadelphia/philadelphia-domestic-worker-bill-of-rights-takes-effect-coronavirus-20200501.html.

52. "New York NDWA & NDWA—We Dream in Black Chapter," *National Domestic Workers Alliance*, https://www.domesticworkers.org/membership/chapters/we-dream-in-black-new-york-chapter, accessed Feb. 7, 2023.

53. "Pennsylvania NDWA & NDWA—We Dream in Black Chapter," *National Domestic Workers Alliance*, https://www.domesticworkers.org/membership/chapters/pennsylvania-chapter, accessed Feb. 7, 2023.

54. This way of casting care work is not without its political detractors. Some, like Premilla Nadasen, who studied the NWRO, argue that the idea that care work is a labor of love obscures its status as labor and contributes to exploitation. See *Household Workers Unite: The Untold Story of African American Women Who Built a Movement* (Boston: Beacon Press, 2016).

55. "We Dream in Black," Eyes Up Here, https://www.eyesuphereproductions.com/we-dream-in-black, accessed Feb. 10, 2023.

56. Eva Feder Kittay, *Love's Labor: Essays on Women, Equality and Dependence* (New York: Routledge, 1999).

57. Women's labor force participation is widely used by social scientists and policy institutions as an indicator of women's empowerment.

58. See Melinda Gates, *The Moment of Lift: How Empowering Women Changes the World* (New York: Flatiron Books, 2019), for a mainstream feminist discussion that attempts to incorporate insights about care and the gender division of labor but focuses on increasing men's responsibilities while saying little about the need for public subsidies and supports for care.

59. Social reproduction theorists, such as Nancy Fraser and Tithi Bhattacharya, argue that employers benefit from the labor of raising children.

60. "We Dream in Black."

61. Chisholm's entire slogan was "unbought and unbossed."

62. Lizzy Ravitch, "Nannies, Caregivers, and House Cleaners in Philadelphia Have Workers' Rights, but Their Employers May Not Know That," *Philadelphia*

Inquirer, Apr. 27, 2023, https://www.inquirer.com/jobs/labor/philadelphia-domestic-workers-rights-nannies-house-cleaners-20230427.html.

63. Stephen Williams, "Domestic Workers Want Better Enforcement of Law and More Protections," *Philadelphia Tribune*, June 14, 2023, https://www.phillytrib.com/news/local_news/domestic-workers-want-better-enforcement-of-law-and-more-protections/article_1df96a5e-fbbc-5d82-a38d-3f4012c7c448.html.

64. Nadasen, *Household Workers Unite*, 61–63.

65. Nadasen, *Household Workers Unite*, 141.

66. Nadasen, *Household Workers Unite*, 140.

67. Anna Lucente Sterling, "New York Could Become First City in Country to Enact Universal Child Care," NY1, July 26, 2022, https://www.ny1.com/nyc/all-boroughs/news/2022/07/25/new-york-could-become-first-city-in-country-to-enact-universal-child-care.

68. Alexandria Ocasio-Cortez, "If Women and Gender-Expanding People Want to Run for Office, We Can't Knock on Anybody's Door—We Have to Build Our Own House," Instagram, June 13, 2018, https://www.instagram.com/p/Bj-ugo0lZod.

69. Lopez, *Not One Less*, 129.

70. In this passage, Lopez criticizes both freedom (or individual autonomy) and "gender inequality, presented as an isolated issue, accepting the logics of social and racial inequality within which it is subscribed" (129). Her argument is effectively that refusing to care about inequalities besides gender inequality is one *cause* of a feminism that will give women individual autonomy but stop short of actual liberation.

INDEX

ableism, 18, 145, 146

abortion: access to, 7, 154; Black female perspectives, 141; focus only on choice, 6, 8, 51, 200n11; intersectional feminist approach, 178–79; laws governing, 157–58, 166–67; organizing around, 147–48. See also *Dobbs v. Jackson Women's Health Organization* (2022)

ActionAid campaign, 183

adoption decision, trivializing, 2, 6, 221n29

Aftershock (Ellis), 146

Against White Feminism (Zakaria), 98

agency, women's, 110–11, 129–32, 140, 167–68, 229n46

Allen, Anita, 153–56

Alvarez, Mariana, 178

amatonormativity, 99, 105, 213n43

Ansari, Aziz, 129

appearance-related norms, 121–24, 132, 203n31. *See also* beauty standards/hierarchies; dress codes/dress-code discipline

Argentina, protections for trans people, 226n16

Bad Feminist (Gay), 112

Bannon, Ian, 64

Barboa, Adriann, 166–68

Barrett, Amy Coney: criticisms of as antifeminist, 7, 119; freedom

feminism of, 3–5, 11, 133; People of Praise, 199n5; safe haven laws, 6, 199n3, 221n29. See also *Dobbs v. Jackson Women's Health Organization* (2022)

Beal, Frances, 19, 142–45, 150, 152–54, 167, 169

beauty standards/hierarchies, 8, 18, 28–29, 31–35, 39–40, 124, 203n31. *See also* appearance-related norms; dress codes/dress-code discipline

Bettcher, Talia, 123, 217n46

Bhattacharya, Tithi, 94

"big tent" feminism, 10–11

the Bimboverse, 137

Blackburn, Marsha, 3

"Black is beautiful" movement, 39

Black Power movement, misogyny in, 152

Black women: care work by, 162–63; coercive sterilization, 143–44; dangers of childbirth/motherhood for, 145–46, 163–64; focus on, and real social change, 165–66, 215–16n27; mass incarceration, 65, 208n34; multiple oppressions experienced by, 19, 146–48, 155, 179; need for "intimate justice," 163; as sexually available, 37, 43; tyranny of low expectations, 12, 52

blaming the victim: for gender violence, 32, 34, 94, 122; for social